THE US AND EU,

AND THE EMERGING SUPPLY CHAIN NETWORK

ISBN Paperback: 978-1-963271-29-4
ISBN Ebook: 978-1-963271-30-0

AMERICAN FOREIGN POLICY COUNCIL

AFPC Press
American Foreign Policy Council
509 C Street NE
Washington, DC 20002

Published by Armin Lear Press, Inc.
215 W Riverside Drive, #4362
Estes Park, CO 80517

THE US AND EU,

AND THE EMERGING SUPPLY CHAIN NETWORK

Politics, Prospects, and Allies

Niklas Swanström
Fredrik Erixon
Mrittika Guha Sarkar

AFPC

CONTENTS

ABBREVIATIONS

5G - Fifth Generation

AI - Artificial Intelligence

API - Active Pharmaceutical Ingredients

ASEAN - Association of Southeast Asian Nations

BRI - Belt and Road Initiative

CBAM - Carbon Border Adjustment Mechanism

CFIUS - Committee on Foreign Investment in the United States

CPTPP - Comprehensive and Progressive Agreement for Trans-Pacific Partnership

DARPA - Defense Advanced Research Projects Agency

DOI - Department of the Interior

EGS - Energy and Geological Survey

EU - European Union

EUA - Emergency Use Authorization

FDI - Foreign Direct Investment

FTA - Free Trade Agreement

G7 - Group of Seven

GCC - Gulf Cooperation Council

GDP - Gross Domestic Product

GHG - Historic Greenhouse Gas

GND - Green New Deal

GSC - Global Supply Chains

HHI - Herfindahl-Hirschman Index

ICT - Information and Communication Technology

ILO - International Labour Organization

IMF - International Monetary Fund

IoT - Internet of Things

IP - Intellectual Property

IPCC - Intergovernmental Panel on Climate Change

LDCs - Least Developed Countries

LED - Light Emitting Diode

MIC 2025 - Made in China 2025

MNC - Multinational Corporation

MRAs - Mutual Recognition Agreements

MSME - Micro, Small and Medium-sized Enterprises

NATO - North Atlantic Treaty Organization

NDCs - Nationally Determined Contributions

NGO - Non-Governmental Organization

NTA - New Transatlantic Agenda

OECD - Organization for Economic Co-operation and Development

OPEC - Organization of the Petroleum Exporting Countries

PV - Photovoltaic

QIS - Quantum Information Science

R&D - Research and Development

RCEP - Regional Comprehensive Economic Partnership

RFP - Request for Proposal

SDG - Sustainable Development Goals

SDR - Special Drawing Rights

SOEs - State-owned Enterprises

STEM - Science, Technology, Engineering, and Mathematics

TEC - Transatlantic Economic Council

TEP - Transatlantic Economic Partnership

TTC - Trade and Technology Council

TTIP - Transatlantic Trade and Investment Partnership

UAV - Unmanned Aerial Vehicle

UN - United Nations

UNEP - United Nations Environment Programme

US - United States

USA - United States of America

USMCA - United States-Mexico-Canada Agreement

WTO - World Trade Organization

ONE
Contextualizing Global Supply Chains

In his 2016 speech at Rutgers University, former President Barack Obama captured the zeitgeist of the modern global economy, asserting that "'We live in an age of global supply chains.'" This statement not only acknowledges the ubiquity of fragmented networks of global production but also sets the stage for a critical examination of their complexities and inherent challenges in today's interconnected world.[1] While not the first to highlight this reality, President Obama's remarks diverged from the usual praise of global supply chains and rather offered a cautionary perspective. He emphasized not their unbridled potential, but the "'legitimate 'concerns" they raise amidst globalization's march, urging a thoughtful approach to 'trade the right way.' This nuanced viewpoint underscores the dual

---

1   "Remarks by the President at Commencement Address at Rutgers, the State University of New Jersey," Obama White House, May 15, 2016, https://obamawhitehouse.archives.gov/the-press-office/2016/05/15/remarks-presidentcommencement-address-rutgers-state-university-new

nature of global supply chains—engines of progress fraught with complexities.

Over the past three decades, Global Supply Chains (GSCs) have evolved from mere logistical achievements to become the bedrock of the global economy. This transformation, driven by rapid technological advances and geopolitical shifts, underscores the critical role of GSCs in shaping economic landscapes and influencing global trade dynamics. This evolution, driven by leaps in transportation technology, communications, and information processing, has fundamentally altered manufacturing's production structures. Since the late 1980s, the meteoric rise of GSCs, albeit at different velocities across various industries, has been fundamentally anchored in the economic principles of specialization and comparative advantage. This strategic dispersion of production processes across nations not only exemplifies globalization's reach but also highlights the nuanced interplay between economic theory and real-world trade practices. By dispersing production processes across nations, GSCs have reshaped the economic landscape. By the late 20th and early 21st centuries there was an unprecedented acceleration in globalization, fueled by advancements in technology and a prior shift towards economic policies that opened markets for trade and global competition. This era was characterized by the reduction of trade barriers, the liberalization of financial markets, and significant investments in transportation and logistics infrastructure. The digital revolution further facilitated this expansion, enabling real-time communication and the seamless transfer of goods and information across the globe. As a result, production became increasingly decentralized, with manufacturing hubs emerging in regions offering competitive advantages, notably East Asia. These developments have generated a transnational and tangled web of interdependence between developed and developing parts of the world. To some extent it is fair to say that the globalization we see today is a product of the growing complexity of the supply chain, but also some of its weaknesses.

Undoubtedly, the fragmentation of production and the emergence of cross-border supply chains have yielded substantial economic and security dividends for both the United States (US) and the European Union (EU). These benefits manifest in various forms, from GDP growth to enhanced household spending power. Through a labyrinth of international supply chains, American and European businesses are intricately woven into the global economy's fabric, international trade representing 26 percent of the US's Gross Domestic Product (GDP). While international trade has been a significant contributor to economic output in the US and the EU since the end of World War II, this new phase of globalization expanded trade with new countries and regions and pulled more countries into a framework based on market-based rules and institutions than ever before. The global economy is no longer an affair predominantly in the Atlantic region, but trade now represents about 60 percent of global GDP.

This interconnection underscores the profound economic and security advantages that GSCs facilitate, illuminating the tangible benefits that extend beyond mere numbers to encompass a broadened reliance on the US and EU for essential goods, services, technology, and ideas. It is beyond doubt that the GSCs are at the core of the economic and security power structures that help keep Americans and Europeans safe and prosperous.

The positive effects are evident if you follow the narrative surrounding GSCs that has predominantly focused on their contribution to economic efficiency, cost reduction, and global GDP growth. This perspective, while highlighting the undeniable benefits of global supply chains, often overlooks the complex web of risks and dependencies they introduce into the global economic system. The fragility of GSCs and their need for undisrupted cross-border supply was thrown into sharp relief by the unprecedented challenges of the COVID-19 pandemic and the geopolitical upheaval following the Russian invasion of Ukraine. These events triggered temporary but severe shortages of essential medical supplies and consumer goods, serving as a wake-up call to the world about the precarious nature of our interconnected supply networks. These crises underscore the pressing need for a more resilient approach to managing various forms of international supply and reliances, including the GSCs. The crises have highlighted the necessity of a holistic approach to GSCs that transcends economic gains and accommodates their strategic and operational vulnerabilities. This comprehensive perspective is vital for crafting policies that safeguard against the multifaceted risks posed by global supply chain dependencies.

The contemporary policy challenge lies in broadening our perspective beyond the conventional metrics of efficiency and cost-effectiveness that have long governed GSCs. Instead, there's a pressing need to incorporate principles of resilience, redundancy, and strategic autonomy into our valuation, ensuring that our supply chains are robust enough to withstand future crises and geopolitical tensions. It requires acknowledging that resilience is a critical component of national and global economic health. Policymakers must contend with the reality that an overreliance on just-in-time supply chains and concentrated sources of supply for strategic and important goods can have dire consequences for economic stability and security. Such an approach demands a strategic pivot towards cultivating diversified, agile, and robust supply networks. These networks must be capable to endure an array of disruptions, be they from geopolitical conflicts or global health emergencies, ensuring a steadfast economic and security posture. This supply chain is not limited to the simple production and transport of products, but ranges from innovation to recycling and could best be described as a process.

The escalating trend of foreign and potentially adversarial states exploiting supply chains as instruments of strategic leverage necessitates a sophisticated dialogue on formulating a comprehensive transatlantic strategy. This strategy must not only counteract such maneuvers but also safeguard the economic and security interests of allied nations in an increasingly complex geopolitical landscape. This strategy must address politicized trade and mitigate malign influences, ensuring economic and security interests are safeguarded. A prime illustration of the geopolitical manipulation of economic dependencies is the Chinese government's strategic use of its trade influence. By weaponizing economic ties, China has pressured states and corporations to adjust their economic and political stances in its favor, a tactic exacerbating the urgent need for a strategic reassessment of GSC vulnerabilities. This is something that has led decision-makers to call for goods, technologies, and supply chains of critical importance to be reshored or nearshored. Nonetheless, such an approach holds the possibility to erode American and European innovativeness, reduce the attractiveness and competitiveness of their products and companies internationally, diminish influence abroad, and likely make the transatlantic economies less resilient. Obviously, a more nuanced approach is needed.

Economic and trade developments over the last thirty years

have exposed the US and the EU, and other democratic market economies, to risks and threats to national security. To be precise, many GSCs came to grow too reliant on countries that have a different character than democratic market economies and, importantly, long-nurtured ambitions to refashion international law and rules in their own image. Dominant among these countries are China and Russia. Both countries expanded over time their importance for Western economies – as countries to make industrial investments and find suppliers of inputs and finished goods, and (as in the case of Russia) to purchase oil, gas, and bulk raw materials.

The US and the EU are now in different positions with different needs for building stable and secure patterns of international economic dependencies, but both share the need for a revitalization of their economies and counter the influence from potentially hostile states. Russia's war on Ukraine has clearly demonstrated the risks of relying on a regime with hostile intentions for the supply of energy and other highly critical goods. Once an import, technology or investment dependency has been established, the exporting country can "weaponize" its supply and condition continued sales to demands of political submission. The resources needed for the importers to substitute for the supply coming from a hostile country are unimaginably high and lead to very big economic, societal and political costs. Europe's problem to wean itself of dependency on Russia's hydrocarbon supply is a cautionary tale.

Russia is not the only country posing these types of dependency risks: China may be an even more significant risk because of its systemic importance for the entire world economy, and the politization of its economic engagement. China's international intentions are increasingly on a collision course with a world order based on freedom, democracy, market economy; the threats to international peace and stability have multiplied under President Xi Jinping. Problematic for a long time, the character of China's regime is now incompatible with the ambitions and interests of nations who want to maintain, if not deepen, the rules-based order for the competitive market economy and protect institutions that are critical for freedom. China is on a path of aggressive economic policies, and its behavior in many areas, including industrial and export subsidies, intellectual property violations, and government procurement discrimination, cause huge unfairness in global competition. Compounding these concerns, China's increasingly assertive and confrontational posture toward its neighbors and Taiwan underscores the peril of Western economies' reliance on China.

Such dependence is not solely about the acquisition of particularly sensitive goods; it extends to a broader deleterious impact on global supply chains, affecting both upstream and downstream states with troubling dependencies on Russia and China. While Russia's role in Western-oriented supply chains may have diminished, with some countries still importing significant quantities of gas and raw materials, China continues to wield considerable influence across various sectors. Some of these sectors may not be strategically important, and if China weaponizes this particular import, it may not have much effect on the strength and security of the US and the EU. Unfortunately, there is also reliance on inputs and goods that are of strategic importance, and in these supply chains, the Chinese government can do significant harm to the resilience and stability of Western economies. Additionally, research and development and future technologies where China has begun to challenge the Western position in ways that exclude fair competition and transparency also raise the bar higher and could in some instances create a future dependency on China that will be concerning.

Furthermore, it is imperative to broaden the analysis concerning the extent of Western economies' exposure to these economic risks. The dependency extends beyond mere importation of goods; Western economies are increasingly intertwined with various sectors of the Chinese economy. To illustrate, consider two pivotal areas of direct reliance. Firstly, there is a growing dependence on Chinese technology—particularly in the realms of green and digital innovations—where the security of technological supply is becoming increasingly precarious. Secondly, both the United States and the European Union are progressively reliant on Chinese human capital and the outputs of Research and Development (R&D), spanning sectors from machinery to batteries and cutting-edge digital technologies. China has invested substantial resources into cultivating a robust human capital base and an R&D infrastructure that, in certain areas, rivals or even surpasses Western capabilities. The prolific generation of new ideas and the cultivation of human capital in the Science, Technology, Engineering, and Mathematics (STEM) fields have positioned China as a formidable competitor on the global stage. With China achieving a leading edge in selected technological domains, the United States and Europe may find their reliance deepening, driven by the superior and more sophisticated technologies offered by Chinese firms and engineers.

Technological advancements have paradoxically enhanced and complicated global trade dynamics. Innovations such as containerization, logistics management software, and digital platforms have significantly increased the efficiency and reach of global commerce. The proliferation of the internet and e-commerce platforms has democratized access to international markets, empowering small businesses to engage globally. Conversely, these technological advancements have also introduced new vulnerabilities. The digitalization of supply chains exposes them to heightened cyber threats and data privacy issues, introducing novel fragilities within the global trade infrastructure. This technological duality—as both a facilitator and a source of risk in global supply chains (GSCs)—underscores the necessity for comprehensive policy measures. Governments and international bodies must strive to capitalize on the benefits of technological advancements while also safeguarding against their risks. This necessitates the implementation of robust cybersecurity protocols, the assurance of data privacy, and the fostering of competition within digital marketplaces. Additionally, there is an urgent need to invest in technologies that bolster supply chain visibility, resilience, and sustainability. For instance, blockchain technology holds promise for securing supply chain data, enhancing transparency, and mitigating fraud. As we navigate the intricacies of the digital era, it becomes evident that technology will persistently influence the configuration of global supply chains. The challenge for policymakers is to cultivate an environment that stimulates innovation and competition while concurrently safeguarding economic security and consumer interests. Achieving this balance is crucial for managing the systemic risks that technological advancements introduce to the global economic framework.

Equally alarming is the increasing reliance on China through more indirect channels. For instance, China has cultivated strong trade relationships with various non-Western economies, becoming more strategically significant to these nations than either the US or the EU. This is evidenced by the magnitude of bilateral trade flows.

As a result, the growing gravitational pull of China's economic orbit has notably diminished the influence of Western economies in fostering good governance and institutional norms internationally. Additionally, China's expanding control over crucial trading routes has empowered it to act in ways that undermine the principles of open seas and jeopardize the stability of international trade infrastructures. Furthermore, China's increasingly aggressive geopolitical stances pose significant risks to American and European trade and technological dependencies on regions beyond mainland China. A pertinent example is Taiwan, particularly its role in the global semiconductor supply. While Taiwan has remained a steadfast partner in upholding key economic institutions and stable trading relationships, the aggressive posture of mainland China toward Taiwan threatens to disrupt the supply of critical technologies. Such dynamics highlight the complex challenges that Western policymakers face in navigating the geopolitical landscape shaped by technological advancements and shifting power balances. This underscores the need for a strategic approach that not only strengthens technological resilience and supply chain security but also addresses the broader geopolitical risks that are increasingly intertwined with global economic dependencies.

China's pivotal role in the global economy is unmistakable, and its refined supply chains and production innovation further amplify this significance. The adage 'If China sneezes, the world economy catches a cold' encapsulates the profound impact China can have. Should China engage in hostile actions prompting Western responses, the resulting decrease in output could plunge both Europe and America into a severe economic downturn. The world economy now hinges on a cooperative and rule-abiding China. When China deviates from international economic norms and fair competition, it inflicts damage on other nations. However, conflict with China is not inevitable. Increased integration and cooperation could be possible if China commits to transparent and fair trade practices and refrains from exerting undue influence through trade. Yet, such a shift seems unlikely in the current geopolitical climate, necessitating preparations to address these challenges.

What if China persists in its current trajectory, ignoring the established rules and norms of the global economic order? Political and business leaders in the EU, the US, and beyond have heightened their awareness of the risks associated with economic engagements with China, particularly post-Covid-19. These risks have been somewhat mitigated by China's economic slowdown and a shift towards economic isolationism, which has decreased the global economic dependence on China. Predictions about China's economic future suggest that its era of rapid catch-up growth is nearing an end. Measures like increased screening of foreign direct investment (FDI) from China have led to a noticeable reduction in investment flows.

However, many recent measures have had limited impact on the core issues and have inadvertently weakened the US and EU's ability to diminish strategic dependence on China. For instance, the US's broad application of tariffs on steel and aluminum has affected European allies as much as it has Chinese exporters. Similarly, provisions in the Inflation Reduction Act aimed at countering economic threats from China also disadvantage European producers. European strategies now emphasize economic autonomy and reducing vulnerabilities, yet many actions disproportionately affect the US and other allies rather than China directly.

This approach is unsustainable. It burdens economies and public finances and undermines any viable economic security strategy that isolates the US and EU from global trade networks, including those with allies. Such isolation only enhances China's role as an economic and security partner to other nations. If the US and EU continue to implement measures that weaken their own economic strength, they risk diminishing the economic foundation necessary to support robust military capabilities and strategic resilience.

Navigating the path forward

Addressing the intertwined issues of strategic dependency and economic vulnerability requires a multifaceted policy response that encompasses diversification of supply sources, investment in domestic capabilities, and international cooperation to ensure a more balanced and secure global economic landscape. The strategic recalibration involves not just reducing dependency on specific geopolitical actors but also enhancing the resilience and flexibility of supply chains to withstand future shocks. This includes fostering innovation, incentivizing domestic industries critical for economic and national security, and building alliances with like-minded nations to counterbalance the influence of geopolitical rivals.

The challenge ahead for policymakers is to navigate these complex waters with a strategy that balances economic efficiency with strategic security, ensuring that global supply chains serve not only as conduits of trade but also as pillars of a stable and secure global order. To create such a "blue" supply chain, in contrast to the China oriented "red" supply chain, it is as much about revitalizing domestic economic dynamism and building new alliances as it is in reducing Chinese and Russian influence in the transatlantic supply chains.

Addressing the complex task of reducing US and EU dependencies on critical goods, services, technologies, and supply lines linked to geopolitical adversaries, this book not only scrutinizes the sources of strategic economic vulnerabilities but also champions a path forward. It advocates for a sophisticated, inclusive strategy that fosters a diverse, competitive, and resilient integration with the global economy. It primarily investigates the sources of strategic economic vulnerabilities and explores impediments to enhancing its domestic production and diversifying away from China-centered supply and networks. The book also seeks to outline how best to resolve the challenges the transatlantic governments are facing to decrease Chinese influence on the economy. The underlying argument is that China has been utilizing its influence over trade to pressure states and companies to rebalance the international system. While acknowledging these challenges, the argument is that it is necessary to devise a broad, inclusive, and sophisticated strategy to ensure a diverse, competitive, and resilient integration with the world economy. Economic isolation will not make the EU, the US, or the international economy strong again, but increased market-economy based trade will be beneficial for most of the international actors.

The post-Cold War economic order have witnessed Western economies entrenching deeper into a dependency on geopolitical rivals, notably China and Russia, for essential goods, services, and energy resources. This interdependence, while fostering economic growth and globalization, has also entailed significant risks, revealing the fragile underbelly of globalized trade systems. China's role as the "world factory" and Russia's position as a critical energy supplier to Europe exemplify this dependency, which has evolved from economic choices aimed at leveraging comparative advantages. However, these dependencies are not merely economic transactions but strategic footholds that these nations can exploit, influencing Western economic stability and policy autonomy.

The economic risks stemming from this dependency are multi-faceted, affecting not only supply chain resilience but also economic sovereignty. The concentration of manufacturing in China and energy reliance on Russia has left Western economies vulnerable to unilateral actions by these suppliers, such as trade restrictions or supply manipulation. This vulnerability was starkly highlighted during the COVID-19 pandemic when disruptions in Chinese manufacturing had ripple effects across global markets, underscoring the precariousness of concentrated supply chains.

The strategic implications of such dependencies extend beyond mere economic considerations, touching upon national security, political sovereignty, and the global balance of power. The reliance on critical inputs and resources from geopolitical rivals gives these nations leverage over Western political and economic decisions, a form of "economic statecraft" that can be used to exert influence and pressure. Economic coercion, a nuanced but noxious tool of statecraft, has been increasingly employed by geopolitical rivals such as China and Russia to assert their influence on the global stage. This approach encompasses a broad spectrum of tactics, from imposing tariffs and trade barriers to leveraging control over critical resources like energy to exert political and economic pressure. The strategic deployment of these tactics underscores a broader intent to reshape international norms and power structures in favor of the coercing state. The implications of economic coercion extend beyond immediate economic impact, challenging the foundational principles of free trade and market openness. This form of coercion tests the resilience of global supply chains, forcing nations to confront the vulnerabilities inherent in their economic dependencies. The response to such coercion necessitates a strategic recalibration of policies to protect national interests while preserving the benefits of global economic integration.

Moreover, the shift of manufacturing bases to China has resulted in the erosion of domestic industries in the West, leading to a significant transfer of technological expertise and a loss of manufacturing capabilities. This not only affects current economic competitiveness but also long-term innovation potential, as the foundation for future technological advancements diminishes.

The erosion of technological leadership, particularly evident in the West's reliance on China in sectors like 5G, Artificial Intelligence (AI), and green technologies, represents a significant strategic risk. This dependency not only undermines the competitive edge of Western economies but also exposes them to potential espionage, data breaches, and other security threats.

External economic policy will play a key role in managing the economic threats from China, but the US and the EU will have to start from a new basis if they ever are going to succeed. First, the best way to manage international economic relations and economic statecraft is to have a strong economy that others want to engage with and fear being excluded from. America and especially Europe represent a rapidly shrinking share of global trade and economic output, and they need to reverse their relative economic decline by boosting rates of productivity and economic growth. The challenge from China can be managed, but if the basic premise is that Western economies will continue to underperform and have low growth rates, the China challenge will be substantially more difficult.

Likewise, the second-best way to manage international economic relations is to have strong domestic companies producing goods, services, and technologies that other countries need, and that there is a superior stream of new ideas and innovation from firms, universities, and the government that other countries want to access. In other words, a core part of a new economic strategy to manage China should be radical expansions of public and private spending on R&D. A third core ingredient is to nurture economic alliances and build new ones. The US and the EU need allies and deep economic partners, and there are many good candidates that has been neglected to some extent. However, general protectionism from the EU and the US, and their unwillingness to deepen economic relations with each other as well as with old and potentially new allies, is undermining their own economic power.

The economic version of the China challenge is thus bigger than just supply chains and can only be responded to effectively with policies that are less about trade. However, it is argued in this book that external economic and trade policies are crucial for an effective response to the threats coming from excessive dependency on the Chinese economy and suppliers. This is especially the case in some strategic goods. Dependencies in such goods and technologies on actors with hostile intentions that control critical, vulnerable, and essential nodes in an economic system are dangerous. This has been strongly reiterated as China discernibly succeeds in securing a key position in the crucial rare earths industry, as one example, which has only helped advance its strategic objectives. As a second example, the world's dependence on Russian oil and agricultural supplies provides Moscow with several opportunities to exploit its crucial position as a critical supplier to its strategic vantage, even as it invades Ukraine.

To that end, this book will examine the transatlantic dependency on China and trace its evolution as dominant player in the global supply chains. It will further analyze the significant challenges and opportunities pertaining to supply lines that are impacting the economy and the security of the US and the EU in a significant way. Lastly, by analyzing approaches like reshoring, nearshoring, and China Plus One strategies, this book will primarily argue for the need to develop a viable alternative to China-oriented supply chains. It will do so by employing a sophisticated portfolio combining off-shored, nearshored, and reshored nodes to strike a balance between economic efficiency and national security. However, at the core is the basic view that the best external economic policy in the EU and the US to reduce dependency on China is to deepen economic relations with allies and friendly nations – and between each other. If there is one low-hanging fruit, it is to advance deeper transatlantic trade relations and ultimately form new trade agreements that free up trade and reduces trade costs between America and Europe.

At the heart of this book is the proposal to establish new Transatlantic leadership for trade and supply chains that put American and Europe in a position of better security, if you will a blue supply chain. Obviously, if both sides could do this on the back of a strong and less overregulated and complacent economy, that would boost their security efforts substantially. The best way to command authority in the global economy is to have high and dynamic growth. We focus on ten points.

1. **New trade alliance.** The EU and the US should establish a new trade alliance for allies and free market democracies that eliminates tariffs and reduces regulatory friction and creates more stable and reliable supply chains. This is the best starting point for establishing new rules that effectively will discriminate Chinese and Russia goods

and services in sectors of strategic importance. While it is unrealistic to go for regulatory harmonization across the board, it is perfectly achievable to establish mutual recognition agreements (MRAs) in selected sectors – building on already existing MRAs between the EU and the US. In the first place, such an agreement would reallocate substantial amounts of trade with China to trade within the new alliance and generally reduce the economic significance of China for partnering countries. Moreover, on the basis of a trade agreement, the EU and the US could also give substantial trade preferences to each other – reducing the risks in a high trade exposure to China and other countries that are hostile to Western economic and security interests.

2. **Constructive trade engagement.** The EU and the US should also seek and deepen constructive trade arrangements with other countries that will not be capable of joining the new trade alliance. It is of particular importance to do this in the Asia-Pacific region and avoid that China takes a leading role in the trade arrangements emerging there. For instance, both the US and the EU should apply to join the Comprehensive and Progressive Agreement for Trans-Pacific Partnership (CPTPP) – once an American initiative – and prevent China from taking up a leadership position in the region's trade policies. Both sides should also deepen the relationship with India in strategic sectors, for instance telecom and energy policies. Signing (or, in Europe's case, approving) new

trade agreements with countries in Latin America and Africa are also part of a programme for constructive trade engagement. The broader point is this: reducing the China threat cannot be done if the EU and the US continue to retreat into economic isolationism because that will only embolden China and make it stronger in the global economy.

3. **A Transatlantic Defense Advanced Research Projects Agency (DARPA) for research and innovation.** The EU and the US should establish a new body to collaborate on research and innovation for future technologies of core importance to national security – including materials, space, computing power, semiconductors, and advanced weapon systems. This initiative should be well-funded and connect researchers across the Atlantic in coordinated and concentrated areas. It can build on already existing initiatives at NATO and generally draw in the NATO infrastructures, including the countries that are close partners of NATO. Moreover, it should include the expansion of universities across borders – for instance having leading US universities being invited to establish in European countries.

4. **Boosting Research and Development (R&D).** The chief long-term strategy to protect economic and security interests is to be at the frontier – ideally leading the frontier – of new knowledge and research. To that effect, the EU, in particular, needs to boost R&D

spending – public and private – and halt the degradation of its universities. It is far away of reaching its goal of total R&D spending of 3 percent of GDP. This was a target established a long time ago, based on an economy that was less knowledge intensive than our current one. A better target now is to have R&D spending at levels of 5 percent of GDP or more by 2040. While the US spends more on R&D, it also needs to rise to the challenge.

5. **Global Gateway initiative.** The EU and the US should coordinate current and new efforts to have better control of key global trading routes and infrastructure. Building on existing resources, they can establish a new investment bank that is well funded to invest in new trade infrastructure in especially the Asia-Pacific and MENA regions. Stronger naval presence is also required in order to command authority over key sea routes – and it is especially important Europe rises to the challenge and become a supplier of protection and order of trading routes.

6. **Security principles for public procurement and system projects.** Both the EU and the US need to become more alert to security threats that are part of sectors strongly influenced by public procurement and system projects, including energy, telecom networks, and biomedicine. Companies that tender for these contracts should, at the minimum, be required to provide full transparency in ownership, links to governments,

and received subsidies. Moreover, there should also be principles that apply to the security of supply for critical products, including demands on when core, auxiliary, or just-in-time facilitates need to exist inside the territory of the procuring countries or close to it. This will add costs to public procurement, but there is no way around the fact that better supply security will entail higher costs.

7. **Ban China's State-owned Enterprises (SOEs) from doing business in the West.** Of particular concern for national security in the economy is the influence of China's SOEs in trade with the EU and the US. There is no reason for Western economies to accept SOEs to operate in their markets and supply chains when it is obvious that they are strongly connected to foreign state interests in countries that are on a collision course with the EU and the US.

8. **Like-by-like mechanism.** China is pursuing aggressive trade policies and closing its markets to Western suppliers. The EU and the US should respond in kind. Reductions in market access in China will immediately be responded to by trade restrictions on Chinese or other exporters. A trade restriction warning system can be established in the EU-US Trade and Technology Council (TTC) to quickly flag new restrictions and coordinate the response. This also applies to cases when China takes coercive action against a single country: the EU and the US will respond collectively and will full economic force.

9. **Trade and climate change.** There is a dire need for the EU and the US to agree on what trade or trade-connected policies that should be allowed for the reduction of carbon emissions. Now the two sides are on collision course, with the US using distorting subsidies and the EU going for carbon tariff-like policies. A Transatlantic trade war is going to emerge in the next ten years unless there is a change of course. An accord on what trade measures that are acceptable, and on what grounds, should include maintained preferential access between each other. If, for instance, the EU is concerned about subsidy discrimination in America, it should also offer the US to be exempt from EU measures in its Carbon Border Adjustment Mechanism (CBAM).

10. **A high-tech alliance.** Finally, it is tremendously important that the EU and the US pursue a high-tech alliance that establishes common standards in key fields of technology. This alliance will have to include cloud, AI and quantum computing, and general rules for how data should be governed. Currently, there is strong divergence in the high-tech field, leading to less capacity for both sides to avoid growing dependence on technology supply from third countries – including China. The EU is shooting itself in the foot by trying to reduce the presence of US technology companies in the EU and eroding the power of industry-driven, bottom-up European Standardization Bodies. Similarly, absence of policies in America and chaotic actions by its agencies create a wedge with all other

countries that are attempting structured policy solutions to new and emerging problems. A new high-tech alliance should deepen current efforts in the TTC to establish better norms and policies on export controls.

TWO
Supply chain challenges and opportunities

Trade, Sourcing and Supply Chains

Establishing itself as an indispensable hub in numerous manufacturing supply chains, China has markedly enhanced its prosperity, economic dominion, and geopolitical sway. Its evolution from a peripheral player to a central pillar of global manufacturing has not only transformed China's internal economic structure but also redefined its interactions on the world stage, amplifying its ability to exert influence across continents. The confluence of favorable production costs, a burgeoning business ecosystem, and strategic policy support has solidified China's status as the linchpin of international manufacturing. This strategic positioning facilitated Beijing's efforts to curtail external influences in sectors it had yet to dominate, showcasing a deliberate push towards self-reliance and increased control over its economic destiny.

On the back of Deng Xiaoping's economic reforms in the late 1970s, China became "the factory floor" of the world. These reforms unleashed a wave of industrialization and opened China's doors to international trade, setting the foundation for its meteoric rise as an economic powerhouse. Many factors contributed to this success: competitive labor costs, a growing business ecosystem, weak regulatory compliance, comparably low taxes and duties, competitive currency practices, and effective supply chains and production networks. They all conspired to make China a good place for outsourced manufacturing and a pivotal node in global supply chains.[2] In an ideal world characterized by transparency and fair play, China's ascent would be seen as a mere shift in global economic dynamics. However, the involvement of State-owned Enterprises (SOEs), coupled with unfair trade practices, political maneuvering, and issues of intellectual property theft, has cast a shadow over China's rise, turning it into a focal point of global concern and debate.[3]

Willy Shih, a distinguished professor at Harvard Business School, emphasizes the global economy's profound reliance on China, stating, '[t]he world is dependent on China for manufacturing.' This observation highlights the pivotal role China plays in sustaining global supply chains, in everything from textiles to advanced electronics to textiles, and underpins the country's notable

2   Prince Ghosh, "The Exodus of Chinese Manufacturing: Shutting Down 'The World's Factory'", Forbes, September 18, 2020, https://www.forbes.com/sites/princeghosh/2020/09/18/the-exodus-of-chinese-manufacturing-shutting-down-the-worlds-factory/?sh=375b3791c2f2. Gann D, Zhang MY, Dodgson M. *Demystifying China's innovation machine: Chaotic order.*; 2022. http://dx.doi.org/10.1093/oso/9780198861171.001.0001.

3   Cai M. Yasheng Huang, "Capitalism with Chinese Characteristics: Entrepreneurship and the State". *Journal of Chinese Political Science.* 2012;17(2):215-216. doi:10.1007/s11366-012-9196-0

trade sector.[4] China's wide array of exports includes half a trillion of exports to the US[5] and 500 billion EUR worth of goods to the EU.[6] In fact, China is the top import source for countries like the US, Japan, Vietnam, South Korea, Germany, Netherlands, the United Kingdom, India, Singapore, Malaysia, Australia, and more, reinforcing Beijing's economic prowess and its deep-seated integration with the global economy.

The economic reforms initiated by Deng Xiaoping marked a seismic shift, propelling China from its traditional agrarian roots into an industrial colossus. This transformation not only reshaped China's domestic landscape but also reconfigured the global economic hierarchy, embedding China firmly at the heart of international trade and manufacturing. The country's GDP grew more than tenfold since 1978 and this transformation was supported by significant investments in manufacturing capabilities, a competitive labor market, and the strategic control of critical raw materials, particularly rare earth metals essential for modern technology. China's ambitious ten-year plan launched in 2015 aimed to further modernize its manufacturing sector to compete globally, underscoring its intention to transition from a quantity-focused to a quality-focused manufacturing giant.[7]

Today, China holds a pivotal role in key global supply chains,

4   Yasmeen Serhan and Kathy Gilsinan, "Can the West Actually Ditch China?", The Atlantic, April 14, 2020, https://www.theatlantic.com/politics/archive/2020/04/us-britain-dependence-china-trade/610615/

5   USTR, "The People's Republic of China" https://ustr.gov/countries-regions/china-mongolia-taiwan/peoples-republic-china, March 2024.

6   "China-EU-international trade in goods statistics", Eurostat, March 2024, https://ec.europa.eu/eurostat/statistics-explained/index.php?title=China-EU_-_international_trade_in_goods_statistics#EU_and_China_in_world_trade_in_goods.

7   Yao K. "China increasingly ambitious with 2023 growth target, may aim for up to 6%". *Reuters*. https://www.reuters.com/world/china/china-increasingly-ambitious-with-2023-growth-target-may-aim-up-6-sources-2023-03-02/. Published March 2, 2023.

extending from critical minerals to pharmaceuticals. Its manufacturing sector produces roughly half of the world's steel, aluminum, and cement, and leads in the production of coal, manganese, lead-zinc, antimony, and tungsten. The strategic importance of China's manufacturing sector is further highlighted by its strong market share in green technologies such as solar cells and wind turbines, aligning with global environmental goals. China's global influence is not limited to manufacturing; it extends to being the largest trading partner for many countries and leading on new trade initiatives like the Regional Comprehensive Economic Partnership (RCEP). This extensive influence grants Beijing significant geopolitical leverage, shaping global economic dynamics.[8]

As a response President Biden introduced in early 2021 an "Executive Order on America's Supply Chains" to examine the country's over-reliance on "competitor country suppliers" and vulnerabilities against global supply chain disruptions while highlighting a need for "a new approach" that would ensure a resilient and sustainable supply chain network.[9] This strategic directive aimed to rigorously scrutinize and address the United States' excessive dependency on suppliers from rival nations, particularly spotlighting the inherent risks and vulnerabilities this poses amidst the ever-present threat of global supply chain disruptions. It highlighted the country's reliance on certain critical supply chains such as semiconductor manufacturing, large capacity batteries, critical minerals and materials, and pharmaceuticals and active pharmaceutical ingredients (APIs), where a majority had a single source risk – China.

---

8   Ibid.

9   "Executive Order on America's Supply Chains", February 24, 2021, The White House, https://www.whitehouse.gov/briefing-room/presidential-actions/2021/02/24/executive-order-on-americas-supply- chains/

Parallel efforts have been undertaken within the European Union to map and mitigate economic vulnerabilities. The European Commission, in a comprehensive analysis, identified 137 products within critical ecosystems where the EU's dependency on imports from non-member countries is particularly pronounced. This initiative reflects a proactive approach to understanding and addressing the complex web of dependencies that characterizes the EU's trade relationships.[10] This was the first in a series of analyses that have taken stock of vulnerable important dependencies in Europe, and the initial work has shown that, out of these imports, 52 percent of the dependent products were imported from China.

While these policy initiatives reflect a strategic recognition of supply chain vulnerabilities, their effectiveness is subject to debate. The complexity of global supply chains and entrenched dependencies on countries like China for critical materials and manufacturing capabilities pose significant challenges, but there is also arguments that the complexity of the supply chains in themselves are the reason for the weakness of the international system and, in liaison with political instability, cause profound risks to the system itself.[11] Research indicates that while the concepts of reshoring and diversifying supply chains hold theoretical appeal, their practical application is fraught with complexity. Achieving the twin goals of independence and resilience through these strategies presents a myriad of challenges, underscoring the intricate nature of untangling established global supply networks that include a large economy like

---

10   "Commission Staff Working Document: Strategic dependencies and capacities", European Commission, May 5, 2021, https://ec.europa.eu/info/sites/default/files/swd-strategic-dependencies-capacities_en.pdf.

11   James Richards, *Sold Out*, Portfolio/Penguin, London 2022.

China.[12] For instance, the COVID-19 pandemic has underscored the fragility of "just-in-time" supply chains and highlighted the need for "just-in-case" strategies that prioritize resilience over efficiency – or at least prompts companies to keep stocks of necessary supplies.[13] However, the transition towards more resilient supply chains is fraught with challenges, including higher costs, the need for significant investment in technology and infrastructure, and the political and economic implications of decoupling from established trade relationships.[14]

Furthermore, integrating sustainability and digital transformation into the fabric of supply chain resilience strategies not only broadens the scope of these initiatives but also introduces a new dimension of complexity. These elements demand substantial investments in cutting-edge technologies, the cultivation of new skill sets, and the establishment of supportive regulatory frameworks, all aimed at fostering environmentally sustainable and technologically advanced supply chains. These include the need for substantial investments in digital technologies, the development of new skills and capabilities, and the creation of regulatory and policy frameworks that support sustainable supply chain practices.[15] Given that

12   Das D, Datta A, Kumar P, Kazancoglu Y, Ram M. "Building supply chain resilience in the era of COVID-19: An AHP-DEMATEL approach". *Operations Management Research.* Published online July 6, 2021. doi:https://doi.org/10.1007/s12063-021-00200-4

13   Li X, Ghadami A, Drake JM, Rohani P, Epureanu BI. "Mathematical model of the feedback between global supply chain disruption and COVID-19 dynamics". *Scientific Reports.* 2021;11(1). doi:https://doi.org/10.1038/s41598-021-94619-1

14   Magableh GM. "Supply Chains and the COVID 19 Pandemic: A Comprehensive Framework". *European Management Review.* 2021;18(3):363-382. doi:https://doi.org/10.1111/emre.12449

15   Xu X, Sethi SP, Chung SH, Choi T. "Reforming global supply chain management under pandemics: The GREAT 3Rs framework". *Production and Operations Management.* 2022;32(2). doi: https://doi.org/10.1111/poms.13885

more than 22 percent of the global GDP is intricately linked to the digital economy, any strategic shift in supply chain management must account for the rapidly evolving digital landscape—a domain where China's influence is progressively expanding. This reality underscores the need for a strategic approach that considers the digital economy's pivotal role in global commerce and China's growing dominance within this sphere.

Analyzing supply chain vulnerabilities requires a broader and more nuanced examination: there lies a significant risk of misdiagnosing the core issues if the analytical focus is either too myopic or overly broad. A balanced and comprehensive analysis is essential to accurately identify and address the multifaceted challenges inherent in global supply chain dependencies. For instance, many of the products where Europe has a vulnerable dependency cannot be called important or strategic. Figures 1 and 2 show the result of the actual import dependency for the EU for more 9000 product categories, taking stock of the extra-EU imports (it is lower in many categories if intra-EU imports are included) and the concentration rate (using the HHI index) in that import. The level of trade dependency is allocated into a quadrant of four categories, with one of the categories (High Dependency) meaning that EU imports are not just high but concentrated to one country. Out of a myriad of products that the EU imports, it has high dependency in a bit more than 280 products. China represents 21 percent of these goods. The list of goods includes many products that are insignificant – e.g. bamboo and ginseng – and that the EU can easily function without in the event that China is weaponizing its exports.

Figure 1: EU import dependency in goods (2022)

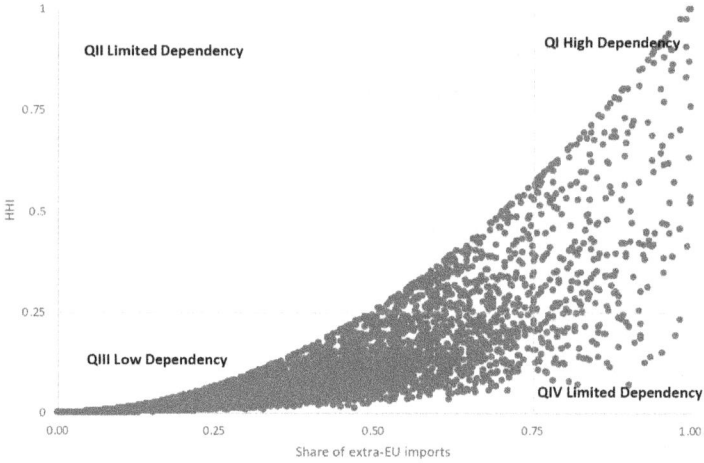

Source: Authors' calculations based on Eurostat

Figure 2: Share of EU imports value of High Dependency Products (QI) in 2022 by country

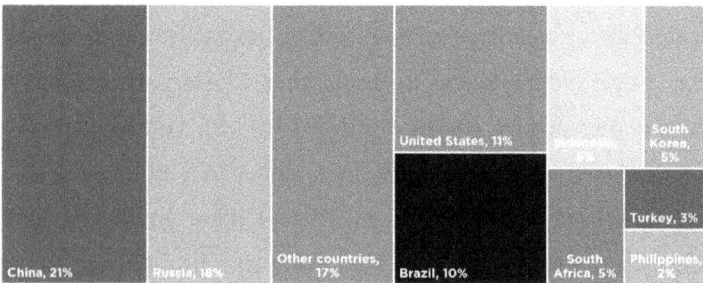

Source: Authors' calculations based on data from Eurostat.

However, this list of goods also includes very important goods that are relevant for economic development and strategy, including chemicals, active pharmaceutical ingredients (APIs), renewables, and – importantly – critical raw materials like rare earths. China has already proven itself capable of using various forms of export restrictions to deny access to such goods for certain countries, and that is a big problem for individual companies as well as for countries. With high levels of trade concentration, it is difficult to diversify imports by buying more from other countries instead of China, and access restriction can ultimately lead to supply restrictions that make it impossible to produce downstream products that are competitive.

It is important to expand the analysis and not just look to trade concentration and dependencies for certain goods. A simple measure like this will not give sufficient understanding of current and potential problems. An expanded analysis will also include what has happened in sectors of Chinese dominance and how Chinese firms came to acquire a dominant position. Moreover, it will look closer at how certain goods are used by those who import it, and what it means for downstream competitiveness. This is where the risks associated with dependence on China start to become more worrying and why we also need to include goods where there is not high dependency on China but where Chinese firms are strong internationally.

While some parts of China's emergence as a global trading power is related to the economics of specialization and opportunity costs, the result of trade concentration is that there is also a reallocation of knowledge, human capital, R&D, and investment. It is not just production that has changed but also who produces and what knowledge they possess about production conditions. These broader aspects of industrial structure and organization are important in light of the more significant need to manage risks related to trade – and societal resilience more generally. China is rarely alone in the global economy of having the knowledge and industrial infrastructure to produce a particular good, but they often represent a share of global output that is worryingly high and there is a concentration of production factors that make it hard for others to start or expand production if this is needed.

In some sectors, China's rise to eminence has also happened on the back of substantial government support and practices that distort free competition. While these factors alone are not sufficient to explain Chinese competitiveness in a sector, they cannot be dismissed and they have helped to force economic reallocation that is not healthy. Medical technology is one example. China has for a long while nurtured domestic companies and helped them to build up a market share in China with subsidies and to export to third markets by dumping prices. Moreover, companies from the US and Europe have been elbowed out from important government contracts or forced to transfer technology in a dangerous way for their long-term competitiveness. The unfair and non-transparent government involvement should be a major concern for government and businesses alike,

Delving deeper into the example of medical technology reveals China's growing influence: between 2015 and 2020, China's importation of medical devices expanded at an annual rate of nearly 9 percent, surpassing global growth rates. This trend not only highlights China's burgeoning role as a critical market for medical technologies but also underscores the strategic importance of this sector within the broader context of global health and innovation. In 2019, the Chinese medical equipment market reached 25 billion euro.[16] China has thus become a market that foreign manufacturers and governments cannot afford to ignore. However, as was outlined above, the medical technology sector, like most sectors of the Chinese economy, is subject to a distinctive regulatory and competitive environment that is crucial for the evolution of this sector, and decidedly controlled by the Chinese government.

American and European firms are global leaders in medical technologies and the main exporters of these goods to China – with Europe representing 34 percent of all Chinese imports, followed by US and Japanese firms with 29 percent and 10 percent of Chinese total foreign purchases of medical technologies, respectively. As can be seen in Figure 3, China's imports of medical technology from the EU have grown significantly: from 0.6 billion euro in 2001 to 6.1 billion euro in 2020 which represents an average annual increase of 14 percent. This increase in exports occurred in a context of growing Chinese imports of medical technologies, rising from 1.9 billion euro in 2001 to 18 billion euro in 2020. Over time, the EU's market share of Chinese imports of medical technology have been relatively stable, albeit rising from 30 percent in 2000 to 34 percent in 2020.

As Figure 3 suggests, something has happened in recent years to change the path of trade in China's medical technology market. Like the growth of EU exports to China, Chinese exports of medical technologies to the EU and the world have also increased, particularly between 2019 and 2020. But Europe's exports to China dropped and China's exports to the EU increased remarkably.

---

16   Fitch Solutions, *Medical Devices Factbook 2021*, Healthcare Expenditure.

Figure 3: EU and Chinese exports of medical technologies (2002-2020, billion euros)

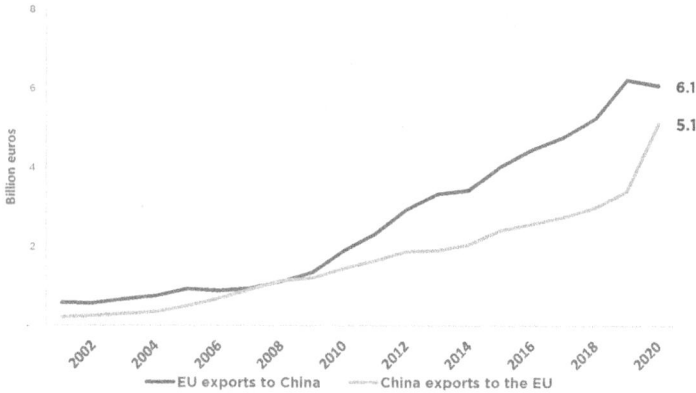

Source: ITC based on UN COMTRADE.

It is important to pay closer attention to what has happened in Chinese imports. Chinese imports of medical technology goods from the EU have declined in the past year. Chinese imports from some other countries such as the United States or Switzerland show a similar trend. What is equally remarkable, if not more, is that the fall in Chinese imports of medical technology can especially be observed in the medical technologies that went through centralized state procurement. Products like syringes, needles, catheters, artificial joints, and pacemakers have experienced a steady fall in their annual growth of imports since 2015. In 2020, it turned negative (see Figure 4). At the same time, Chinese total exports of these products between 2015 and 2020 showed positive growth. These figures indicate that Chinese companies are not only substituting foreign goods for domestic production, but they are also gaining market shares abroad. This is, for instance, the case of Chinese manufacturers of pacemakers that, whilst representing a small share of global sales, saw their global exports between 2015 and 2020 grow by 110 percent while sales of foreign manufacturers of pacemakers to China increased by just 2 percent during the same period.

So, what has happened? New products and innovation in the medical sector cannot explain this change. One key explanation is that China started to use a different policy for government procurement of medical technologies and moved to a system of volume-based pricing that clearly advantages local firms that can supply more volumes and at lower costs because they receive subsidies. Forced price cuts made it impossible for many European and American firms to continue selling their products and being part of various tenders by local, regional and central government in China. In a stroke, China could improve its international market position in medical technology in a remarkable way.

Figure 4: Chinese global trade balance for medical technology goods subject to centralized state procurement (2001-2020, billion euros)

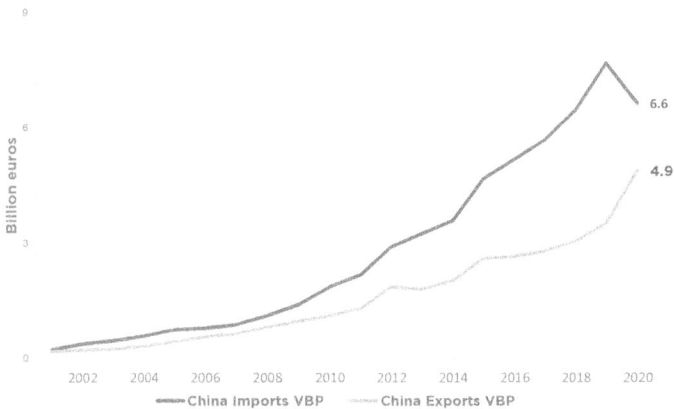

Source: ITC based on UN COMTRADE.

A poignant example of China's strategic industrial policy is evident in the solar panel sector. Although Chinese manufacturers are renowned for their efficiency and competitive pricing, it's imperative to recognize that their position on the global stage has been significantly bolstered by substantial government support.[17] This state support has not only facilitated China's dominance in the renewable energy market but has also raised concerns about market distortions and the implications for international competition. It used to be a strong sector for Europe, with many countries in the region having competitive producers that had invested a lot in R&D and technology. Now the sector has largely been hollowed out and Europe is completely dependent on Chinese manufacturers for the supply of solar panels. This development was not entirely the result of free and fair competition: it cannot be understood without the subsidies handed to solar panel manufacturers by Beijing and provincial governments. True, a substantial part of this supply comes from Chinese manufacturers that have invested in Europe to have local assembly there, driving down the actual import dependency. While Chinese firms that have invested outside of China are more difficult for Beijing to use for trade manipulation, they are still susceptible to the political influence of the country. In other words, a country can be dependent on China even if it does not look that way in import data.

Some numbers add more concern, as in the solar panel example. The market for these products was taken over by Chinese manufacturers which saw their share of global exports increase from 4 percent in 2002 to 42 percent in 2019. Currently, China is the most important global exporter of solar panels, exporting 21 billion euro

---

17   Nahm, J. (2023), *How Solar Developed from the Bottom-up in China*, University of California Institute on Global Conflict and Cooperation.

of these products in 2019. As a result, the Chinese solar panel industry has become an indispensable partner for the decarbonization of electricity in many developed countries. In 2019, the EU and Japan imported 45 percent and 62 percent, respectively, of their solar panels from China.

The Chinese success in this sector did not come from business prowess alone. In its 11th Five Year Plan (2006-2010), the Chinese Government provided subsidies and favorable access to credit in order to help Chinese solar companies to become leaders in the global solar market. In addition to subsidies and credits, the Chinese Government encouraged joint ventures with Western companies and tightened its control over Chinese raw materials that were essential in the production of solar panels. Meanwhile, between 2010 and 2019, EU export of solar panels declined by 63 percent and EU's market share on world exports of this product went from 23 percent to 10 percent. The EU has been fully aware that Chinese subsidies have damaged Europe's solar industry and imposed anti-dumping measures.[18] The emphasis on photovoltaic (PV) technology development, supported by substantial R&D investments, has led to considerable advancements in solar cell efficiency and production techniques. Chinese firms have contributed to setting new benchmarks for solar cell efficiency, pushing the global industry towards more sustainable and cost-effective solar energy solutions. The rapid technological evolution within China's PV sector underscores the

---

18   Solar panels are defined as "Photosensitive semiconductor devices, including photovoltaic (PV) cells whether or not assembled in modules or made up into panels; light emitting diodes" which corresponds with 854140in HS-2002 nomenclature.

country's ambition to lead in global renewable energy technology.[19] The trend is similar in large parts of the green sector, even if the EU and the US is not a dependent on all sectors, the Chinese are pushing forward a technological development that could create a new dependency.

This path towards higher value-added and local content has led to Chinese manufacturers exporting goods like machinery and machine tools that were mainly exported by European, American and Japanese companies in the past. For instance, Chinese exports of machinery and equipment in 2019 equaled 227 billion euro and it has increased by 208 billion euro since 2002.[20] Chinese exports of machinery and equipment now represent 17 percent of global exports and China is now the main foreign supplier of these products for many countries, like the European Union and Australia. Furthermore, government subsidies have been a key ingredient behind the growth in foreign sales in the country's machinery industry.[21]

The trajectory toward increased global dependency on China is poised to intensify with the 'Made in China 2025' (MIC 2025) initiative. Launched in 2015, this ambitious program is designed to catapult Chinese firms to the forefront of high value-added manufacturing sectors, positioning them as global leaders. This strategic pivot not only signifies China's intent to ascend the value chain but also underscores the potential for reshaping global trade dynamics and competitive landscapes. In 2020, President Xi Jinping vowed

---

19   Zhao F, Bai F, Liu X, Liu Z. "A Review on Renewable Energy Transition under China's Carbon Neutrality Target". *Sustainability*. 2022;14(22):15006. doi:https://doi.org/10.3390/su142215006

20   ISC Rev 3. Manufacture of Machinery and Equipment N.E.C. Code 29.

21   Szamosszegi, A., Anderson, C., & Kyle, C. (2009). "An Assessment of China's Subsidies to Strategic and Heavyweight Industries". Washington, DC: United States-China Economic and Security Review Commission.

that the government would be doing more to support strategically important sectors – specifically robotics, biomedicine and medical technology.[22] Implied by the name 'Made in China', this initiative puts an emphasis on industrial policy that is preferential to Chinese domestic producers, while often discriminating against foreign manufacturers. China's industrial policy has already been widely criticized for distorting free and fair competition, and the impacts of it can be seen in the shrinking role of the EU in global value chains. While EU trade integration with China is increasing, the EU's external competitiveness has been undermined in several sectors.[23]

In response to the profound reliance on China, a critical debate has emerged within the US and the EU regarding strategies to mitigate this dependency. Central to this discussion is the concept of reshoring critical supplies through the establishment of domestic processing operations. This strategic consideration reflects a growing recognition of the vulnerabilities inherent in current supply chain configurations and the need for a more resilient and self-sufficient approach to securing essential goods and services. However, considering the financial and technical infeasibility and how China has utilized price dumping as a strategy to remain in a central position,[24] Washington and Brussels have been in a difficult spot to address the question of how to address the vulnerabilities in the event of a major supply disruption. The US and the EU face significant hurdles

---

22 Xinhua News (2020, March 23rd), "Xi stresses Covid-19 scientific research during Beijing inspection". https://www.tsinghua.edu.cn/en/info/1399/9816.htm

23 Garcia-Herrero, A. and Martinez Turegano, D. (2020, November 27th) "Europe is losing competitiveness in global value chains while China surges." Bruegel. Accessed at: https://www.bruegel.org/2020/11/europe-is-losing-competitiveness-in-global-value-chains-while-china-surges/

24 "China's Dumping Undermines free and fair International Trade?", Aegis Europe, February 2016, http://www.aegiseurope.eu/news/chinas-dumping-undermines-free-and-fair-international-trade.

in mitigating vulnerabilities against major supply disruptions. This predicament underscores the complexity of reconfiguring supply chains that are deeply entrenched in the current global manufacturing paradigm, necessitating innovative approaches to enhance resilience. China's strengthened regulation of critical industries, as well as the practice of encouraging SOEs to purchase key companies internationally to control technology, suggests a coordinated effort to control the flow of strategic material. Against this backdrop, the urgency for the US and EU to offset potential vulnerabilities is greatly enhanced.

Further, the viability of an open and unrestricted approach and how best to approach the central position China now occupies within the global supply chain network has also been the subject of debate. This has touched not only on production and transportation but has also put light on dependencies in services. For instance, the Australian government has already commissioned a vital study of Vulnerable Supply Chains.[25] This report looks at the nature and sources of risks for supply chains and takes a broad approach in outlining how Australia can increase the country's national security. Unsurprisingly, the study's findings indicate that dependency on *single sources of production* have increased Australia's vulnerability and lends credibility to the notion that other countries have been subjected to similar developments.

For its part, Beijing has already begun to increase its supply chain security and enforced new regulations forcing companies and provincial officials to be cautious and reduce certain dependencies – especially on the United States. Moreover, the country's

---

25 Australian Government, "Production Commission, Vulnerable Supply Chains", Production Commission Interim Report, March 2001, Canberra.

dual circulation strategy underpins future growth plans and seeks to develop domestic production and supply system in critical areas to offset vulnerabilities, affecting the seamless functioning of foreign business within its territory and impacting international supply chains.

The US, along with other countries, has also long criticized China over its trade policies. The US Trade Representative's report in March 2018 elucidated China's continued "unfair, unreasonable, and market-distorting practices", which were at the heart of the US-China trade conflict.[26] China's sustained practice and support for cyber theft of US intellectual property and continued discriminatory technology licensing has attracted significant attention amidst the imposition of tariffs by Washington. US-China economic relations have been marked by transfers of technology and manufacturing capacity to China, substantial financial investment in China, and the emergence of an unbalanced bilateral trade relation. These developments have contributed to American economic and national security concerns and have had an immense impact on the global supply chains, leading manufacturers to divert trade in search of tariff-dodging workarounds. These have called for the development of a sophisticated strategy by collaborating with countries that can take up labor intensive assembly activities in a cost-effective manner while bringing back some vital production to the US.

Another major challenge to effectively developing a successful alternative to China is the divide within the EU. Despite growing

---

26 Findings of the Investigation into China's Acts, Policies, and Practices Related to Technology Transfers, Intellectual Property, and Innovation Under Section301 of the Trade Act of 1974, , OFFICE of the UNITED STATES TRADE REPRESENTATIVE EXECUTIVE OFFICE of the PRESIDENT, March 22, 2018, https://ustr.gov/sites/default/files/Section%20301%20FINAL.PDF

suspicion of Beijing, there has been resistance, not least from some parts of the business community, to jeopardize economic interests in China. China's deep-seated economic relations with the EU have been enhanced as China has overtaken the US to become the EU's main trading partner in goods.[27] In fact, the bilateral trade between European countries like the Netherlands, Germany, France, Italy, Spain and China, concurrently highlights the monumental difference between the EU's trade with China and with the US, with the balance shifting towards the former.

It is crucial, when trying to shape new supply chains, to examine the major economies of Europe and their business communities. Conversations with German parliamentarians in 2021 suggested that the lack of credible alternatives or "models" was the primary reason for German reluctance to further distance themselves from China and move closer to the US. Similar responses were given in Paris and to a certain degree in Brussels, but the tone has changed significantly after the Russian full-scale invasion of Ukraine in 2022. There is now a greater understanding that dependencies on countries with markedly different economic models and potentially hostile intentions towards Europe and its partners cannot continue as they were. This said, the US and EU are not on the same page when it comes how they view China as an economic partner.

Credibility, sustainability and predictability will need to be included in discussions of alternative supply systems. It is imperative to understand that the European divide is not between the so called 17+1 Framework, that has turned into 14+1 to the dismay of China, and western Europe, or between China's major destinations of

---

27   "China overtakes US as EU's biggest trading partner", BBC, February 17, 2021, https://www.bbc.com/news/business-56093378.

investments in Europe (Germany, France, Sweden, and Italy) and the less "fortunate".[28] The current situation results from a complicated combination of factors, both political and economic, understanding the nuances of which is vital for an effective engagement. To be sure, China is having problems in Europe, but it is far from counted out as a business partner, and events in the US that threatens the security of European states have the effect of moderating China critics.

Another major, and often neglected, challenge to the reliance on China and other non-democracies is the relative economic decline of the US and the EU in favor of China and other emerging economies.[29] It will be essential for Europe and the US to prevent further relative decline by improving their economic competitiveness, but also their innovation ability. The Eurozone is particularly lagging, something that could potentially increase the rift between the US and the EU over time if Europe's declining growth make it to turn inwards and become hostile to deeper Transatlantic integration. That said, the US economy is also expected to decline relative to the Asian economies, both in terms of growth and innovation and it is not feasible to point to external challenges without considering the internal related to the supply chain security.

China's strong role in global supply and supply chain speaks to the country's noteworthy economic growth, which has coexisted

28 Laurens Cerulus, "Coronavirus Forces Europe to confront China dependency", Politico, March 6, 2020, https://www.politico.eu/article/coronavirus-emboldens-europes-supply-chain-security-jawks/; Patricia Van Arnum, "The EU's API Supply Chain Under Focus", May 19, 2021, ValueChainINSIGHTS, https://dcatvci.org/7143-the-eu-s- api-supply-chain-under-focus; Svante Cornell & Niklas Swanström, "Compatible Interests? The EU and China´s Belt and Road Initiative", Swedish Institute for European Policy Studies, Report no. 1, Stockholm, January 2020. https://www.sieps.se/en/publications/2020/compatible-interests/

29 Robert Kappel, "The Decline of Europe and the US: Shifts in the world Economy and in Global Politics", GIGA Focus, International Edition, Number 1, 2011, https://www.files.ethz.ch/isn/127602/The%20Decline%20of%20Europe%20and%20the%20US%20-%20Shifts%20in%20the%20World%20Economy%20and%20in%20Global%20Politics.pdf

with its inherently "undemocratic capitalist" nature. This has led to both admiration and concern, particularly regarding Beijing's true intentions.[30] Speculation about intentions has only grown with the onset of the Covid-19 pandemic, which drew greater attention to over-dependence on China-centered supply chains, not least in the medical field. The Covid-19 pandemic intensified the calls for diversifying supply chains away from China, particularly in the US and the EU, which was already gaining momentum as a result of the US-China trade conflict.[31]

However, this process has not been uncontroversial. Some American and European companies prefer a status quo scenario, at least in the short-term, of continued unrestricted engagement.[32] There are also good reasons for ensuring remaining sales by European and American firms in China. For instance, telecom companies have lobbied for the Chinese company Huawei to be allowed to participate in Europe's 5G rollout in an effort to protect European sales in China, this despite the already existing restrictions on foreign firms in China. This has somewhat changed after the Russian invasion of Ukraine in 2022, and there is a growing realization in most business sectors that dependency on China and Russia needs to decrease.

---

30 David Zweig, "Undemocratic Capitalism: China and the Limits of Economism", The National Interest, No 56, 1999, pp- 63-72; Jonathan Fenby, "Is lack of democracy a problem for China?", BBC, 19 January 2015, https://www.bbc.com/news/world-asia-china-30780040

31 Elaine Dezenski & John Austin, "Secure US Supply Chains With Allies, and Move Out of China", Barron's, 1 December, 2020,https://www.barrons.com/articles/secure-u-s-supply-chains-with-allies-and-move-out-of-china-51606860404

32 Andy Purdue, "Supply-chain restrictions on China actually hurt American companies", *Fortune*, May 9, 2021, https://fortune.com/2021/05/09/supply-chains-semiconductors-huawei-us-china/

Russia, the Global Supply Chains and the Ukraine Crisis

Russia, too, occupies a pivotal role in certain global supply chain networks, especially in hydrocarbons and some minerals and agricultural supplies. The geopolitical tensions and economic sanctions resulting from Russia's actions in Ukraine have further spotlighted the fragility of these supply chains, underscoring the need for strategic diversification and resilience planning to mitigate the risks of overreliance on a single country for essential commodities. In the last years, the already fragile and sensitive supply chains have faced tremendous challenges in the aftermath of the second Russian invasion of Ukraine in 2022.

Among the most pressing vulnerabilities is an overreliance in Europe on natural gas and crude oil from Russia, as well as dependence on Russia for key agricultural commodities (for example, fertilizers). Up to 40 percent of Europe's gas has come from Russia, and even while supplies to the US were low (about 3 percent of the country's supply), the effects remain substantial as the international prices skyrocketed.[33] According to the Food and Agriculture Organization of the United Nations, Russia and Ukraine account for more than 25 percent of the world's trade in wheat and for more than 60 percent of global sunflower oil and 30 percent of global barley exports. Russia is also a major global exporter of fertilizers, which

---

33 "How important is Russian oil and how high could prices go?", The Guardian, March 7, 2022, https://www.theguardian.com/business/2022/mar/07/how-important-is-russian-oil-and-how-high-could-prices-go.

means any supply shortages, or restricted access, could impact crop yields globally.[34]

It's not just oil and agricultural commodities that are under stress. As Deloitte noted in a recent report, "The principal reason that Russia plays above its weight is that it is a major exporter of some of the world's most important commodities."[35] Russia is a significant source of many of the 35 critical minerals that the US Department of the Interior (DOI) deems vital to the nation's economic and national security interests, including 30 percent of the globe's supply of platinum-group elements (including palladium), 13 percent of titanium, and 11 percent of nickel. Russia is also a major source of neon, used for etching circuits on silicon wafers. Palladium, a critical component of catalytic converters for cars, has climbed as much as 80 percent in price since the conflict started.

In fact, according to a report by Dun & Bradstreet, the international domino effect of global dependencies on businesses in the Russia-Ukraine region was felt immediately after the start of the war.[36] The report observed that, "Businesses around the globe continue to grapple with inflation brought on by the pandemic as well as commodity price increases brought on by disruptions to the supply chain. Furthermore, the report concludes that "Amidst this ongoing volatility are the new consequences arising from the Russia-Ukraine crisis that could leave the world facing extended reductions to energy

---

34 Jim Kilpatrick, "Supply chain implications of the Russia-Ukraine conflict", Deloitte, March 25, 2022, https://www2.deloitte.com/us/en/insights/focus/supply-chain/supply-chain-war-russia-ukraine.html.

35 Ira Kalish, "How sanctions impact Russia and the global economy", Deloitte Insights, March 15, 2022, https://www2.deloitte.com/us/en/insights/economy/global-economic-impact-of-sanctions-on-russia.html.html

36 "Global Business Impacts: Russia-Ukraine Crisis", Dun & Bradstreet, March 2022, https://www.dnb.com/content/dam/english/dnb-data-insight/DNB_Russia_Ukraine_Crisis.pdf.

supply, severe sanctions that will likely impact food security as well as rare metal supplies needed to sustain production of key technologies.

Where do we go from here?

Given the backdrop of these multifaceted challenges, the future landscape of Global Supply Chains (GSCs) stands at a crossroads. The path forward requires a concerted, multi-stakeholder effort to reconstruct supply chains that are not only resilient but also adaptable to the rapidly changing geopolitical and economic conditions. This entails a strategic blend of diversification, technological innovation, regulatory support, and international collaboration to forge supply chains capable of withstanding future disruptions while promoting sustainable and inclusive growth. The complexity and interconnectedness of modern supply chains require a comprehensive, multi-stakeholder approach to build resilience. By diversifying supply sources, embracing technological advancements, providing regulatory support, fostering collaborations, and investing in human capital, both governments and businesses can enhance their supply chain resilience. International collaboration will be a cornerstone of these efforts, as shared challenges necessitate shared solutions. Together, these strategies can mitigate the risks associated with current supply chain dependencies and capitalize on emerging opportunities for global supply chain restructuring, ensuring that supply chains are not only resilient but also sustainable and equitable in the face of future disruptions.

In the event of no change in the current China and Russia-dominated supply chains, the GSCs would likely be exposed to further vulnerabilities, both in critical and essential areas of national security. With supply chains remaining heavily dominated by China and, to a lesser extent, Russia, the global economy could find itself increasingly susceptible to a spectrum of vulnerabilities. These range from geopolitical leverage exerted by these countries to disruptions stemming from unilateral actions or broader conflicts. Such a scenario accentuates the urgent need for a strategic recalibration of global supply chains, emphasizing resilience, diversification, and the reduction of dependency on any single nation. As the pandemic has already exposed the risks of complex GSCs built on manufacturing practices controlled by China, and Russia's war worsened the situation further, a continuation of the current state of affairs might push the global economic infrastructure towards greater dependence on Beijing's and Moscow's political ambitions, particularly in the context of critical sectors like health, technology, military equipment, and more. Furthermore, owing to Chinas manufacturing capabilities, deep-seated economic integration, and developed production infrastructure, the sustenance of the current scenario would prevent companies from finding economic alternatives in the future. Russia on the other side is economically backward, with their strength in natural resources and sales of military equipment to second rate armed forces.

With the calls for moving away from China and Russia-centered supply chains picking up speed, one scenario could also be a complete decoupling, a strategy already explored in the case of Western relations to Russia. However, fully decoupling from China is a pipe dream because it would entail a severe decline in both global and Western living standards. It would also impede innovation and resource allocation in American and European economies. It would further threaten economic growth and business competitiveness, affecting global attractiveness and outreach. From a business point of view, complete reshoring of supply lines is bound to face challenges, such as a limited vertical ecosystem - in which particular the tooling capabilities might not be available locally and the skill base for certain kinds of manufacturing, like apparel production, might have waned. Problems such as not being able to meet projected cost reductions and automation challenges might further make the products less competitive.[37]

In the event of a "China Plus One" or a "Russia Plus One" economic strategy,[38] which some companies have already employed in response to the US-China Trade War in 2018, diversification would be a more plausible scenario. Nearshoring may occassionaly work with the Americas for the US, and Eastern Europe, Caucasus, the Middle East, and North Africa for the EU, allowing companies to adapt their production process to global markets by relocating some of their operations to a location closer to their final markets.

Identifying a viable 'plus one' destination presents its own set of challenges. The success of this strategy hinges on selecting a location with the necessary infrastructure to support immediate production needs or the agility to quickly adapt and develop new industrial practices. This decision-making process must carefully weigh the potential of each candidate against the strategic objectives of diversification and resilience. The new landscape would need to have a favorable political climate; for instance, a challenge faced by companies desiring to shift supplies to Vietnam has been corruption,

---

37 "Introduction to right-shoring", *Arrkgroup*, https://www.arrkgroup.com/thought-leadership/introduction-to-right- shoring/

38 China Plus One, sometimes referred to as Plus One, is business strategy aiming at avoiding investing solely in China and to diversify into other states to decrease dependency and reliance on the Chinese market.

lack of accountability, low transparency, and the challenges of dealing with a burdensome bureaucracy. Further, a new site would need to contain an emerging market and the ability to attract major customers. Moreover, this strategy, too, could undermine innovation, which could then hurt economic effectiveness and commercial impact. With this in mind, decoupling from China is neither possible nor in the interest of the transatlantic economies, but diversification of strategic and sensitive industries are definitely possible and necessary.

Many scholars have tried to make sense of the possibilities stemming from the call for diversifying away from China-centered supply chains. The Covid-19 pandemic interrupted many of the diversification strategies that had emerged before 2020. While some of the focus has been on the business sector's ability to diversify away from China, the discussion has brought in another dimension into the demand to diversify: the significance of supply chain resilience and the ability to adapt to unforeseen systemic shocks.[39] These changes have been spurred by federal and state law-making, as over-dependence of critical industries, such as technology, defense, and pharmaceuticals have begun underpinning national security implications, while some countries, particularly the US and in the EU have started to plan for greater control over critical supply chains.[40]

Another major approach that has been discussed as a response to over-dependence on the China-centered supply chains is reshoring, a practice of bringing manufacturing and services back home

---

39 Kenneth Rapoza, "New Data Shows US Companies Are Definitely Leaving China", *Forbes*, April 7, 2020, https://www.forbes.com/sites/kenrapoza/2020/04/07/new-data-shows-us-companies-are-definitely-leaving- china/?sh=79b3674640fe

40 Sarah Rathke "Do you expect a resurgence in reshoring to the United States? Why or why not?", Inbound Logistics, February 28, 2021, https://www.inboundlogistics.com/cms/article/do-you-expect-a-resurgence-in- reshoring-to-the-united-states-why-or-why-not/.

from overseas. This concept is not new. In their book *Bringing Jobs Back to the USA* from 2014, Tim Hutzel and Dave Lippert discussed five companies that chose to bring manufacturing back home due to not-so-positive experiences with offshoring.[41] Considering the market, delivery expectations, intellectual property, quality demands, shipping costs, currency exchange rates, and labor rates as factors, companies like Caterpillar, Master Lock, Neutex, General Electric, and Windstream Technologies started to employ a reshoring strategy. By and large, their strategies seem to have worked out well.

Examples of similar approaches can also be found in Europe, particularly in the wake of Covid-19. The European Parliament, for its part, examined the strategy for reshoring production back to Europe and put down its findings in a report.[42] It notably cast light on European companies already in the process of reshoring, for instance the Italian company DiaSorin which relocated part of its manufacturing back to Italy due to the risk exposure and supply disruptions. Fondazione Atagamma, an Italian association of 107 brands operating in the high-end of fashion, jewelry, design, food, hotels, automotive, and wellness industries has also decided to bring a significant part of its production back home. In a similar vein, the French Federation of Health Industries also documented similar developments.[43]

---

41 Tim Hutzel and Dave Lippert, *Bringing Jobs Back to the USA: Rebuilding America's Manufacturing through Reshoring*, CPC Press, Taylor and Francis Group: Boca Raton, June 12, 2014.

42 "Post Covid-19 value chains: options for reshoring production back to Europe in a globalized economy," European Parliament, March 2021, https://www.europarl.europa.eu/RegData/etudes/STUD/2021/653626/EXPO_STU(2021)653626_EN.pdf.

43 Paolo Barbieri, Albachiara Boffelli, Stefano Elia, Luciano Fratochhi, Matteo Kalchscmidt and Danny Samson, "What can we learn about reshoring afterCovid-19?", *Operations Management Research*, (13), August 11, 2020, pp. 131-136.

In essence, proponents of this approach acknowledge the core weaknesses of a lean global supply chain model overly relying on China and propose the localization of industries and their component supply chains to offset vulnerabilities, particularly in light of systemic crises. Andrew Fish and Honora Spillane of the Brookings Institution have argued that reshoring could not just address supply chain challenges, but also increase employment growth across industries and develop opportunities for US regions with economic fundamentals conducive to manufacturing.[44] There are also examples of successful nearshoring. For instance, Inditex, a Spanish apparel company nearshored 10 percent of its production to Morocco and Turkey,[45] while Whirlpool, an American multinational manufacturer, nearshored its operations to Mexico back in 1987.[46] Similarly, Boeing decided to nearshore its aircraft wiring plant to Mexico in 2020, while Toyota Motors, a Japanese automotive manufacturer, nearshored its second production to Thailand in 1996.[47] Under the Biden administration, the US has already incentivized "Made in USA" by pledging to support reshoring through a 10 percent tax credit for companies that create American jobs. The US Inflation Reduction Act has been premised on the same objective.

44 "President Biden to Sign Executive Order Strengthening Buy American Provisions, Ensuring Future of America is Made in America by All of America's Workers", *The White House*, January 25, 2021, https://www.whitehouse.gov/briefing-room/statements-releases/2021/01/25/president-biden-to-sign-executive-order- strengthening-buy-american-provisions-ensuring-future-of-america-is-made-in-america-by-all-of-americas- workers/.

45 "Fast fashion is turning into ultrafast fashion-report", *Inside retail*, May 29, 2017, https://insideretail.asia/2017/05/29/fast-fashion-is-turning-into-ultrafast-fashion-report/

46 "Electronics Manufacturing in Tijuana and Mexico: Advantages of Nearshoring in Mexico, Key Highlights and 2016 Industry Overview", *Co-Production International, Inc*, May 2016, https://www.coastlineintl.com/wp- content/uploads/2017/12/White_Paper_-_Electronics_Manufacturing_in_Mexico_-_CPI_- 01-11-2016.pdf.

47 "Boeing Aircraft Parts to be Manufactured in Mexico", *Airline Geeks*, July 16, 2020, https://airlinegeeks.com/2020/07/16/boeing-aircraft-to-be-manufactured-in-mexico/.

However, reshoring as a core strategy is neither easy nor cheap.[48] It just cannot happen across many sectors simultaneously because there is a shortage of key resources like labor. If, for instance, the US should nearshore a significant part of its manufacturing imports, it would have to reallocate labor from sectors that generate higher value added, better salaries and more prosperity. Nearshoring is not a value or a sustainable strategy in itself: it is a component in a broader development that has as its objective to cut dependence on hostile countries and riskful trade flows.

In other words, nearshoring would require enhanced production skills, significant investment of time and money, and it might not improve resilience.[49] A report by the European Parliament also concludes that the success of reshoring policies in Europe, the US and Japan have been modest, and promoting a proactive policy to mitigate security concerns regarding supply disruptions should be imperative. Thus, a more viable approach, as suggested by some, might be "rightshoring" rather than focusing only on reshoring, through "distributed manufacturing" or having several production units around the world, or as the study proposes, concentrating on "focused manufacturing" to prioritize focus on certain sectors and diversify accordingly.[50]

Returning to the "China Plus One" Model, which aims at reducing dependency on China but not breaking relations, it is notable

---

48 Enda Curran, "APEC Sees Challenges in Reshoring as Pandemic Hits Supply Chains", *Bloomberg*, May 27, 2021,https://www.bloomberg.com/news/newsletters/2021-05-27/supply-chains-latest-weighing-costs-and-benefits-of-reshoring

49 Willy Shih, "Bringing Manufacturing Back to the USIs Easier Said Than Done", *Harvard Business Review*, April 15, 2020, https://hbr.org/2020/04/bringing-manufacturing-back-to-the-u-s-is-easier-said-than-done

50 Brian Groom, "Reshoring: bringing manufacturing home", *Raconteur*, August 22, 2018, https://www.raconteur.net/manufacturing/reshoring-manufacturing-home/.

that many already practice this strategy. An increasing number of Western firms outsource from China because of security concerns or China's diminishing cost advantages, Thus, companies have been in pursuit of opportunities in emerging Asian markets while not completely decoupling from China. Western companies have been considering branching out to Asian countries like Vietnam, Indonesia, Thailand, or Myanmar, owing to a possible cost control, risk diversification, and new market access.

Southeast Asia has emerged as a compelling focal point for the 'China Plus One' strategy, attributed to the region's diverse economic landscape and specialized industrial capabilities. This strategic diversification aims to mitigate risks by complementing China-based operations with alternatives in Southeast Asia, thereby reducing dependency on a single market while leveraging the unique strengths of countries within this vibrant region. For instance, popular sportswear brands like Nike and Adidas have re-allocated the vast majority of their manufacturing and footwear base from China to Vietnam.[51] Thailand has also seen an increase in exports of about 19.7 % to the US, particularly in food, beverages and natural rubber manufacturing. Indonesia, and other Asian countries like India, as well as Mexico and Brazil, have witnessed increased attention through this approach.

Stuart Witchell and Philippa Symington take a similar approach but also point to the challenges each new country presents, making the pursuit of a reliable partner difficult.[52] In a similar vein, a study

---

51 Marc Bain, "To see Asia's manufacturing map is being redrawn, look at Nike and Adidas", *Quartz*, May 10, 2018, https://qz.com/1274044/nike-and-adidas-are-steadily-ditching-china-for-vietnam-to-make-their-sneakers/.

52 Stuart Witchell and Philippa Symington, "China Plus One", *FTI Journal*, February 2013, https://www.fticonsulting.com/~/media/Files/us-files/insights/journal-articles/china-plus-one.pdf

for the United Nations Conference on Trade and Development discusses the China Plus One strategy to be having the capability to strengthen regionalization of supply chains, while not underestimating the difficulties establishing a "plus one".[53] One problem in having plus ones is that most candidates have considerably smaller markets in relation to China. Other challenges abound: relatively underdeveloped infrastructure, relocation costs, unfamiliar local conditions, and additional operational costs.[54] These difficulties were especially noteworthy in efforts to do business in Vietnam, particularly while dealing with a complicated tax system, doing business in a country which maintains a cash-dependent economy, as well as major challenges with bureaucracy and transparency with lack of regulations, corruption, and notoriously weak intellectual property protection rights.[55] These issues were further aggravated by Vietnam's manufacturing sector suffering from supply chain problems due to Covid-19, which delayed the production of new phones for Samsung Electronics Co.[56] Thus, while the "China Plus One" strategy remains a significant approach to offset overdependence on China, this strategy alone will not sufficient for solving the purpose for all kinds of businesses and might require it to be combined with other approaches.

53 Peter Enderwick and Peter Buckley, "Rising regionalisation: will the post-COVID-19 world see a retreat from globalization?", *Transnational Corporations*, Vol. 27, no. 2, 2020, pp 99-112.

54 "Top challenges of doing business in Vietnam", *TMF Group*, February 15, 2019, https://www.tmf- group.com/en/news-insights/articles/2019/february/top-challenges-business-vietnam/

55 Kotaro Hosokawa, "Samsung Galaxy faces delays on Vietnam entry limit", Asia Nikkei, March 20, 2020, https://asia.nikkei.com/Business/Companies/Samsung-Galaxy-faces-delays-on-Vietnam-entry-limit

56 Daniel Runde and Sundar Ramanujam, "Recovery with Resilience: Diversifying Supply Chains to Reduce risk in the Global Economy", *CSIS*, September 2020, https://csis-website-prod.s3.amazonaws.com/s3fs- public/publication/200904_Ramanujam_GlobalSupply_v4.pdf

The most recent approach has been to prescribe collaboration between entities across the globe to ensure the resilience of GSCs. Daniel F. Runde and Sundar R. Ramanujam have outlined some ideas for this approach, working around the call to diversify sourcing, production, and distribution to countries and allies with similar interests and greater security.[57] This analysis prescribes considering countries like Bangladesh, India, Indonesia, and Vietnam for supply chain engagement, considering their economic transformation fostering openness and industrialization. It also provides a Five-Point plan of action, including: "The building of consensus through coordination, emphasis on diversification of sourcing, production, and shipping, develop capacity for new country alternatives, invest in trade facilitation initiatives, and ease Micro, Small and Medium sized Economies (MSME) transition with development finance."

Most of the above approaches include the need for greater diversification to avoid supply chain disruptions while suggesting an imperative to improve collaboration, which is global and not just restricted to Asia. The consensus among these strategies underscores the critical need for enhanced diversification and strategic collaboration to preempt supply chain disruptions. This dual focus not only aims to spread risk across a broader spectrum of sources and partners but also encourages innovation and agility within supply chain management practices, ensuring a dynamic response to global economic and geopolitical shifts. However, there remains a dearth of analysis that explores the possible collaborations in detail as an answer for resilience in supply chains which is deprived by disruption. Scholarship focusing on supply chain networks lacks analyses on current supply chain vulnerabilities and the possible solutions

---

57   Ibid.

to address risks, especially when combining these with geopolitical analysis. The solution is neither a pure openness regime nor a protectionist response, but a combination of policies to ensure national security and encouraging market-based change in business activity.

THREE

The US and the EU in a Changing Economic and Geopolitical Environment

The United States and Europe remain pivotal allies, in security policy and economic matters, supporting each other's market stability, economic foundations, and security frameworks. Their economies are intricately linked, with the transatlantic relationship fostering an economic powerhouse that generates over $6 trillion in commercial sales each year, supporting employment for approximately 16 million individuals in highly integrated job markets. This economic interdependence signifies not just a mutual reliance but also a shared commitment to sustaining the free world's economic and security order. It is the largest and wealthiest market in the world, accounting for half of the total global personal consumption and close to one-third of world GDP in terms of purchasing power.[58] Due to the Covid-19 pandemic, inflationary challenges, congested supply

---

58 "The Transatlantic Economy", *US Chamber of Commerce*, March 22, 2022, https://www.uschamber.com/international/trade-agreements/the-transatlantic-economy-2022.

chains, and war in Ukraine, the two sides of the North Atlantic are poised for remaining economic challenges throughout the 2020s, especially on the European side of Atlantic. That said, transatlantic trade and investment continue to grow, and sales through foreign subsidiaries have grown substantially too.[59]

The Biden administration brought new impetus to strengthening the transatlantic security alliance, marking a departure from previous tensions. Upon entering office, President Biden committed to revitalizing US alliances, emphasizing diplomacy and international collaboration as cornerstones of his foreign policy strategy. This pledge to mend and fortify the bonds with European allies was a significant step towards re-establishing the United States' role on the global stage as a leader committed to collective security and mutual respect.[60] Here, the Biden administration drove a significant focus toward the European countries, agreeing also to continue establishing a new form of bilateral economic and technological collaboration between the two sides in the Transatlantic Trade and Technology Council.

The full-scale invasion of Ukraine by Russia critically heightened the importance of transatlantic security cooperation. This event has not only underscored the geopolitical threats at Europe's doorstep but also catalyzed a deeper strategic partnership between the US and Europe, underscoring the urgent need for a unified stance against external aggressions and affirming the indispensable value of the NATO alliance. Policymakers in the Trump administration

---

59 Ibid.

60 Amanda Macias, "Biden vows to restore US alliances and lead with diplomacy in his first foreign policy address", *CNBC*, February 4, 2021, https://www.cnbc.com/2021/02/04/biden-vows-to-restore-alliances-in-first-foreign-policy-address.html.

had already acknowledged and recognized the prominent role that the European nations would play in a competition with China and help maneuver through an uncertain economic and security environment, where economics and technology would have to be given equal weightage as military balancing.[61] Despite successful groundwork laid in domains from trade agreements to 5G technology development, signaling the onset of a broader spectrum of competitive collaboration, the transatlantic partnership continues to confront substantial challenges. These hurdles range from regulatory divergences to philosophical differences on privacy, data protection, and digital taxation, illustrating the complex nature of US-EU relations in adapting to new economic and technological realities.

The transatlantic relationship has encountered turbulence due to significant divergences, particularly inflamed by the imposition of tariffs and persistent trade frictions. Moreover, regulatory developments within Europe, aimed at the digital services sector, have notably strained relations as these regulations seem all too often have been targeting American tech companies. These actions have not only spotlighted the regulatory and trade policy differences but also underscored the need for a harmonized approach to digital governance and trade practices that respect mutual interests and promote equitable market access. Further complicating the transatlantic dynamic are the differing strategies on addressing China's ascendancy on the global stage and managing the belligerence of an emboldened Russia. While the United States has adopted a more

---

61   Andrew Small, Bonnie Glaser, and Garima Mohan, "Closing the Gap: US-European Cooperation on China and the Indo-Pacific", *The German Marshall Fund of the United States*: Policy Paper, February 2022, https://www.gmfus.org/sites/default/files/2022-02/Small%20et%20al%20-%20China%20Indo-Pacific%20-%20paper%20NEW.pdf.

confrontational stance towards China's strategic ambitions, European approaches have varied, oscillating between engagement and caution. Similarly, responses to Russia's aggression have necessitated a delicate balance between deterrence and diplomacy, revealing a spectrum of perspectives within the transatlantic alliance on navigating these geopolitical challenges.

More importantly, there seems to be an increasing alienation between the US and the EU regarding the fundamentals of the transatlantic partnership, both at the levels of elites and mass opinions, and it is not certain that the transatlantic partnership will remain strong. Crucially, there's a growing sense that the foundational principles of the US-EU partnership are eroding.

This drift is not merely about policy disagreements but touches on deeper questions about the future direction and values of the transatlantic alliance. Whether it concerns security commitments, trade policies, or diplomatic strategies, there is an urgent need for reinvigorated dialogue and mutual understanding to arrest the divergence and renew the commitment to a shared transatlantic vision. In this context, how can the US and EU mobilize and align their policy and business interests to collaborate and reinvigorate the trans-Atlantic partnership? This chapter will delve into the imperative for the European Union to reinforce its partnership with the United States, building on their shared values of democracy, pluralism, and adherence to a rules-based international order. In an era marked by economic uncertainty and security concerns, this exploration is not just timely but essential. It will illuminate the strategic alignment and collaborative potential between the EU and the US, underscoring the importance of revitalizing their alliance to navigate the complexities of the contemporary geopolitical landscape effectively.

It would, most importantly, stress the need for an alternative blue supply chain focusing on trans-Atlantic cooperation.

Chalking out the Fundamental Challenges

The Transatlantic relationship is a cornerstone of the modern geopolitical and economic order, playing a pivotal role in upholding the principles of liberal democracy. This alliance, forged in the aftermath of World War II, has evolved into a multifaceted partnership that extends beyond mere geopolitical interests, underpinning the global economic system, ensuring collective security, and promoting democratic values and human rights. In an era marked by rising authoritarianism and complex global challenges, the resilience and adaptability of this transatlantic bond are more crucial than ever. Indeed, a fundamental necessity for the transatlantic partners has been to structure the Euro-American economic relationship with an eye to the emerging Chinese order and the growing Russian threat. However, a greater imperative for the US and EU has been to re-examine the evolving dynamics of the transatlantic trade and investment while addressing the deep-rooted structural challenges between the two partners, impacting the strategic dimensions of the alliance.

Notably, these challenges have been overshadowed by the discussions on exterior challenges of the transatlantic partnership. For over five decades, economic tensions have simmered between Europe and the United States, manifesting in disputes that span a wide array of issues from agricultural practices, such as the use of chlorinated chicken, genetically modified organisms (GMOs), and hormone-treated beef, to contemporary concerns over digital taxation and data privacy regulations. These conflicts highlight the underlying challenges in harmonizing regulatory standards and trade policies between two of the world's largest economic powers, reflecting broader debates over consumer protection, technological sovereignty, and the balance between free trade and regulatory oversight. Arguably, these flashpoints have emerged because of the deepening economic link across the Atlantic and have threatened to sour diplomatic relationships rather than reinforce them.[62]

These flashpoints were most visible and even strengthened during the Trump era and his "America First" approach to foreign policy. More so, unlike his predecessors, Trump, during the course of his presidency, rejected key foundations of the liberal international order as evidenced by his contempt for multilateral organizations, his deep mistrust in US traditional allies, and his unilateralist and transactional view of security and trade alliances. These were reflected, for instance, in Trump's 2019 Trade Policy Agenda,[63] which highlighted a few crucial points. First, the Trump administration defined the global trading system as "deeply flawed" and grounded on "outdated and imbalanced trade agreements" such as the North American Free Trade Agreement (NAFTA), which reduced US economic growth and market competition, thus harming US workers and businesses. Moreover, the international trade law embodied by the World Trade Organization (WTO) was deemed "failing" and inefficient because

---

62   Elmar Hellendoorn, "How the US and Europe should rethink their Economic Relationship in the Biden years", *The Atlantic Council*, December 17, 2020, https://www.atlanticcouncil.org/blogs/new-atlanticist/how-the-us-and-europe-should-rethink-their-economic-relationship-in-the-biden-years/.

63   "2019 Trade Policy Agenda", *Executive Office of the President of the United States, Office of the United States Trade Representative*, March 2019, https://ustr.gov/sites/default/files/2019_Trade_Policy_Agenda_and_2018_Annual_Report.pdf

of the difficulties the WTO faced in concluding rounds of multilateral trade negotiations".[64]

During President Trump's tenure, the United States took a dramatic turn away from its longstanding commitment to international cooperation, either withdrawing from or threatening to exit key international treaties and institutions that have been foundational to the rules-based global order. Actions such as abandoning the Paris Agreement on climate change, reneging on the landmark nuclear deal with Iran, and initiating a withdrawal from the World Health Organization amid a global pandemic, signal a shift towards a unilateral approach to foreign policy, raising concerns about the future of global governance and collaborative efforts to address common challenges.[65]

The Trump administration also outright declared that its ultimate goal was to rebalance all America's trade relationships to serve the US interests better. Specifically, this strategy also included pulling the US out of trade agreements deemed to be disadvantageous for America, such as the Trans-Pacific Partnership (TPP). Further, on June 1, 2018, President Trump imposed a 25% tariff on steel imports and a 10% tariff on aluminum imports from the EU under Section 232 of the Trade Expansion Act of 1962. This section allows the US President to request an investigation by the Department of Commerce about the effects of specific imports on the US national security. If any such effects are discovered, the President is allowed to take action to adjust the level of imports by increasing tariffs or

---

64 Ibid.

65 Alice Tidey, "How did US President Donald Trump impact Europe during his four years in office?", *Euronews*, January 19, 2021, https://www.euronews.com/2021/01/19/how-did-us-president-donald-trump-impact-europe-during-his-four-years-in-office.

imposing quotas.[66] In reaction to Trump's tariffs, the EU imposed retaliatory tariffs on selected US products.[67] In a major speech in the summer of 2018, former EU Trade Commissioner Cecilia Malmström argued that the EU "had no choice but to respond" to the US actions while stressing that the EU wanted to de-escalate tensions and return to the trade status quo as of January 2018, before the execution of punitive trade sanctions by the Trump administration.[68] This type of retaliatory actions between the US and EU does not only decrease the chances for cooperation and economic growth, but plays into the hands of China, who can present itself as a more stable trading partner.

Even if the Biden Administration changed the tone towards the transatlantic partnership, the EU-US economic relations have continued to feel the impact of the diplomatic and policy amendments that were imposed under Trump.[69] In fact, the Biden administration has reinforced some parts of this strategy, for instance by its actions under the Inflation Reduction Act that threatened to introduce heavy discrimination of European auto manufacturers. Undoubtedly, these developments altered the EU's perception of

66 "Section 232 Investigation on the Effect of Imports of Steel on US National Security", US Department of Commerce, March 18, 2018, https://www.commerce. gov/issues/trade-enforcement/section-232-steel; "Section 232 National Security Investigation of Steel Imports Information on the Exclusion Process", *Bureau of Industry and Security*, March 8, 2018, https://www.bis.doc.gov/index.php/232-steel.

67 "US tariffs: EU response and fears of a trade war", *European Parliament*, 2018, https://www.europarl.europa.eu/RegData/etudes/ATAG/2018/623554/EPRS_ATA(2018)623554_EN.pdf; Frances P. Hadfield, Brian McGrath and Walter Boone, "EU Places Retaliatory Tariffs on $4 Billion in US Goods", *Crowell*, November 20, 2020, https://www.cmtradelaw.com/2020/11/eu-places-retaliatory-tariffs-on-4-billion-in-u-s-goods/.

68 Anna Dimitrova, "The State of the Transatlantic Relationship in the Trump Era", *The Foundation Robert Schuman*, February 4, 2020, https://www.robert-schuman.eu/en/doc/questions-d-europe/qe-545-en.pdf;

69 Erik Brattberg, "Transatlantic Relations After Biden's First 100 Days", *Carnegie Endowment for International Peace*, May 6, 2021, https://carnegieendowment. org/2021/05/06/transatlantic-relations-after-biden-s-first-100-days-pub-84472

America as a leader of the liberal order and as trusted ally, while the transatlantic relations remain fraught with thorny issues of trade, technology, China, and Russia.

Europe has not been an innocent bystander. The EU has arguably grown even more envious and harmful of the supremacy of US Big Tech and sought ways to limit their role in the European market – sometimes by proposals including outright discrimination. With a growing leadership role in the EU for France and President Emmanuel Macron, old French and Gaullist ideas about mercantilism and isolationism have flourished – driving a strong wedge between the two sides in their economic approach to each other. Nor have attempts to seek a permanent settlement on trade frictions (e.g. the tariffs related to steel) been successful. Unfortunately, the EU and US have all too often looked like an old couple nearing the point of a breakup because they have grown tired of each other, not observing all the good things they have together.

The China Wedge between US – EU Partnership

While the transatlantic partnership remains important, albeit with challenges, one of the major sources of friction is the often-divergent US and EU perceptions of and relations with China. In retrospect, the transatlantic relationship between the United States and its European allies has been one of the world's most robust since World War II, and it held together throughout the Cold War when facing the threat from the Soviet Union. However, the alliance appears less unified on the issues of collectively pressuring Beijing, while the divergent perceptions stimulate the already prevalent divisions in the transatlantic partnership. The US' foreign policy towards China, since long, has fluctuated between, on the one hand, containing a strategic rival and preventing it from acquiring the technological sway to challenge the incumbent influence of the US through direct and indirect sanctions and trade impediments, and on the other hand, trying to incorporate China, as an emerging power, into the US led international system by integrating a promising new sphere of trade and investment into the global economy.[70] In the last few years, in particular, the American foreign policy has increased its view of China as a strategic rival and has been choosing a confrontational approach rather than a cooperative one. Such an approach was heightened during the Trump administration, which seems to be continuing under Biden too, and could be accelerated during a second term under Trump.

The European perceptions, on the other hand, have been resting on an important policy strategy paper by the EU introduced in March 2019, which dubbed China as "simultaneously a cooperation partner, an economic competitor in pursuit of technological leadership, and a systemic rival promoting alternative models of governance."[71] For the EU, China is, simultaneously, in different policy areas, a cooperation partner with whom the EU has closely aligned objectives, a negotiating partner with whom the EU needs to find a balance of interests, an economic competitor in the pursuit of technological leadership, and a systemic rival promoting alternative models of governance. The dominant approach in Europe was to see China as a challenging economic partner with whom engagement would produce positive

---

70   Jon Bateman, "The Evolution of US Thinking and Policy", in *U.S.-China Technological Decoupling: A Strategy and Policy Framework*, Carnegie Endowment for International Peace, April 25, 2022, https://carnegieendowment. org/2022/04/25/evolution-of-u.s.-thinking-and-policy-pub-86898

71   "EU-China Strategic Outlook", *European Commission*, March 12, 2019, https:// ec.europa.eu/info/publications/eu-china-strategic-outlook-commission- contribution-european-council-21-22-march-2019_en.

results. European policymakers rejected the American view of China as overly securitized and believed that China was well on its way to becoming a responsible stakeholder in the international order, a view that has a bitter aftertaste today among many European states. This was reflected throughout the first half of the last decade as Germany took the lead in framing its relations with China as "a comprehensive strategic partnership" in 2014. UK Prime Minister David Cameron and his Chancellor of the Exchequer, George Osborne, declared the beginning of a "golden era" in Britain's relations with China when President Xi Jinping made a state visit to their country in 2015.[72]

Primarily, there has been a naive view in Europe that suggests a balance between economic interests and systemic contradictions with China, keeping business and politics separate. Subsequently, there has been a call for strategic autonomy, mainly featuring in EU's global strategy doctrine in 2016, which focused on EU's ability to operate independently across all fronts and a balance between China and the United States.[73] These were chiefly reflected during the Trump administration, as despite the considerable pressure by the US on Europe to limit its engagement with China, particularly on sensitive matters like the role of Chinese telecoms giant Huawei in European 5G wireless infrastructure, European governments, including the UK, primarily ignored this pressure, judging the economic

---

72   Tom Phillips, "Britain has made 'visionary' choice to become China's best friend, says Xi", *The Guardian*, October 18, 2015, https://www.theguardian.com/uk-news/2015/oct/18/britian-has-made-visionary-choice-to-become-chinas-best-friend-says-xi.

73   Amber Wang, "Dangers for China in the EU drive for strategic autonomy: analyst", *South China Morning Post*, December 14, 2021, https://www.scmp.com/news/china/diplomacy/article/3159657/dangers-china-eu-drive-strategic-autonomy-analyst?module=perpetual_scroll_0&pgtype=article&campaign=3159657.

benefits from engagement with China to outweigh the risks.[74] This was not the case in all countries in Europe, Sweden as one example banned Huawei from bidding on the 5G network, despite that some Swedish business's actively lobbied for China, mainly out of fear of being locked out of a Chinese market they paradoxically are already severely restricted from.

Further, a previous Italian government, which included the nationalist-populist party Lega (Lega Nord per l'indipendenza della Padania), signed a memorandum of understanding with Beijing on the Belt and Road Initiative (BRI), becoming the first G-7 country to join the initiative, much to Washington's dismay.[75] [76] Similarly, Czech President Miloš Zeman also declared that the Czech Republic hoped to become "an unsinkable aircraft carrier of Chinese investment expansion" in Europe, reflecting China's growing economic ties with the Eastern European nation.[77] Further, in 2019, Greece joined China's "16+1" forum with Central and Eastern European nations — including 11 European Union member states and an additional five Balkan countries, and primarily seen as divisive by the EU — turning it into the 17+1.[78]

This trend hit a reef and the unsinkable aircraft carrier that the

---

74   David E. Sanger and David McCabe, "Huawei is Winning the Argument in Europe, as the US Fumbles to Develop Alternatives", *The New York Times*, February 17, 2020, https://www.nytimes.com/2020/02/17/us/politics/us-huawei-5g.html.

75   Giovanna De Maio, "Playing with Fire: Italy, China, and Europe", *Brookings*, May 2020, https://www.brookings.edu/research/playing-with-fire/.

76   In the summer of 2018, 27 EU ambassadors signed a statement criticizing BRI as mainly beneficial for China, lacking transparency and causing unsustainable debt relations.

77   David Barboza, Marc Santora and Alexandra Stevenson, "China Seeks Influence in Europe, One Business Deal at a Time", *The New York Times*, April 12, 2018, https://www.nytimes.com/2018/08/12/business/china-influence-europe-czech-republic.html?auth=login-googletap&login=googletap.

78   Emilian Kavalski, "China 16+1 is Dead? Long Live the 17+1", *The Diplomat*, March 29, 2019, https://thediplomat.com/2019/03/chinas-161-is-dead-long-live-the-171/.

Czech Republic was supposed to become signed up for service with the US, and today the Czech Republic together with Lithuania are two of the most China critical states in Europe.[79] The once hyped 17+1 turned into a crippled 14+1 in 2022 when Lithuania, Estonia and Latvia left, and the structure currently suffers today from a lack of real impact in Europe. Since then, the Beijing format of cooperation has been further weakened, not least because of the changes in geopolitical perceptions that followed on the heels of Russia's full-scale invasion of Ukraine.

A Divided Europe and its Challenges

Since the end of World War II, European countries have sought to deepen their integration in pursuit of peace and economic growth. As a result, the institutions that became the European Union have steadily expanded and strengthened their authority as member states have passed more and more decision-making power to the union. However, the EU has been buffeted by a series of crises in recent years that have tested its cohesion, including the 2008 global financial crisis, an influx of migrants from Africa and the Middle East, Brexit negotiations,[80] and the economic fallout of the COVID-19 pandemic. While these incidents tested the EU integration from time to time, two particular developments enabled the internal divisions to lay bare respectively strengthen: the divide on China challenge and the EU's strong support for Ukraine.

---

79   Svante Cornell & Niklas Swanström, "Compatible Interests? The EU and China's Belt and Road Initiative", *Swedish Institute for European Policy Studies*, Report no. 1, Stockholm, January 2020. https://www.sieps.se/en/publications/2020/compatible-interests/

80   James McBride, "What Brexit Means", *Council on Foreign Relations*, July 22, 2019, https://www.cfr.org/backgrounder/what-brexit-means.

In this context, the China challenge is not confined to a wedge between the transatlantic partners; it has also roused the structural divide in the EU while the development of a successful alternative to China becomes a major challenge. In particular, despite the growing suspicion of Beijing amongst the EU nations, there has been resistance, not least from the business community, to jeopardizing economic interests in China. China's deep-seated economic relations with the EU have been enhanced as China has overtaken the US to become the EU's leading trading partner (see figure 5).[20] Figure 5 outlines bilateral trade between European countries like the Netherlands, Germany, France, Italy, Spain, etc,. and China, concurrently highlighting the monumental difference between the EU's trade with China and the US, with the balance shifting towards the former. Additionally, as been noted before, it is not only a question about China. With a more anti-European policy from the US, China could be an alternative to many European states, arguably not a good alterative but a trading partner that potentially could have a moderating impact on Russia. This would be a short-sighted strategy, that would be detrimental to both the US and EU positions over time.

Figure 5: US and China Trade with EU Countries (2023)

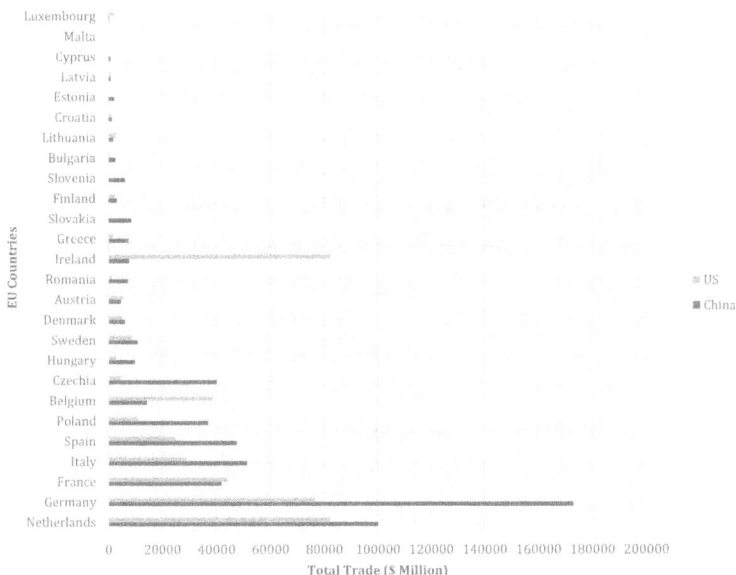

Source: OEC World

It is crucial, when shaping new policies on trade and supply chains, to examine the major economies of Europe and their business communities' views of China. Conversations with German parliamentarians have suggested that the lack of credible alternatives or "models" was the primary reason for German reluctance to distance itself from China further and move closer to the US. Similar responses were given in Paris and to a certain degree in Brussels. It is imperative to understand that the European divide is not between the 14+1 Framework and western Europe or between China's major destinations of investments in Europe (Germany, France, Sweden and Italy) and the less "fortunate".[21] The current situation results from a complicated combination of factors, both political and economic, understanding the nuances of which is vital for an effective engagement with global supply chains.

In the current scenario, while an increasingly anxious Europe is waking up to the threat of economic dependence that has been on display since the Russian war on Ukraine, the clear European support for Ukraine has paved the way to a unified response and an acceptance of Ukraine's bid to join the EU.[81] In retrospect, a very different situation ensued in 2014 when Russia exploited the conflict to pursue their geopolitical and economic agendas such as the takeover of Crimea.[82] In the current scenario, the EU has been divided over how the Ukraine war should play out and, most importantly, how to implement sanctions on Russia's lucrative energy sector over its invasion of Ukraine, but the disgust of the Russian breaches of international law has brought closer cooperation within EU and also with the US

Many European countries have been heavily dependent on Russian oil and gas. The EU imported roughly 40% of its gas and 25% of its oil from Russia in 2021. A clearer picture of the EU's dependence on Russian energy exports is presented in figures 6 and 7.

---

81 "The EU's unity over Ukraine has given it surprising heft", *The Economist*, March 26, 2022, https://www.economist.com/europe/the-eus-unity-over-ukraine-has-given-it-surprising-heft/21808306

82 Gleb Zhukov, "A divided Ukraine diving Europe", *Gateway House*, June 2014, https://www.gatewayhouse.in/a-divided-ukraine-dividing-europe/

Figure 6: Top 10 Countries Importing Crude Oil from Russia (2021)

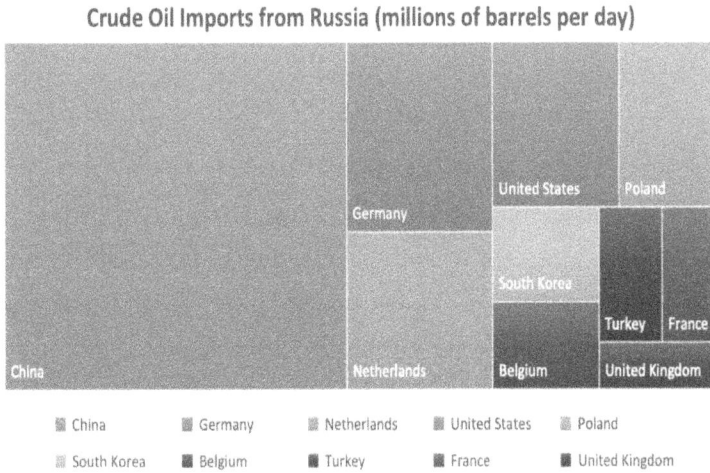

Crude Oil Imports from Russia (millions of barrels per day)

Source: iea.org

Figure 7: Largest Importers of Russian Oil in the EU and UK (2021)

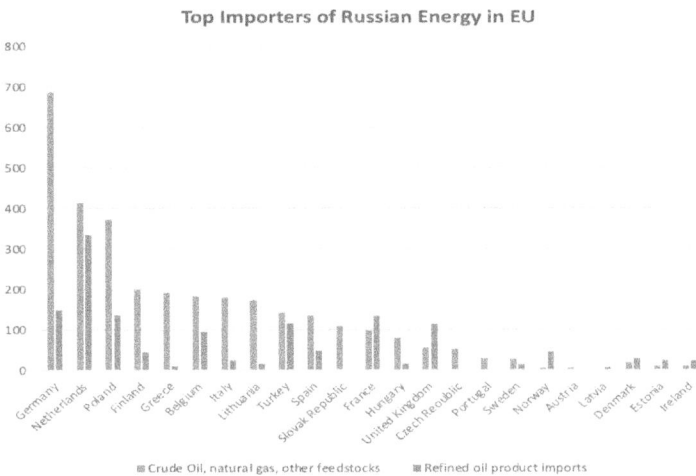

Top Importers of Russian Energy in EU

Source: iea.org

Germany has been the top EU importer of Russian oil. Germany was also the largest EU importer of Russian pipeline crude.[83] Further, the Netherlands, Europe's key trading hub, was the second largest importer of Russian crude and the EU's top importer of Russian refined products. Their dependencies only added to the challenges in ensuring a common EU strategy against Russia's invasion of Ukraine, as many EU nations remain perplexed between national interest and values, but the result has been surprisingly positive and coordinated as a result of the Russian slaughter of Ukrainian civilians.

The EU has reached an agreement to ban some Russian oil. Engaged in a deadlock for months over the feasibility of such a ban, the 27-member bloc decided that by the end of 2022 that no Russian oil would arrive on EU shores by sea route. Still, imports of Russian oil via pipeline have continued, with a gradual plan to wean dependent nations off this source as well. However, internal divisions within the EU continue to play a role, with for example Hungary demanding a complete exemption from the European Union's plans to ban Russian oil imports, citing national interest. Notably, Hungary and Slovakia received 75 and 100 per cent of their respective oil imports from Russia in 2022. If anything, Russia's energy exports continue to fuel the war in Ukraine, and the EU's inability to end its dependency on Russian oil and gas has been perceived by many as an embarrassing failure in holding the Kremlin accountable.

Moreover, even as the EU decided to phase-out the Russian oil, it remains a challenge for the European nations to find a suitable replacement for the Russian supply. Considering the above situation, the EU situation vis-à-vis the Russian oil supply only enhances the

---

83   Ingrid Melander & Sabine Siebold, "EU Split on Russia oil sanctions, mulls other steps", *Reuters,* March 22, 2022, https://www.reuters.com/world/europe/eu-mull-russian-oil-embargo-with-biden-set-join-talks-2022-03-21/

call for a democratic, pluralistic, and liberal rules-based alternative supply chain, mainly focusing on transatlantic cooperation. EU companies have been signing deals with Middle Eastern and Atlantic refiners, forging new supply ties ahead of the Russian oil freeze. The EU is also looking at the Americas, Africa, the Middle East, and India for its needs. It is also turning inward, stressing local energy production.[84] While such a search might not provide overnight results, the inception of a common transatlantic strategy would undoubtedly provide more extensive results. However, the result has to be connected to new sources of energy outside of the oil and gas sources, such as renewable and green technology that have been unable to cover the deficits in energy.

Uncertain Economic and Security Environment: Over-dependence on China

Over the years, the world has witnessed both changes and continuities in US policies and actions vis-a-vis the EU These have underpinned the goals of ensuring that the EU doesn't help China enhance its military and technological capabilities in a way which hampers the US security; attaining greater leverage over China through joint actions with EU; strengthening free-market democracies; establishing a stronger trans-Atlantic partnership in the Indo-Pacific; and ensuring Chinese influence does not adversely affect its sway in Europe.[85]

However, the US private sector and public policy approach has long prioritized efficiency and low costs over security, resilience, and

---

84 "Russian oil: EU agrees compromise deal on banning imports", *BBC*, 31 May, 2022, https://www.bbc.com/news/world-europe-61638860

85 Ibid.

sustainability, pushing the US towards more significant supply chain risks. It has come to acknowledge its overdependence on China, which has not just had economic implications, but political and security repercussions too. For the EU, too, there have been shared concerns regarding Chinese presence in Europe, even if their goals have not directly mirrored those of the US. If anything, disengaging from the Chinese economy has become a focus of strategic debates in the US, EU, as well as Asia. Furthermore, as instances of China's increasingly assertive and authoritarian behavior in the regions proliferate, coupled with Beijing's unilateral measures, the need to bolster the call for diversification away from China-centric global supply chains strengthens further. Still, a minimum of analysis has focused on how a combined force of democratic states could function as a powerhouse when it comes to taking a new approach on supply lines. In this context, the primary aim should be to examine the patterns surrounding the emerging alternate global supply chain nexus and its implications and prospects for democratic powers like the US and the EU as a whole and other like-minded nations across the globe.

While the EU has expressed skepticism towards a "tariff war" against China, it is on course to introduce a host of different trade and market measures that ultimately seek to counter malign Chinese practices in markets. These policies include public procurement, foreign subsidies and coercion practices by foreign governments.

Institutions being the difference?

What is then the difference between economic engagement between China and the transatlantic partners and the intra-transatlantic cooperation? Institutions always come up as central in the construction of cooperative behavior and international institutionalization, but it is not only the formal creation of institutions, but their role, legitimacy, mandate, and capacity that matter.[86] The mushrooming of international institutions is not really transferable to effective cooperation and conflict management/resolution, and arguably many international institutions tend to be less effective than projected.[87]

Transatlantic institutions tend to be more effective than both broader institutions, or institutions initiated, for example, by China, India, or Russia. This is due to a great extent to shared norms, and values as well as continuously tested institutions that provide predictability, something that is often lacking in many other regional and international arrangements. The international critique that the EU and the US have more trade conflicts between each other than with any other partner has validity, but more importantly, these conflicts are managed in institutions that both parties have a great deal of confidence in. To some extent, the management of conflicts increases the trust and confidence between the conflicting parties and creates institutional stability over time despite not being perfect in any way.

Jointly they have also introduced quasi bodies for negotiating shared policies of interest and defuse problems – for instance, the US-EU Dialogue and the US-EU Trade and Technology Council. The latter pledged to renew the Transatlantic partnership and set up a "Joint Transatlantic Agenda for the post-pandemic era", along with establishing six working groups focusing on technology

---

86 Rebecca Steffenson, *Managing EU-US Relations: Actors, Institutions and the New Transatlantic Agenda*, Manchester University Press Manchester, 2005, pp- 4-5

87 Niklas Swanström, *Regional Cooperation and Conflict Management: Lessons from the Pacific Rim*, Dissertation, Department of Peace and Conflict research, Uppsala University, 2002, https://isdp.eu/content/uploads/publications/2002_swanstrom_regional-cooperation-and-conflict-management.pdf

standards cooperation (including on AI, Internet of Things, among other emerging technologies), climate and green tech, ICT security and competitiveness, data governance and technology platforms, the misuse of technology threatening security and human rights, export controls, investment screening, promoting SMEs access to, and use of, digital technologies, and global trade challenges. It also included a working group on reviewing and strengthening our most critical supply chains. Further, the Transatlantic partners are committed to building a US-EU partnership on the rebalancing of global supply chains in semiconductors to enhance US and EU respective security of supply as well as capacity to design and produce the most powerful and resource-efficient semiconductors.[88]

This dialogue was renewed with a Second High-Level Meeting of the US-EU Dialogue on China, where both the sides reiterated that:

> "United States' and EU's respective relations with China are multifaceted and emphasized the importance of the United States and European Union maintaining continuous and close contacts on our respective approaches as we invest and grow our economies, cooperate with China where possible, and manage our competition and systemic rivalry with China responsibly."

They also reaffirmed the importance of protecting and building economic and technological resilience, diversifying and strengthening supply chains, and addressing economic coercion. Further, they

---

88 "US-EU Summit Statement", *The White House*, June 15, 2021, https://www. whitehouse.gov/briefing-room/statements-releases/2021/06/15/u-s-eu-summit-statement/.

stressed on the importance of close US-EU cooperation to uphold the rules-based international order, including securing a level playing field for all countries. They also emphasized the importance of protecting intellectual property rights, critical infrastructure, and sensitive technologies, as well as information-sharing on tools to strengthen economic resilience, reduce loopholes and vulnerabilities, and shield against risks, including non-market practices. Lastly, the countries emphasized the importance of results-oriented engagement on key transnational challenges, such as the climate crisis and health security.[89]

Similarly, the US-EU Trade and Technology Council (TTC) targeted establishing ten working groups in key areas of concern.[90] These are surrounded Technology Standards, Cooperation, Climate and Clean Technology, Secure Supply Chains, Information and Communication Technology and Services Security and Competitiveness, Data Governance and Technology Platforms, Misuse of Technology Threatening Security and Human Rights, Export Controls, Investment Screening. Promoting Small- and Medium-Sized Enterprises (SME) Access to and Use of Digital Tools Global Trade Challenges. The formation of TTC came at a pivotal period for the US-EU relations, particularly when the partnership was witnessing low levels of cooperation and rising geopolitical tension. Thus, this initiative was an attempt to rebuild the transatlantic relationship and leverage that relationship to address global challenges, most notably the rise of China.

---

89 "U.S.-EU: Joint Press Release by the EEAS and Department of State on the Second High-Level Meeting of the U.S.-EU Dialogue on China", *US Department of State*, December 2, 2021, https://www.state.gov/u-s-eu-joint-press-release-by-the-eeas-and-department-of-state-on-the-second-high-level-meeting-of-the-u-s-eu-dialogue-on-china/.

90 "EU-US Trade and Technology Council Inaugural Joint Statement", *European Commission*, September 29, 2021, https://ec.europa.eu/commission/presscorner/detail/en/STATEMENT_21_4951

These initiatives have undoubtedly set the stage for a reinvigorated Transatlantic partnership in the face of increasing geopolitical
and geo-economic uncertainties. These two dialogues were also
important at underscoring the differing goals and approaches of
the US and EU towards the region, and particularly towards China
while highlighting the shared values of openness, fair competition,
transparency, and accountability. Yet, the EU and the US have been
unable to chalk out a common strategy which would benefit from
an open economy regulated by fair standards and strong cooperation
with like-minded states. This is to ensure that innovation, ideas, and
investments strengthen the economies and do not create further
instability, as well as take account of the distinct goals, approaches
and domestic compulsions of the US and the European nations.

In fact, the TTC is not the first attempt to align the United
States and European Union more closely. Before the TTC, there
was the 1995 New Transatlantic Agenda (NTA), which was followed
by the 1998 Transatlantic Economic Partnership (TEP), the 2007
Transatlantic Economic Council (TEC), and most recently, the
Transatlantic Trade and Investment Partnership (TTIP). Unfortunately, the NTA, TEP and TEC – all efforts to coordinate policy
across the Atlantic and deepen ties – fell victim to enduring regulatory differences between the EU and the United States and domestic
sensitivities.[91]

This provides a need to develop a viable alternative to a China-oriented supply chain, the so-called "red supply line". At the heart
of such an initiative should be efforts to reduce barriers and trade
costs across the Atlantic. Such measures would also have an impact

---

91   Jennifer Hillman, "Can the U.S.-EU Trade and Technology Council Succeed?",
     Council on Foreign Relations, October 29, 2021, https://www.cfr.org/blog/can-us-
     eu-trade-and-technology-council-succeed.

on reducing trade with China and the country's role in the supply chains of the EU and the US. Take the machinery sector as an example. It is a sector that mostly run on the principle of zero tariffs: the EU and the US have over the years taken away such industrial tariffs and, as a result, increased their trade with China. However, tariffs are only one part of the protection against Transatlantic trade and, for a long time now, they have not been a significant cost for firms. What generate significant costs, however, are regulatory divergences.

There is a Mutual Recognition Agreement (MRA) between the EU and the US that dates back to the late 1990s. This MRA operates on the principle that Conformity Assessment Bodies (CABs) in either the EU or the US can certify compliance under each other's regulatory frameworks.[92] Expanding this MRA to include machinery and electrical equipment would be a straightforward and effective policy to deepen EU-US economic integration, gain economic security and lower the cost of climate change policies. Furthermore, extending the scope of the current MRA could lay the groundwork for future integration of additional sectors and products subject to conformity assessment. For our purposes, it would also rebalance trade with China.

Currently, China takes up a significant market share in the EU and the US in these industrial goods sectors. Figure 8 lays out the development of trade market shares. About 20 years ago, the EU represented 14 percent and China 17 percent of US imports of machinery, electrical equipment and relevant green goods. Today, China has a 30 percent trade market share while Europe's has declined to 7

---

92 "Agreement on mutual recognition between the European Community and the United States of America - Joint Declaration". L31/3. (1999); also see: "Summaries of EU legislation" (n.d.) EUR-Lex. https://eur-lex.europa.eu/EN/legal-content/summary/eu-united-states-of-america-mutual-recognition-agreement-mra.html#keyterm_E0002

percent. In other words, China has nearly doubled its trade market share in twenty years while the EU has halved its trade market share. Figure 9 shows the same development in the US market, and the results are broadly similar – although with an even more significant development for China's trade market share.

Figure 8: EU, China, and other countries' share of US imports of machinery, electrical equipment and green goods belonging to machinery and electrical equipment (share, 2002-latest year)

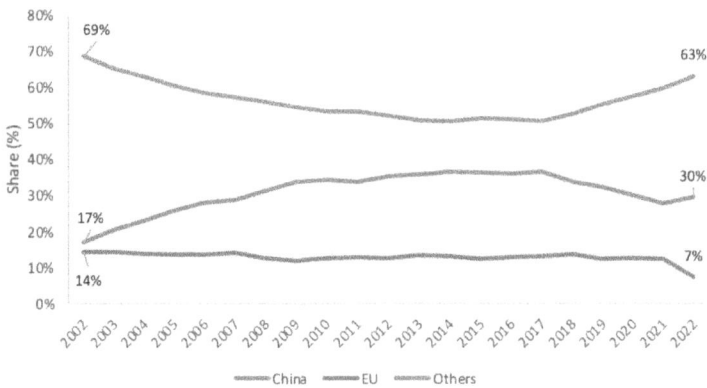

Source: UN Comtrade, authors' calculation.

Figure 9: US, China, and other countries' share of EU imports of machinery, electrical equipment and green goods belonging to machinery and electrical equipment (share, 2002-2022)

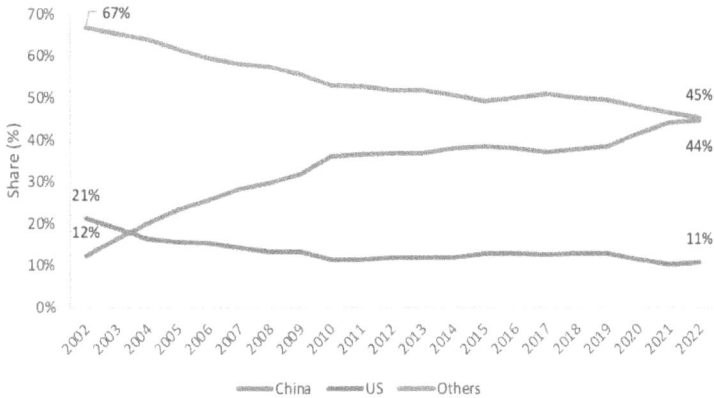

Source: UN Comtrade, authors' calculation.

An MRA agreement alone would have an impact on this trade and lead to much more Transatlantic trade and much less trade with China. Figure 10 presents the result of a simulation of the results of an extension of the current MRA agreement. The actual effects depend upon by how much trade costs would go down if there would such an agreement between the EU and the US. Assuming bilateral trade costs would be reduced by 6 percent, bilateral Transatlantic trade would go up significantly in all three sectors while, simultaneously, trade with China would go down significantly. Bilateral trade in machinery would increase by almost 50 billion US dollars, which would be a 40 percent increase from current levels.

Figure 10: Change in EU, US and Chinese trade as a result of EU-US MRA on conformity assessment for machinery and electrical equipment resulting in a 6 percent reduction in EU-US bilateral trade costs

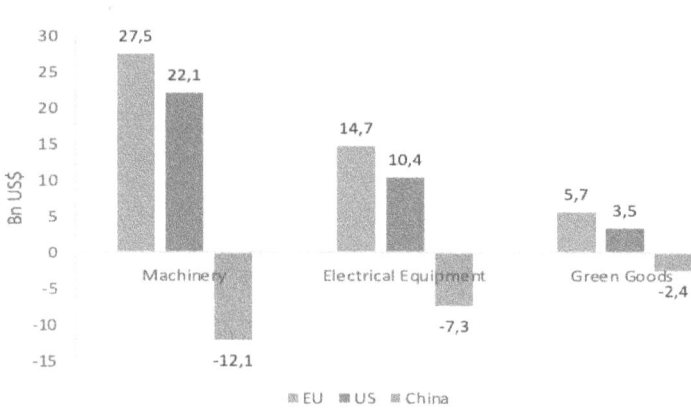

Source: Authors' calculations using GTAP.

The US and EU, and their ability to address pressing global challenges

Both the EU and the US have an interest in addressing pressing global challenges in a concerted fashion. Climate change is likely to be the animating global issue for US–EU relations over the longer term.[93] The Biden administration has already signaled a major change of course on this front with a return to the Paris Climate Accord. John Kerry's March 2021 visit to Brussels to meet EU climate policy counterparts was among the first high-level in-person

---

93 "EU-US: A new transatlantic agenda for global change", *European Commisson*, December 2, 2020, https://ec.europa.eu/commission/presscorner/detail/en/ip_20_2279.

transatlantic meetings for the new administration.[94] During this time, at the center of this agenda were three principles: First, green investments are no longer seen as a cost but an engine for jobs and growth. Second, the creation of wealth must take place within planetary boundaries. This requires the decoupling of economic growth from resource consumption. Third, none of this can succeed without a genuine commitment to international solidarity and justice. Meaningful financial and technical support to developing countries is urgently needed.[95]

However, there have been global skepticism of US climate commitments. Particularly, as it would be extremely difficult for the Biden administration to achieve his desired emission cuts solely through executive action and without the Congress making Biden's new target legally binding. Such an approach would be in line with legally binding targets set by the European Union, United Kingdom and Canada.[96]

Thus, cooperation around green economic recovery and a post-carbon future will be central to the future of transatlantic relations and will influence policies in other critical areas, from trade to infrastructure. This is one of the points in which international policy has a direct connection to the concerns of citizens. For the next generation, in particular, cooperation on climate will be an increasingly important test for the worth of the transatlantic relationship.

---

94 "Joint Statement following the visit of US Special Presidential Envoy for Climate John Kerry to the European Commission", *European Commission*, March 9, 2021, https://ec.europa.eu/commission/presscorner/detail/en/STATEMENT_21_1093

95 "Kerry calls for enhanced cooperation on climate between EU and US", *Euronews*, March 09, 2021, https://www.euronews.com/my-europe/2021/03/09/kerry-calls-for-enhanced-cooperation-on-climate-between-eu-and-us

96 Coral Davenport, "Biden's climate plan faces global skepticism", *The New York Times*, October 22, 2021, https://www.nytimes.com/2021/10/22/climate/biden-climate-plan.html.

One of the simplest ways for the Biden administration to lock in goodwill from foreign governments — without having to get a climate target passed through Congress — is to help fund small and poor countries to fortify themselves against the effects of climate change. "The debt of small states has risen to unsustainable levels, because of repeated borrowings to rebuild and recover from natural disasters, arising from climate change," said Prime Minister Gaston Browne of Antigua and Barbuda, representing the Small Island Developing States alliance.[97] Biden, in April 2021, launched a US International Climate Finance Plan that was light on financial details. He promised to "double, by 2024, our annual public climate finance to developing countries relative to the average level during the second half of the Obama-Biden Administration."[98]

In this context, it would be imperative of the EU and the US to join forces, considering Europe's focus on green development and environmental sustainability. In fact, the EU has been leading the demands and driving the focus on green development and environmental sustainability, focusing on the threats of climate change and environmental degradation. Thus, it initiated the European Green Deal, aimed at transforming the EU into a modern resource-efficient and competitive economy.[99] This has been acknowledged and comprehended by China, which has embarked on an EU-China

---

97 Fiona Harvey, "Wealthy nations 'failing to help developing world tackle climate crisis", *The Guardian*, April 24, 2021, https://www.theguardian.com/environment/2021/apr/24/wealthy-nations-failing-to-help-developing-world-tackle-climate-crisis

98 Ryan Heath, "Danger ahead as Biden plays climate catch-up", *Politico*, April 23, 2021, https://www.politico.com/newsletters/global-translations/2021/04/23/danger-ahead-as-biden-plays-climate-catch-up-492579.

99 "A European Green Deal", *European Commission*, https://eur-lex.europa.eu/legalcontent/EN/TXT/?qid=1576150542719&uri=COM%3A2019%3A640%3AFIN

Cooperative green partnership,[100] on the foundations of environmental governance through cooperation in air pollution control, climate change, green growth, circular economy and other fields. Given the role assigned to green development, the EU would expect any plans for a supply network to include this aspect.

Thus, the challenge argues for building of a Green Supply Chain Network – which will be discussed in greater detail in the subsequent chapters. This is not predicting an environmental crisis or that Europe and the US is dependent on China in all segments, but to ensure that the US and EU takes the lead in the technological development that comes with the green economy, which de facto has become a major component of world trade. It would further delve into the nexus of trade and environmental sustainability, domains of climate change, green policies, energy efficiency through renewable energy, and the extent to which the network could contribute to sustainable growth.

Transatlantic Partnership beyond the Transatlantic

Importantly, Transatlantic relations are not just about the Washington–Brussels/Berlin axis. The transatlantic community has a responsibility to think more creatively across latitudes. Many of the most pressing global challenges, from public health to the environment and from migration to the future of trade and finance, cannot be tackled effectively without cooperation with the global south. Even in strictly transatlantic terms, there is a need to work more closely with Atlantic societies in Africa, Latin America and

---

100 Yanzhu Zhang, "EU-China Green Partnership for Better Global Governance", *Konrad Adenauer Stiftung*, https://eur-lex.europa.eu/legal-content/EN/TXT/?qid=1576150542719&uri=COM%3A2019%3A640%3AFIN.

the Caribbean. The lessons from the pandemic are very clear about the value of a broader geographic approach, especially in confronting issues at the confluence of domestic and international concerns.

Here, Asia deserves a special mention, as a region which has the potential to attract overseas investment as companies look to diversify their production and distribution. This region comprises emerging markets, favorable and cost-effective labor forces, resource-abundant locations, an economically advantageous geographical location, as well as regions which are incrementally witnessing increasing geopolitical gravity. Likeminded countries in Asia have also been focusing on strengthening their supply chain resilience against disruptions through the 'Supply Chain Resilience Initiative', while countries like India and Japan, strategic partner and ally to the US, respectively, and both maintain strategic partnerships with the EU, can play a significant role in the trans-Atlantic supply chain strategy. Similarly, like minded countries like Thailand, Malaysia and Vietnam have reiterated their potential as alternative destinations for investments. These countries have started to witness increasing amounts of FDI applications, while nations like Vietnam have already been considered a key part in the "China plus one" strategy by many companies.[101] For instance, many Asian economies have been forecast to play a dominant role in apparel manufacturing in the coming decade.[102]

In this context, while most Asian nations might have

---

101 Sara Hsu, "Which Asian Nations Can Benefit from the 'China Plus One' Strategy?", *The Diplomat*, June 11, 2021, https://thediplomat.com/2021/06/which-asian-nations-can-benefit-from-the-china-plus-one-strategy/

102 "Asia to remain dominant player in garment manufacturing in coming decade: Report", *The Economic Times*, July 14, 2020, https://economictimes.indiatimes.com/industry/cons-products/garments-/-textiles/asia-to-remaindominant-player-in-garment-manufacturing-in-coming-decade-shows-report/articleshow/76963643.cms?from=mdr

infrastructures that lag far behind China's and are home to less favorable manufacturing landscapes, these locations might still gradually emerge as an attractive alternative for downstream manufacturing. Moreover, considering the aim to propose a "focused manufacturing" looking at critical supplies and less essential supplies to be reshored and nearshored, Asian countries could fit in the picture for manufacturing non-essential supplies.

Thus, filling the gaps of the geopolitics of supply chains, this book will deep dive into the prospects for the US collaborating with Europe as well as other likeminded powers to ensure a sophisticated, sustainable, and resilient trans-Atlantic supply chain network with the fundamentals of mutual complementarities, while not undermining underlying reservations. It will look at how to build solutions that would maximize commercial profit and reduce risks, as well as how to manage national security for the US and EU Concurrently, it will focus on how a new supply chain network will be able to fill the gaps that China dominated supply line system has missed out on, such as transparency, credibility, sustainability and predictability. Some of these aspects also need to be strengthened between the US, EU, and its allies.

FOUR

US-EU-China Triangularity
and the Supply Chain Challenges

Previous chapters have emphasized that the EU and the US depend on China for many critical products, and that this dependency has incrementally become a vulnerability. This as the Chinese government does not shy away from using its influence over trade and supply chains and trade to pressure other states and companies to effect favorable behavior. Scales and volumes have increased remarkably. In the last few decades, trade between the United States and China and the European Union and China has risen dramatically and is now vital to all the three entities. Both United States and EU import more from China than any other country, and China is one of the greatest export markets for US and EU goods and services today.[103] This trade has benefited the US and the EU by lowering consumer prices and increasing corporate profits, but it has also

---

103 Theresa Fallon, "The Impossible Triable: China, the US, and the EU", *Observer Research Foundation*, May 05, 2021, https://www.orfonline.org/expert-speak/the-impossible-triangle-china-the-us-and-the-eu/.

incurred expenses, both economically and politically.[104] Companies has competed with each other how much they can outsource to cut every corner and save money, but the outsourcing has proven to have hidden costs.

In this context, this chapter will draw from the China challenge faced by both the EU and the US and explore the Chinese investment and trading patterns in both regions, identifying the trends in Chinese outreach. It will further try to analyze the extent to which China's assertive economic policies have and can further mobilize the US and EU forces. Lastly and more importantly, the chapter will delve into the grey zones of the US-China dynamics and the EU's changing, but not united, China Policy, which remains likely to significantly impact a common strategy pertaining to supply chains between both the entities. This is not to argue that the EU and the US can, or even should, cut trade relations with China in all areas but there is a strong case for both to accelerate a selected reduction of trade dependencies in critical areas and industries that could extend over time to a broader base.

Trade between the United States and China

The link between the United States and China's economy is intricately intertwined. The total trade has grown from $503.2 billion in 2011 to $748 billion in 2022. While China has been the US's largest trading partner, it is also the US' third-largest commercial partner behind Canada and Mexico, remaining the source of the majority of

---

104 Winston Ellington Michalak, "Triangular Economic Relations: China, the EU, and the United States", *Harvard Kennedy School, Belfer Center*, March 16, 2020, https://www.belfercenter.org/publication/triangular-economic-relations-china-eu-and-united-states.

its imports. Exports from China to the United States have shifted away from low-value, labor-intensive goods in recent decades to high-tech areas with high value impact. A wide range of items now have a Chinese or American component as a result of China and the United States being involved in multiple global supply chains, so the solution to the reduction of supply chain security is much more complicated than simply focusing on, as one example, semiconductors, as they are an integrated part of a wider trade network that is needed to finalize end-products such as computers and cars.

However, the US has faced major trade barriers, unfair practices, and a lack of reciprocity in many critical areas. Concerns about China's state-controlled economic, trade, investment and technological activities have been raised by a number of lawmakers. China, in particular, continues to demand the transfer of important US assets in order to operate in strategic areas. Chinese companies are expanding in sectors where the US places or are confronted with restrictions. Many of China's activities distort markets and impede free and fair competition both within China and in third markets – using trade instruments (e.g., antidumping and antitrust, standards and procurement),[105] economic coercion and espionage. In other words. the Chinese government have continuously benefited its enterprises and advanced China's industrial agendas, but also their political and military agendas, through commercial policy. As a result of the state's expanding role in commercial activity, including an intensification of industrial policies and the implementation of a set of interrelated

---

105 "China's Recent Trade Measures and Countermeasures: Issues for Congress", *Congressional Research Service,* December 10, 2021, https://crsreports.congress. gov/product/pdf/R/R46915.

national economic security policies and data restrictions since 2020, the risks inherent in US commercial ties with China have risen.[106]

To be sure, there are significant economic benefits to the US from its trade with China. For instance, Economists Xavier Jaravel and Erick Sager have estimated that increased trade with China boosted the annual purchasing power of the average US household by $1,500 between 2000 and 2007.[107] In a similar vein, the US-China Business Council has shown that the bilateral trade between both countries have created roughly 2.6 million jobs in the US across industries dealing with cars and trucks, construction equipment, and semiconductors.[108] Besides, many US companies have been benefiting substantially on annual basis from sales in China, even if the US suffers from a large trade deficit defined by its unbalanced macroeconomic position. Chinese companies have invested tens of billions of dollars in the United States, though this investment has dwindled in recent years amid heightened US government scrutiny. China has invested in the US in the field of wholesale trade, manufacturing, and information services.

---

106 Ryan Hass and Abraham Denmark, "More pain than gain: How the US-China trade war hurt America", *Brookings*, August 7, 2020, https://www.brookings.edu/blog/order-from-chaos/2020/08/07/more-pain-than-gain-how-the-us-china-trade-war-hurt-america/.

107 Xavier Jaravel and Erick Sager, "Despite job losses, lower prices from trade with China have left US households massively better off", *LSE US Centre*, https://blogs.lse.ac.uk/usappblog/2019/08/14/despite-job-losses-lower-prices-from-trade-with-china-have-left-us-households-massively-better-off/

108 ttps://www.uschina.org/sites/default/files/Oxford%20Economics%20US%20Jobs%20and%20China%20Trade%20Report.pdf; "How Trade with China Benefits the United States", *The US-China Business Council*, https://www.uschina.org/how-trade-china-benefits-united-states,

Figure 11: Foreign Direct Investment between US and China

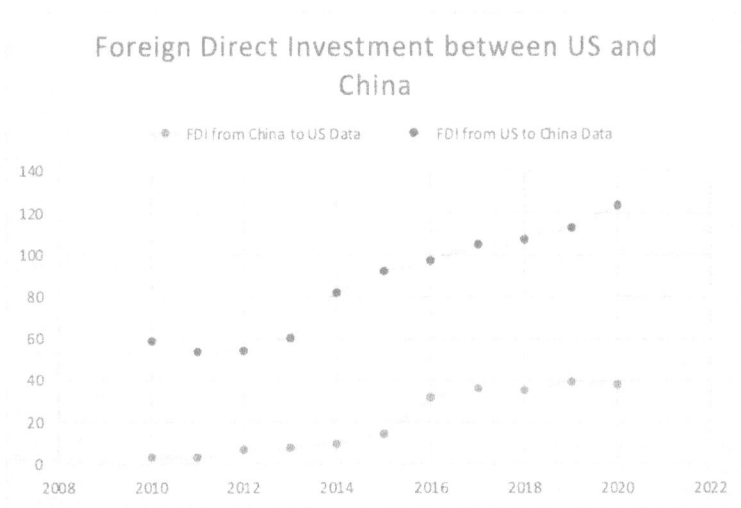

Foreign Direct Investment between US and China

- FDI from China to US Data
- FDI from US to China Data

Source: Statista

Further, trade with the United States has reaped enormous rewards for the Chinese economy as well. With that in mind, trade ties are considerable, but remain uneven; China sells 3-4 percent of the value of goods the US exports to China. A Bank of America survey in 2021 further revealed that 16 percent of Fortune 500 companies rely on China for at least 5 percent of their income, while some of these companies rely on China for more than 20 percent of their revenue. In actuality, even after several years of a trade war and supply disruptions, the US trade deficit with China remains at very high levels.

US policymakers have been looking for solutions to reverse the decades-long shift in American manufacturing to China and the associated loss of industrial capacity and jobs. US corporations are re-evaluating their sourcing risks in light of China President Xi

Jinping's potential to shut down shipments to the United States at any time, which has prompted the government to rebuild domestic production, particularly of critical items, and reduce reliance on an increasingly hostile strategic rival.[109] The strengthened US support of Taiwan, in light of the increased Chinese aggressions against Taiwan has increased the risks for Chinese hostile actions against American companies. This is something that has created concerns among both companies and the government alike, even if the conclusions drawn have at times been different.

In recent years, China's commitment to Green Supply Chain Management (GSCM) has emerged as a pivotal element reshaping its trade relations with global partners, including the US and EU. The adoption of GSCM practices reflects a broader shift towards environmental sustainability, marking a significant transition in China's approach to international trade and economic development. This movement towards green supply chains is not merely a domestic policy shift but has far-reaching implications for global supply chain dynamics, particularly in the context of US-China trade relations.

The research conducted by Li *et al* provides insightful analysis into the nuances of GSCM in Chinese firms, highlighting how market and export pressures significantly influence GSCM practices. [110] This shift towards environmental sustainability within supply chains underscores China's response to global environmental concerns and its role in setting new standards for international trade.

109 Thomas Hout, "A New Approach to Rebalancing the US-China Trade Deficit", *Harvard Business Review*, December 2021, https://hbr.org/2021/12/a-new-approach-to-rebalancing-the-u-s-china-trade-deficit.

110 Li G, Li L, Choi T, Sethi SP. Green supply chain management in Chinese firms: Innovative measures and the moderating role of quick response technology. *Journal of Operations Management*. 2019;66(7-8). doi:https://doi.org/10.1002/joom.1061

The study illuminates how these practices are not only enhancing environmental performance but are also reshaping the competitive landscape, with implications for both cost and efficiency within global supply chains.

The incorporation of GSCM practices signifies China's strategic move to align its economic ambitions with environmental sustainability goals. This alignment is particularly relevant in the context of the US-China trade relationship, where environmental standards and sustainability practices increasingly factor into trade negotiations and agreements. As China advances its GSCM capabilities, it sets a precedent that could encourage or compel US firms to adopt similar practices, potentially leading to a greener global supply chain ecosystem.

Moreover, the transition towards GSCM in China reflects a strategic adaptation to the evolving demands of global markets, where consumers and regulatory bodies are increasingly prioritizing environmental sustainability. This trend offers an opportunity for the US and EU to engage with China on environmental issues within the framework of trade discussions, potentially fostering a collaborative approach to sustainability in global supply chains.

Investments

Technology licensing, research, venture capital, and financial investments, which are not included in data on foreign direct investments (FDI), have grown since 2016. Net FDI flows from the United States to China in 2020 were $9.3 billion, and net FDI flows from China to the United States were $4.3 billion, according to the Bureau of Economic Analysis (BEA). Chinese and American foreign direct investment shares totalled $123.9 billion and $54.9 billion respectively, on an ultimate beneficiary ownership basis (UBO). As of 2020, China's FDI stock in the United States amounted to around 1% of the entire FDI stock in the United States. In December 2020, according to estimates from the United States government and private sector, US investors held $1.15 trillion in Chinese stocks and bonds while Chinese investors held $1.4 trillion in US debt and $720 billion in US equities. China was the second-largest foreign holder of US Treasury securities behind Japan as of November 2021, with holdings totalling $1.08 trillion and $235 billion, respectively (offshore financial centres are not included in this set of statistics).[111]

China has now surpassed the United States as the world's top recipient of foreign direct investment (FDI), defying earlier predictions that foreign companies would seek to reduce their reliance on China as a key part of their supply chains in the wake of new tariffs on trade between China and the United States.[112] Foreign companies that had halted or even withdrawn their investments in China as the country's economy began to recover began to pour more money into the country as China's recovery continued and the rest of the world deteriorated, allowing foreign companies to see China as a production base and a critical growth market for their products. In 2023 there has been a halt in FDI to China with the slowest growth since 1993, but this do not indicate a complete drying up of investments.

For instance, Walmart Inc. announced during a city government-hosted investment conference in Wuhan, the city that was the first hub of the pandemic, that it will invest 3 billion yuan ($460

---

111 "US-China Trade Relations", *Congressional Research Service*, March 2, 2022, https://crsreports.congress.gov/product/pdf/IF/IF11284

112 Paul Hannon and Eun-Young Jeong, "China Overtakes US as World's Leading Destination for Foreign Direct Investment", *Wall Street Journal*, January 24, 2021, https://www.wsj.com/articles/china-overtakes-u-s-as-worlds-leading-destination-for-foreign-direct-investment-11611511200.

million) in Wuhan over the following five years.[113] Kunshan, a city in China's eastern province of Jiangsu, has also been chosen as the location for Starbucks' new roasting factory and innovation park.[114] Tesla, on its side, is increasing production capacity at its Shanghai plant and constructing a new research centre,[115] while, despite a drop in visitors for the second year in a row, Walt Disney Co. is moving ahead with the construction of a new theme area at Shanghai Disneyland.[116] It is increasingly apparent that engagement with China is not declining as much as it was hoped for in Washington[117], despite the new trend in 2023. A large majority, 83 percent, of the surveyed US companies mentioned to the same report that they are not considering relocating from China, a result that will call for government regulations if there will be a change.

The strategic imperative for diversifying supply sources has gained unprecedented momentum in the wake of China's dominant position in the supply chains of critical materials, notably rare earth elements, which are indispensable for a wide range of high-tech industries. This dependency has been a point of vulnerability for both the U.S. and EU, spotlighted by geopolitical tensions and the

---

113   Tobias Hoonhout, "Walmart Says It Will Invest $425 Million to Expand Presence in Wuhan over the Next Five Years", *Yahoo*, April 9, 2020, https://www.yahoo.com/news/walmart-says-invest-425-million-155324623.html.

114   Reuters Staff, "Starbucks to invest $130 million for roasting plant in China's Kunshan", *Reuters*, March 13, 2020, https://www.reuters.com/article/us-china-starbucks-idUSKBN2100LM.

115   "Tesla plans new Shanghai plant to more than double China capacity – sources", *Reuters*, February 24, 2022, https://www.reuters.com/business/autos-transportation/exclusive-tesla-plans-new-shanghai-plant-more-than-double-china-capacity-sources-2022-02-24/.

116   "Shanghai Disneyland theme park re-opens after three-months", *WION*, June 30, 2022, https://www.wionews.com/photos/in-pics-shanghai-disneyland-theme-park-re-opens-after-three-month-493301#theme-park---last-to-reopen-493293.

117   Tanner Brown, "US Firms in China Aren´t Leaving. They´re Just Not Investing More, According to This Study", *Barron´s*, March 8, 2022, https://www.barrons.com/articles/u-s-firms-in-china-arent-leaving-theyre-just-not-investing-more-according-to-this-survey-51646752612

realization that supply chain resilience is paramount to national security and economic stability.

Research by Mancheri *et al* underscores the strategic vulnerability associated with over-reliance on a single source for critical materials and highlights the importance of diversification strategies.[118] The study explores the dynamics of rare earth element supply chains and delineates the consequences of policy interventions by China, which controls a significant share of the global market for these materials. The findings emphasize that without a diversified supply chain, economies remain at risk of supply disruptions, which can have far-reaching implications for industrial sectors reliant on these materials.

The push towards diversifying supply sources is not merely a reactive measure to geopolitical tensions but reflects a broader strategic recalibration towards ensuring supply chain resilience. This involves exploring alternative sources of critical materials, investing in domestic production capacities, and fostering international partnerships to secure a more stable and reliable supply chain network.

For the US and EU, the challenge of diversification extends beyond merely finding alternative suppliers. It encompasses the need to innovate in supply chain management, invest in research and development to reduce dependence on critical materials, and engage in diplomatic efforts to secure access to alternative sources. This multi-faceted approach signifies a profound shift in how supply chains are conceptualized, moving from a cost-minimization model to a resilience-oriented framework.

---

118 Mancheri NA, Sprecher B, Bailey G, Ge J, Tukker A. "Effect of Chinese policies on rare earth supply chain resilience". *Resources, Conservation and Recycling.* 2019;142:101-112. doi:https://doi.org/10.1016/j.resconrec.2018.11.017

China's Trading Positions and Issues for the US Government

For their part, the Chinese government has used trade restrictions and protectionism to effect an impact on the US- China trade relation. While Beijing considers it important to have access to open markets abroad, it does not apply the same principle for its home market. In fact, Beijing is very active to reduce the competition for many US firms in the Chinese market. A new trade strategy has emerged in the wake of China's industrial policies, such as Made in China 2025,[119] which aims to benefit Chinese exports while substituting imports in key sectors with domestic produce. China is working to open global markets and set standards for digital trade and emerging technologies, all the while restricting foreign firms from operating legally in these sectors in its own country. Current government plans highlight China's power to define global trade standards, extend the reach of its legal, Intellectual Property and digital and antitrust authorities, and fight US policy moves with their countermeasures. Since joining the Regional Comprehensive Economic Partnership (RCEP) and seeking to join the Comprehensive and Progressive Agreement for Trans-Pacific Partnership (CPTPP), China has implemented export controls, foreign investment restrictions, as well as extraterritoriality blocking measures.[120]

---

119 James McBride and Andrew Chatzky, "Is 'Made in China 2025' a Threat to Global Trade?", *Council on Foreign Relations*, May 13, 2019, https://www.cfr.org/backgrounder/made-china-2025-threat-global-trade.

120 Jing Zhang , Tamer A. Soliman , Paulette Vander Schueren , Margaret-Rose Sales , Heng Li , Edouard Gergondet , Yoshihide Ito , Thomas So and Jason Hungerford, "China Issues Legislation To Block Unjustified Extra-Territorial Application Of Foreign Legislation And Measures", *mondaq*, January 15, 2021, https://www.mondaq.com/china/export-controls-trade-investment-sanctions/1026174/china-issues-legislation-to-block-unjustified-extra-territorial-application-of-foreign-legislation-and-measures.

The Belt and Road Initiative (BRI), launched by China, represents a monumental global development strategy that aims to enhance regional connectivity and embrace a brighter economic future through building a trade and infrastructure network that mirrors the ancient Silk Road trade routes. The BRI's influence on global supply chains is profound and multifaceted, substantially affecting trade patterns, investment flows, and economic development across continents.

A pivotal study by Kohl sheds light on the BRI's significant impacts on supply-chain trade for numerous economies, particularly emphasizing the initiative's ability to reduce trade costs through infrastructural enhancements and the establishment of free trade agreements. [121] The findings underscore an asymmetric advantage accruing mainly to China, Russia, and Southeast Asian countries, stemming from expanded access to the European market. This asymmetry suggests that while the BRI is positioned as a mutually beneficial economic partnership, the strategic benefits are disproportionately in favor of China and its closest allies.

Furthermore, the BRI serves as a strategic tool for China to cement its role as a central hub in global supply chains, extending its influence beyond mere trade to encompass geopolitical and strategic dimensions. Through the BRI, China is not only facilitating easier and more efficient trade routes but is also embedding itself deeper into the economic fabric of participating countries. This integration presents both opportunities and challenges for the global economy, particularly for the US and EU, as they navigate the complexities of their dependencies on China amidst growing geopolitical tensions.

121　Kohl T. "The Belt and Road Initiative's effect on supply-chain trade: evidence from structural gravity equations". *Cambridge Journal of Regions, Economy and Society*. 2019;12(1):77-104. doi:https://doi.org/10.1093/cjres/rsy036

The BRI's capacity to shift global trade dynamics underscores the need for a strategic response from the US and EU. It highlights the importance of understanding the comprehensive implications of China's initiatives on their economic security and supply chain resilience. As the US and EU assess their trade policies and supply chain strategies, incorporating a nuanced understanding of the BRI's effects on global trade architecture will be crucial. This entails not only mitigating potential vulnerabilities but also exploring new opportunities for cooperation and development in a rapidly changing global economic landscape.

China's Trade Coercion

According to an investigation conducted by the US Trade Representative (USTR) under Section 301 of the Trade Act of 1974, China has for long been engaging in forced technology transfer, cyber-enabled theft of USIP and trade secrets, discriminatory and nonmarket licensing practices, and state-funded strategic acquisitions of US assets.[122] Chinese statist policies and Beijing's lack of response to long-standing US concerns have probably exacerbated the situation. In the US Congress, some legislators are alarmed by the imbalances, the United States' participation in China's industrial policies, ties to PRC firms that violate human rights, and China's practices that could force or unfairly encourage the transfer of American technology and data to China. There are growing concerns about how China's demands for business ties may threaten US competitiveness, national security, and leadership in international affairs.[123]

---

122 "Section 301 of the Trade Act of 1974", *Congressional Research Service*, May 26, 2022, https://crsreports.congress.gov/product/pdf/IF/IF11346.

123 Michael J. Green and Scott Kennedy, "US Business Leaders Not Ready for the Next U.S.-China Crisis", CSIS, May 16, 2022, https://www.csis.org/analysis/us-business-leaders-not-ready-next-us-china-crisis.

One possibility that the US Congress has considered is to tighten international trade regulations, compel reciprocity, engage with allies to address China trade concerns, and expand ties with like-minded countries in commercial, technological, and research fields.

Technology Transfers

As the Chinese government works to achieve its industrial policy goals and strengthen its military through the acquisition of US technology, Washington policymakers are growing increasingly concerned about this trend.[124] Forced technology transfer is a term coined by the United States to describe the practice of Beijing pressuring American companies doing business in China to surrender their proprietary technologies. For instance, the Justice Department in the US charged Chinese telecommunications giant Huawei in 2020 with racketeering and stealing trade secrets from US firms for over two decades. The indictment accuses Huawei of building its empire on the backs of other companies, including six US firms, by copying intellectual property and then selling it in products around the world.[125]

To aid their Chinese counterparts, Chinese hackers have allegedly also stolen vast amounts of intellectual property from American corporations, allegations that resembles concerns raised in the EU and other advanced economies in the world.[126] In 2020,

---

124 Reuters, "China theft of technology is biggest law enforcement threat to US, FBI says", *The Guardian*, February 6, 2020, https://www.theguardian.com/world/2020/feb/06/china-technology-theft-fbi-biggest-threat

125 Steven Overly, "US charges Huawei with decades long theft of US trade secrets", *Politico*, February 13, 2020, https://www.politico.com/news/2020/02/13/us-charges-huawei-with-racketeering-and-theft-114912.

126 Jethro Mullen, "How China squeezes tech secrets from US companies", *CNN Business*, https://money.cnn.com/2017/08/14/news/economy/trump-china-trade-intellectual-property/index.html

Chinese investment in high-tech and key infrastructure in the United States has been viewed with skepticism by US regulators, partly because of direct and indirect examples of cyber theft. In some cases, actors have acted for their own financial advantage, while in others, for the benefit of the Ministry of State Security (MSS) or other Chinese government agencies. US networks were put at risk by the sophisticated and prolific danger that the hackers stole terabytes of data.[127] The full spread of cyber theft will never be known as the Chinese authorities are not cooperating with the US authorities.

Concerns about China's ability to obtain or soon gain access to sensitive and critical technologies that underpin American military superiority and economic power have been raised by the recent investment of billions of dollars in the US technology industry by Chinese private sector companies and state-owned enterprises. An older report from 2014 by the Asia Society and Rhodium Group found that US high-tech sectors are becoming increasingly attractive targets for Chinese investment.[128] The report indicated that Chinese companies have invested in a wide range of American technology sectors, including automobiles and medical gadgets. As China moved up the product and technology value chain, it also gained greater latitude for private businesses, which made up the vast majority of outbound investments in US high-tech. More than 25,000 employments have been generated or supported by Chinese investments,

---

127 "Two Chinese Hackers Working with the Ministry of State Security Charged with Global Computer Intrusion Campaign Targeting Intellectual Property and Confidential Business Information, Including COVID-19 Research", *The United States Department of Justice*, July 21, 2020, https://www.justice.gov/opa/pr/two-chinese-hackers-working-ministry-state-security-charged-global-computer-intrusion

128 Thilo Hanemann and Daniel H. Rosen, "High Tech: The Next Wave of Chinese Investment in America", *Asia Society*, April 2014, https://asiasociety.org/files/China_Hi_Tech_Report.pdf

both in the form of new greenfield projects and acquisitions, according to new research. In recent years, China has also taken advantage of the generally open US economy by freely investing in the United States while maintaining trade controls and exhaustively reviewing investments and acquisitions on its own shores.[129]

Subsidizing China's state-owned enterprises and its impacts

Creating "national champion" enterprises has been another objective of the Chinese government's massive infusion of subsidies into a variety of industries. While government subsidies are a poor tool for boosting competitiveness, the enormous scale of subsidies in China have been disruptive for other countries that cannot compete with such levels of state support. State-owned firms in China have been accused by the US of being government controlled and not following market principles like their private sector counterparts. All governments, including the United States, provide subsidies to domestic businesses, such as support for farmers, tax credits for certain investments, and incentives for corporations like Amazon to locate in certain federal states.

However, in addition to the full scale of central and provincial subsidies in China, business there are also the recipients of indirect support through low lending rates from banks and reduced energy prices. This is particularly the case for high-tech companies and critical industries such as oil and gas exploration.[130] Additionally, many of the subsidies are hidden and aimed at strengthening the

---

129 Jyh-An-Lee, "Forced Technology Transfer in the Case of China", *Boston University*, August 22, 2020, https://www.bu.edu/jostl/files/2020/08/3-Lee.pdf

130 Capital Trade Incorporated, "An Assessment of China's Subsidies to Strategic and Heavyweight Industries", *US-China Economic and Security Review Commission*, https://www.uscc.gov/sites/default/files/Research/AnAssessmentofChina'sSubsidiestoStrategicandHeavyweightIndustries.pdf

political impact of the Chinese government, rather than transparent and aiming to strengthen a certain industry or sector in the national economy. There are many other interventions too, like protectionist trade policies and requirements that international companies form joint ventures with native Chinese companies as a condition for market access. So-called "forced technology transfer," in which international corporations' hand over innovative technology as a condition for investing and producing in China, is a frequent requirement.[131] Many economists will also claim that, for some time, China artificially manipulated its currency to boost exports. That proposition can be debated. What is clearer is that China's regulation of financial markets and services, and capital controls, have had the effect of closing out foreign firms from China's finance sector.

Trade between the EU and China

China's most important trading partner is not the US but the European Union. Since China's entry into the WTO in December 2001, EU exports of goods and services to China have increased by an average of more than 10% annually.[132] At the same time, China's exports to Europe have grown faster. Figure 14 shows one example of this. As a result, the EU now has a $220 billion trade deficit with China. While bilateral trade deficits are of little relevance, and the EU's trade deficit with China is substantially lower than the US trade deficit with China, a large and growing trade deficit can nevertheless be a sign of non-reciprocal trade conditions.

---

131 "How Chinese Companies Facilitate Technology Transfer from the United States", *US-China Economic and Security Review Commission*, May 06, 2019, https://www.uscc.gov/research/how-chinese-companies-facilitate-technology-transfer-united-states

132 "How Influential is China in the World Trade Organization?", *China Power CSIS*, https://chinapower.csis.org/china-world-trade-organization-wto/.

Figure 12: EU Trade with China

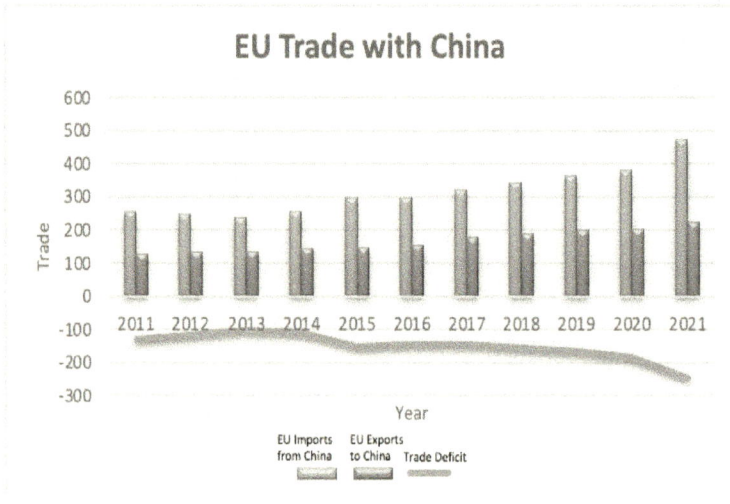

Source: Eurostat

Figure 13: EU Trade with China by Product Group (2011-2021)

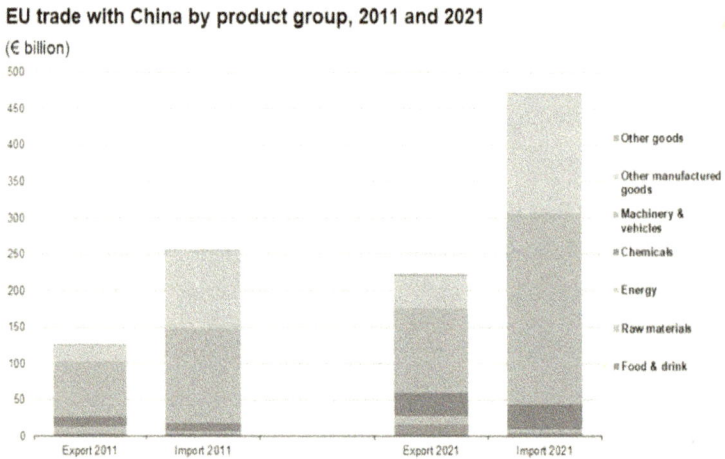

In terms of sectors, the EU's trade with China is concentrated to certain industrial goods. In 2021, EU exports of manufactured goods (86 percent) had a higher share than primary goods (12 percent). The most exported manufactured goods were machinery & vehicles (52 %), followed by other manufactured goods (20 percent) and chemicals (15 percent). In 2021, EU imports of manufactured goods (98 percent) also had a higher share than primary goods (2 percent). The most imported manufactured goods were machinery & vehicles (56 percent), followed by other manufactured goods (35 percent) and chemicals (7 percent).[133] These datapoints highlight the growing dependence of the EU on China in certain manufacturing sectors.

Contrary to popular belief, EU member states have become increasingly dependent on China for intermediate goods as the intra-EU value chain has decreased.[134] The European Commission noted already in 2018 that the EU´s global share of the manufacturing chain declined from 27 percent in 2000 to 16 percent in 2014.[135] The analysis suggested that 60% of the decline could be explained by the shifts in demand and 40% on the loss of competitiveness. While Chinese firms are competitive, there has also been a complacent attitude in Europe with regard to advanced manufacturing, leading to decline in investments and the expansion of relevant

---

133 "China-EU - international trade in goods statistics", *Eurostat*, February 2022, https://ec.europa.eu/eurostat/statistics-explained/index.php?title=China-EU_-_international_trade_in_goods_statistics#:~:text=In%202011%2C%20the%20EU%20had,2011%20(%E2%82%AC%20127%20billion).

134 Huiyao Chen and Changyuan Luo, "EU-China trade and intra-EU trade: Substitute or complementary?", *Journal of Economic Surveys*, 36(3), pp. 558-585, https://onlinelibrary.wiley.com/doi/10.1111/joes.12471?af=R.

135 "EU losing share in global manufacturing value chains", JRC Science for Policy Brief, European Commission, , June 2018.

human capital.[136] For the EU to increase its competitiveness, it is not only a question of improving the intra-regional value chain but also to boost skills, investment and innovation. Garcia-Herrero and Martines Turègano have suggested that EU has lost 1 million jobs between 2000 to 2014 due to EU´s declining participation in the manufacturing value chain.[137]

Investments

EU investment into China has been decreasing recently. There have been several complaints from European companies about the difficulties they confront in China, including insufficient investor protection, inconsistent and often arbitrary market access. In several industries, joint venture requirements have been a major concern. Investing in Chinese operations has become less appealing due to the prevalence of intellectual property transfers to Chinese peers. China's inclusion in the ranks of the world's most powerful investors has also sparked concerns about the country's state-run economy. This concept has the potential to produce an unfair playing field. The EU's biggest challenge is ensuring that EU companies doing business in China are treated equally with Chinese counterparts and that Chinese companies doing business in the EU are not given preferential treatment by the Chinese government. SOEs in particular may be affected, but private businesses may also be included in this category.

---

136 Alicia Garcia-Herrero & David Martines Turègano, "Europe is losing competitiveness in global value chain while Cina surges", Bruegel, 27 November, 2020, https://www.bruegel.org/blog-post/europe-losing-competitiveness-global-value-chains-while-china-surges

137 Alicia Garcia Herrero, David Martínez Turégano. "The economic rationale for reshuffling global value chains". *Medium*, January 19, 2021. https://1556865737385.medium.com/the-economic-rationale-for-reshuffling-global-value-chains-bebd1984d847

Chinese and American corporations now share the top spot on the Fortune 500 list, making them key competitors for European firms. In addition, many significant Chinese corporations are owned by the government, which presents unique issues in terms of governance and financial support. It has been exacerbated by the fact that Chinese companies are now operating in high value-added markets – increasingly operating in areas where European companies are competitive. The challenge is that the European Union, as well as the US, is becoming more linked to the Chinese market and firms, while China is becoming more vertically integrated and less dependent on foreign companies.

The Belt and Road Initiative and the EU

Although China's BRI is frequently connected with Central and East Asia, China's BRI has attracted a growing number of European countries, including two-thirds of the EU's 28 members. BRI's flagship European project, Hungary's Budapest-Belgrade railway,[138] has received major investment from China, as well as Greece's Piraeus port,[139] Portugal's energy sector,[140] and the port of Sines.[141] BRI-affiliated companies have also invested heavily in Greece, Portugal,

138 Andreea Brînză, "China and the Budapest-Belgrade Railway Saga", *The Diplomat*, April 28, 2020, https://thediplomat.com/2020/04/china-and-the-budapest-belgrade-railway-saga/.

139 Momoko Kidera and Shin Watanabe, "China bolsters Europe foothold with Belt and Road expansion", *Nikkei Asia*, November 14, 2019, https://asia.nikkei.com/Spotlight/Belt-and-Road/China-bolsters-Europe-foothold-with-Belt-and-Road-expansion

140 Mat Youkee, "How Long Can Portugal Continue to Play Both Sides of the U.S.-China Rivalry?", *World Politics Review,* November 25, 2020, https://www.worldpoliticsreview.com/articles/29246/how-long-can-portugal-continue-to-play-both-sides-of-the-u-s-china-rivalry

141 Samuel Wejchert, "Port of Sines: The Atlantic End of the New Silk Road?", *European Institute for Asian Studies*, July 2021, https://eias.org/wp-content/uploads/2021/07/Port-of-Sines-The-Atlantic-End-of-the-New-Silk-Road.pdf.

and Hungary in the past few years.[142] More than two-thirds of the EU's member nations have signed on as formal partners with it. More recently, there is a growing realization that BRI is not delivering the economic benefits that was promised and comes with a frowning political luggage.[143] European members are increasingly distancing from Chinese economic initiatives, partly because of human rights abuses and political pressure, but mainly because the economic benefits are simply not there. The 16+1 mechanism is an example of this, where Beijing used this to influence EU economically through what it defined as Europe's soft belly. However, this soft belly partially turned out to be both critical of China and ready to stand up against Chinese abuses. Today, all the Baltic states have left the mechanism and growing dissatisfaction threatens to further decrease the role of the 16+1 (now 14+1) mechanism.

The BRI has been failing in EU, and it was highly symbolic when Italy left as BRI member in late 2023. Italy's decision to join the BRI had been opposed by European and American leaders, especially as the EU developed a new strategy for dealing with Beijing, labelling it "an economic competitor in the pursuit of technical leadership and a systemic opponent that promotes alternative kinds of governance."[144] Italy's decision to join also hastened EU-wide legislation for screening FDI, and Italy leaving has resulted in stronger polices against China and less influence.

---

142 Valbona Zeneli, "Italy Signs on to Belt and Road Initiative: EU-China Relations at Crossroads?", *The Diplomat,* April 03, 2019, https://thediplomat.com/2019/04/italy-signs-on-to-belt-and-road-initiative-eu-china-relations-at-crossroads/.

143 Svante Cornell & Niklas Swanström, "Compatible Interests? The EU and China´s Belt and Road Initiative", *Swedish Institute for European Policy Studies*, Report no. 1, Stockholm, January 2020. https://www.sieps.se/en/publications/2020/compatible-interests/

144 *European Commission*, Commission reviews relations with China, proposes 10 actions, Press Release March 12, 2019,

BRI's push into Europe initially made it harder for the EU to craft a united approach to China or to keep some aspiring Eastern European entrants to the bloc on board. This too has changed, and even more so after the Russian invasion of Ukraine in 2022 and the Chinese *de facto* support of Russia. European BRI beneficiaries like Hungary and Greece did push back on EU attempts to criticize China as a bloc, but never took this very far for obvious reasons. Austria, Hungary, and initially Greece resisted efforts to ban Chinese 5G provider Huawei. In Serbia, China has been funding projects that violate EU environmental regulations, something that has impacted on Serbia's bid to join EU.[145]

An important reason for concern about the BRI is China's economic model of state capitalism and the need for China to find new markets for its excess capacity. Excess capacity is a natural consequence of China's model, which for long was based on over-investment to keep growth going, and is strengthened by the government's industrialization and infant-industry support. Also, without market principles, the recipient countries run the risk of engaging in too many projects, which is likely to be unprofitable in the long run, casting doubts on the sustainability of BRI projects. There has already been some argument over debt traps related to some BRI projects, such as the failure of Sri Lanka to make repayments against loans given by China to construct Hambantota Port, and the subsequent 99-year lease given to China in place of payment. The situation has been exacerbated by most BRI projects being long-term and carrying large uncertainty politically as well as economically, which intrinsically bears high risk.

---

145 Phillippe Le Corre, "Europe's mixed views on China's One Belt, One Road initiative", *Brookings*, May 23, 2017, https://www.brookings.edu/blog/order-from-chaos/2017/05/23/europes-mixed-views-on-chinas-one-belt-one-road-initiative/.

The European Union is also concerned about the reciprocity and access to the Chinese market for European businesses. Some investment protections were due to come with the negotiated Bilateral Investment Treaty, but this agreement was put in the freezer after heavy-handed sanctions by China of Members of the European Parliament.[146] The European Chamber of Commerce in China continues to document the policy-based restrictions that European firms face in China – and this list keeps growing year by year. The challenges are growing and the Chinese legislation is making it increasingly difficult for foreign companies to compete on equal terms in China, but they have a more a level playing field in Europe which further skews free and fair competition.

In addition, because of the unilateral nature of the BRI and the lack of global collaboration, most of the projects fall short of, for example, Organization for Economic Co-operation and Development (OECD) transparency standards. Although China has made an effort to establish a multilateral institution – the Asian Infrastructure Investment Bank (AIIB) – it has not fully addressed external concerns. The situation has become more complicated because of China's growth model, with a strong government role and weak domestic institutional development. The lack of trust in the BRI poses challenges. In fact, according to a survey published by the European Union Chamber of Commerce in China, a lack of information and transparency were top barriers for European

---

146 "EU-China FDI: Working towards more reciprocity in investment relations", *MERICS*, April 17, 2018, https://merics.org/en/report/eu-china-fdi-working-towards-more-reciprocity-investment-relations

companies seeking involvement in China's market.[147] Further, only 20 out of 132 firms polled said they have bid for projects related to the BRI, and of them, only 10 percent got wind of the project through publicly available information. While about a quarter of respondents said the BRI – which was launched in 2013 – was improving in transparency, quality and fairness, this trend was less even less pronounced when it comes to access to projects.[148]

Owing to these issues, the EU in September 2021 announced a plan to mobilize 300 billion Euros in public and private infrastructure investment around the world, which has been analyzed by many as a response to China's BRI strategy. Termed as "Global Gateway",[149] it will be bringing together resources of the EU, member states, European financial institutions and national development finance institutions.[150] However, to develop an initiative which is truly global, the EU would need a more coordinated and collaborated approach in tandem with its development, environmental and trade efforts. This holds greater cruciality considering the estimates by the Global Infrastructure Hub, a G20 initiative, pronouncing the global investment infrastructure deficit of $15 trillion by 2040.[151] In this

---

147 "European Chamber Report Identifies Profound Lack Of European Involvement In China's Belt And Road Initiative, And The Scheme's Dampening Effects On Global Competition", *European Chamber*, January 16, 2020, https://www. europeanchamber.com.cn/en/press-releases/3110/european_chamber_report_ identifies_profound_lack_of_european_involvement_in_china_s_belt_and_road_ initiative_and_the_scheme_s_dampening_effects_on_global_competition

148 "China's Belt and Road projects lack transparency, say European firms", *Business Standard*, January 16, 2020, https://www.business-standard.com/ article/pti-stories/lack-of-transparency-in-china-s-belt-and-road-projects-eu-firms-120011600166_1.html

149 "Global Gateway", *European Commission*, https://ec.europa.eu/info/strategy/ priorities-2019-2024/stronger-europe-world/global-gateway_en

150 AFP, "EU plans $300 billion infrastructure fund to counter China's BRI", *The Hindu*, December 1, 2021, https://www.thehindu.com/news/international/eu-plans-300-billion-infrastructure-fund-to-counter-chinas-bri/article37795447.ece

151 "2021 G20 Infrastructure Investors Dialogue", *OECD*, June 3, 2021, https://www. oecd.org/finance/g20-infrastructure-investors-dialogue-2021.htm.

context, a trans-Atlantic effort towards sustainable global development might be more viable. In fact, the Global Gateway initiative could work in partnership with the initiatives already in place by the US, such as the Build Back Better World (B3W) as well as UK's Clean Green Initiative.[152]

EU-China Relations after Russia's Invasion of Ukraine

A more united front against China is long overdue, but the EU has been unable to speak with one voice due to a variety of foreign policy differences among Member States as well as their disunited economic interests. However, since March 2021, when the European Parliament uniformly stopped the ratification of the Comprehensive Agreement on Investment (CAI)[153] over human rights concerns, both economies have been at loggerheads. Relations between EU and Russia have deteriorated dramatically since Russian troops invaded Ukraine on February 24, and the following tacit support of Russia from China. There appears to be little hope for a quick peaceful resolution of the war in Ukraine, and the effects of the war will be lingering on decades after a resolution of the war is found.

The EU has been dissatisfied with Beijing for failing to speak out against Russia's military aggressiveness in Ukraine. An effort to ensure peace had been expected from China since the beginning of the conflict, but a meeting on April 1 in 2022 between EU leaders

---

152 James Norris, "For it's Global Gateway to succeed, the EU must learn the art of partnership", *China Dialogue*, March 17, 2022, https://chinadialogue.net/en/business/for-its-global-gateway-to-succeed-the-eu-must-learn-the-art-of-partnership/; "The Build Bank Better Framework", *The White House*, https://www.whitehouse.gov/build-back-better/

153 "EU-China Comprehensive Agreement on Investment: Levelling the playing field with China", *European Parliament*, March 2021, https://www.europarl.europa.eu/RegData/etudes/BRIE/2021/679103/EPRS_BRI(2021)679103_EN.pdf

and China's President Xi Jinping crushed those hopes. However, the conflict in Ukraine has compelled Europe to re-examine its geopolitical strategy, something it hadn't done since 1991.

More plans are in the works that aren't specifically aimed at China but provide resources for a protracted conflict. It is being discussed in EU institutions how to analyze trade partners' industrial subsidies and levy tariffs to make up for the lost revenue. China, which has massively subsidized a number of its export-oriented domestic businesses, could probably use this against Brussels. Imports created employing forced labor will be prohibited from entering the EU under a new trade mechanism. This, too, might provide trade regulators with a flexible tool with which to increase pressure on Beijing.

Beyond the immediate geopolitical responses, the EU's strategy towards China in the post-Ukraine invasion era must also grapple with the broader trend of de-globalization, a movement accelerated by the pandemic and heightened by ongoing US-China trade tensions.

The restructuring of Global Value Chains (GVCs) has emerged as a critical strategic response amidst the escalating trade tensions between the US and China. This reconfiguration is driven by a need to mitigate vulnerabilities exposed by over-reliance on concentrated supply sources and to adapt to the shifting sands of global geopolitics and economic policies. The research conducted by Gopalakrishnan *et al* provides a comprehensive analysis of this phenomenon, illuminating the implications of such restructuring for global trade and economic resilience. [154]

The study highlights how GVCs, integral to the modern global

---

154 Gopalakrishnan BN, Vickers B, Ali S. *Analysing the Effects of the COVID-19 Pandemic on Medical Supply Chains in Commonwealth Countries.* Commonwealth iLibrary; 2022. Accessed February 28, 2024. https://www.thecommonwealth-ilibrary.org/index.php/comsec/catalog/book/943

economy, are being reevaluated in light of the need for greater supply chain security and economic sovereignty. The US-China trade tensions serve as a catalyst for this reevaluation, prompting both economic powerhouses and their global partners to reconsider the configuration of their supply chains. The potential shift towards more regionalized or localized production models is a significant outcome of this process, aiming to reduce dependency on any single country or region and enhance the flexibility and resilience of supply chains.

For the EU, this restructuring of GVCs presents both challenges and opportunities. On one hand, the EU must navigate the complexities of reducing its own dependencies on Chinese manufacturing and supply chains without compromising its economic interests or disrupting existing trade relations. On the other hand, the EU has the opportunity to strengthen its internal market, foster closer economic ties within the bloc, and explore new trade partnerships that diversify its supply sources and economic alliances.

The implications of GVC restructuring extend beyond mere supply chain logistics to encompass broader economic, strategic, and policy considerations. For instance, the push towards regionalization may encourage the development of new industrial capacities within the EU, promoting innovation, sustainability, and competitiveness. Furthermore, this shift may also catalyze closer cooperation between the US and EU as they seek to align their strategies on trade, technology, and security in response to common challenges posed by China's economic policies and geopolitical ambitions.

Integrating this expanded discussion into the discussion enriches the narrative on EU-China relations by placing the restructuring of GVCs within the context of broader geopolitical dynamics and economic strategies. It underscores the need for strategic foresight and collaborative action between the US and EU to navigate the complexities of global trade in an era of heightened tensions and uncertainty.[155]

The EU's view of China has clearly been affected by Russia's war and emerging geopolitical conflicts caused by these authoritarian regimes. As the EU deepens the policies at its disposal to counter hostile economic influences by China, the EU is also growing closer to the US approach to China.

155 Gopalakrishnan BN, Chakravarthy SL, Tewary T, Jain V. "Isolating China: Deglobalisation and its impact on global value chains". *Foreign Trade Review*. 2021;57(4):001573252110454. doi:https://doi.org/10.1177/00157325211045463

FIVE

Back to the Basics –
Human Resources, Innovation, and Mining

The US-China trade war and the Covid-19 outbreak have disrupted international trade and brought Western overreliance on China's economy to the forefront. Businesses are now compelled to re-evaluate their global supply chains and make them more secure, and both the EU and the US are intensifying policies that are reducing their exposure to trade and supply-chain risks emanating in China. Historically, supply chains were structured to reduce costs and inventory levels. Now, however, supply chains are being redesigned to lessen the likelihood of future disruptions, even though doing so incurs additional expenses. Given that China is the world's largest exporter of goods and manufacturing inputs, and is engaged in a trade war with the United States, supply chains passing through China may be among the most susceptible to future disruption. The rerouting of supply chains for high-tech and research-intensive commodities will undoubtedly play a role in the narrative. However, the process of supply chain restructuring is neither easy nor cheap, and rebuilding them independently of China will have to start at the very bottom of the pit, literally and metaphorically.

China's Rise up the Value Chains

China's climb up the value-added chain has been fast by historical standards. Starting in light manufacturing such as textiles, it moved into machinery, electronics, and other more advanced industries. As a result, China's role in labor-intensive trade has increased remarkably. It has been estimated that China's share of labor-intensive exports increased from 13.9 percent in 2000, the year before it joined the World Trade Organization, to 26.9 percent in 2018, roughly the same as in the four years prior. This percentage is greater than the following five largest exporters of labor-intensive items combined.[156] In this regard it should be noted that Europe's participation in labor intensive manufacturing have decreased significantly, partly as a result of low-cost competition, partly as a result of technological change. The trend is very much the same in Japan and the US: industrial output has been growing but not at a fast pace while industrial employment has declined as technology has substituted for labor.

Like other catch-up economies before it, China has moved into higher value-added production as productivity and prosperity has gone up. The massive program for government investment has also made many companies to deepen capital and technology a lot faster than in other historical examples, leading to many industrial sectors in China being technologically sophisticated. At the same time,

---

156 "World Trade Statistical Review: 2019", https://www.wto.org/english/res_e/statis_e/wts2019_e/wts2019_e.pdf.

low-costs advantages have been maintained by relocating production from coastal regions to inland regions where salaries are lower,
and the level of development is vastly different. This combination
has enabled China to maintain its production of labor-intensive
commodities.

The export data in recent years, however, have begun to suggest
that this trend is slowing down and that China has entered a new
structural phase – of either plateauing industrial growth or a reallocation of production factors from industry to other sectors. China is to
a growing extent a state-run economy, but such economies are more
bound by the metrics of economics than market economies. With
the gradual shift away from its model of investment-led growth and
strong focus on real estate, the Chinese economy is confronted by
structural problems that are costly to manage and that do not allow
for strong growth of labor and capital flowing into the industrial
sector. These problems have led the government to focus more on
using third markets to help support its industrial sector.

Further, instead of manufacturers relocating from high-cost to
low-cost regions, workers had relocated from low-wage rural areas
to high-wage urban areas, with over 150 million migrant laborers
employed in the eastern provinces. Typically, migrant workers had
been given low pay and received limited benefits, which allowed
exporters to remain competitive in these otherwise high-cost regions.
In recent years, however, salary growth for migrant workers has
accelerated, and the number of migrant workers employed in eastern
provinces has decreased, especially in the main exporting regions.[157]

Nonetheless, China's productivity increase in the past thirty

---

157 "The end of cheap China", *The Economist*, March 10, 2012, https://www.
     economist.com/business/2012/03/10/the-end-of-cheap-china.

years is one of the strongest reasons for why China has remained anchored in the industrial sector. Notable productivity gains in the labor-intensive sectors of textiles, apparel, and footwear have compensated for wage rise in manufacturing in the main exporting coastal regions between 2010 and 2016, at least.[158] Between 2010 and 2016, manufacturing wages in China's three major exporting provinces increased between 11 and 14 percent annually. China's textiles, garment, and footwear productivity increased between 14 and 15 percent during the same time frame. More importantly, its overall labor productivity growth has been strong and growing, especially in the market-based sector.[159]

It is not only a question of what China has done, but it is equally a question of what the US and EU has (not) done. Generally, by importing more from China and deepen technology, all developed economies have been able to gradually reallocate labor and other production factors into higher value-added output. But this is not the only story – especially not in some strategical important sectors of industry like minerals. Due to the initial high costs of extraction of minerals, environmental concerns, and geopolitical complacency, the EU and the US hollowed out important industries and allowed themselves to become dependent on China for critical raw material supply. This has put the transatlantic economies, as well as Japan and Australia, in a dependency position to an authoritarian state that has been known for using economic coercion to gain political advantages. The short-term gains have superseded the long-term environmental,

---

158 Michael Wolf, "Chain reaction: The China Link in Global Supply Chains", *Deloitte*, December 05, 2020, https://www2.deloitte.com/xe/en/insights/economy/asia-pacific/china-supply-chain.html.

159 "China Labour Productivity Growth", *CEIC*, https://www.ceicdata.com/en/indicator/china/labour-productivity-growth.

geopolitical, and economic objectives, resulting in what are now costly efforts to regain control over especially rare earth minerals access. The growth of dependence on China for minerals and some other important industrial products has become a big concern.

However, China's competitive advantages are not the only factor that has contributed to the global reliance on Chinese manufacturing. China's ascension to economic superpower status is preceded by a precarious system of just-in-time production and considerable offshore production. At the end of the 1970s, the concepts of keeping small inventories and outsourced production gained popularity. This occurred during the same decade that important components of the global system for delivering commodities from producer to final destination were deregulated, leaving the world with a more sophisticated but less unified logistics system. Often, the supply chain's links were not adequately connected. While just-in-time production has been important to drive increased efficiency, and generally helped to rebalance dependencies away from often unreliable domestic supply structures, there has been a huge underinvestment in ensuring these global supply chains are safe. This is particularly the case in light of China – an authoritarian state with strategic ambitions hostile to many Western interests – becoming the chief node in the supply chains.

There are variations between industrial sectors, but in some of them the structural change in manufacturing – through trade and technology – had the effect of pushing resources away from R&D and innovation. An efficiency paradigm grew supreme. Lean supply chain management practices demanded controlled release processing with low inventory volumes, leveled and just-in-time production, and accurate scheduling of transport for cross-docking operations, resulting in more cost-effective and responsive supply chains. Unfortunately, the push to reduce costs partly resulted in the outsourcing and offshoring of numerous R&D and innovation activities, too, also in sectors that are strategically important.[160]

Innovation

China has now arisen to be an innovation nation: it contributes significant innovation in many industrial sectors. Decades of fast economic expansion have allowed China to spend in important innovation-driving areas, including research and development and the creation of new intellectual property. China's GII rating has increased as a result of these investments, allowing it to compete with sophisticated economies such as the United States and Europe.

Figure 14: Gross Spending on R&D

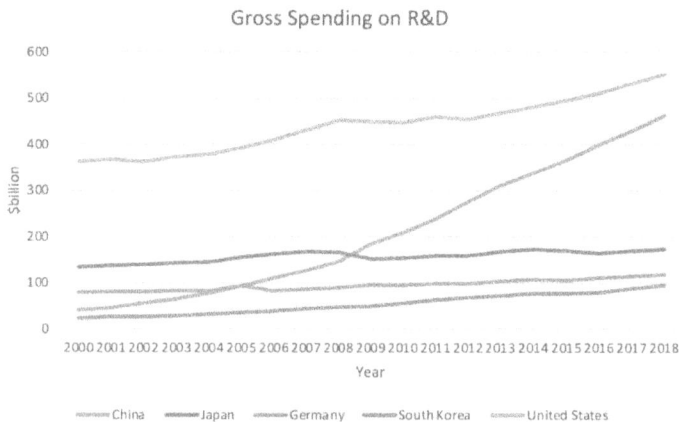

Source: China Power Project, Center for Strategic and International Studies.

---

160 K. Katsaliaki, P. Galetsi, and S. Kumar, "Supply chain disruptions and resilience: a major review and future research agenda", *Annals and Operations Research*, 2021, https://link.springer.com/article/10.1007/s10479-020-03912-1.

China's acceleration as an innovation nation has been remarkable. As shown in Figure 14, China's R&D expenditures were comparatively low around the turn of the century, only topping those of South Korea. However, its R&D expenditures have increased from 1.71 percent of its GDP in 2010 to 2.40 percent in 2020. Although it is less than average OECD spending on R&D (which is about 2.7% of GDP), China's economy is very big and this percentage increase leads to substantial effects on nominal spending. The acceleration started in the late 2000s and continued throughout the 2010s, leading to a frontier position for China. China's R&D spending is currently second only to the United States and, in a decade, it will likely have surpassed US R&D spending. Add to those other strategies – focus on R&D to strategic sectors (e.g. telecom, materials, defense, and biomedicine), huge growth in patent filings, intellectual property theft, and more – and it becomes clearer that China is a serious power in R&D and innovation intense sectors. This also includes Artificial Intelligence.[161]

Assessing the role of business in China's R&D spending is complicated because of the prominence of state-owned firms in countries and non-transparent policy. Numerous SOE executives hold positions inside the government and Chinese Communist Party, and it is obvious that R&D activities backed or mediated

161   Jon Bateman, U.S.-China Technology "Decoupling": A Strategy and Policy Framework, *Carnegie Endowment of International Peace*, April, 2022, https://carnegieendowment.org/2022/04/25/countering-unfair-chinese-economic-practices-and-intellectual-property-theft-pub-86925

by SOEs frequently align with government-funded initiatives.[162] Additionally, SOEs have preferential access to bank loans from state-owned banks, which reduces the cost of borrowing and gives SOEs a stronger financial position that has also been observed to fuel certain R&D activities.[163]

China is also running fast on the accumulation of patents and establishing itself as an innovator. China has increased its efforts over the past five years to become an intellectual property superpower. During this time period, it has granted more than 2.53 million patents, with an average annual growth rate of 13.4%.[164] China rose from 22nd in 2017 to 12th in the World Intellectual Property Organization's Global Innovation Index for 2021. It topped the rating for middle-income nations, surpassing developed nations such as Japan, Israel, and Canada. Moreover, according to the "Outline for Building an Intellectual Property Rights Powerhouse (2021-35)" presented by the Communist Party's Central Committee and the State Council, China plans to increase this figure to 13% by 2025. Moreover, by

---

162 Xiankun Jin, Liping Xu, Yu Xin & Ajay Adhikari, "Political governance in China's state-owned enterprises", *China Journal of Accounting Research*, Vol. 15, Issue 2, June 2022, https://www.sciencedirect.com/science/article/pii/S1755309122000168 ; CNB Editor, "State-owned Enterprise Reform Steps up Role of Chinese Communist Party in Corporate Governance", *China Banking News*, August 19, 2021, https://www.chinabankingnews.com/2021/08/19/state-owned-enterprise-reform-steps-up-role-of-chinese-communist-party-in-corporate-governance/

163 "Is China a Global Leader in Research and Development?", *CSIS*, https://chinapower.csis.org/china-research-and-development-rnd/.

164 Zhang Yangfei, "China makes headway in IP industry", *The State Council*, The People's Republic of China", April 25, 2022, https://english.www.gov.cn/statecouncil/ministries/202204/25/content_WS6265f45dc6d02e5335329e0b.html.

2035 – the strategy said – China would be a global leader in intellectual property rights.[165]

The United States may have led the world in innovation, research, and technology development since World War II, but this leadership is now in jeopardy.[166] Federal support and funding for research and development have been stagnant for decades. The private sector has not increased its share of R&D by much either – even if there has been significant R&D spending in some sectors. But private sector investment is not a substitute for publicly sponsored research and development oriented at basic and strategic research. Other factors such as a poor domestic education system confound America's research status, too. A persistent cultural divide between the technological and policymaking sectors jeopardizes national security by making it more challenging for the Defense Department and intelligence agencies to acquire and utilize sophisticated technologies from the private sector and to recruit technical expertise.[167]

In terms of R&D spending and technological innovation, Europe is behind not just the United States and Japan, but also China. China has recently surpassed the EU in research and development spending, which is equivalent to 2.1% of GDP. EU-based universities have fallen significantly in international university rankings. Currently, none of the world's 15 largest digital enterprises

---

165 "China's 2021-2025 Five-Year Plan – An Outlook To China's Planned Future For IP", *Spruson*, July 29, 2021, https://www.spruson.com/patents/chinas-2021-2025-five-year-plan-an-outlook-to-chinas-planned-future-for-ip/.

166 "James Manyika, William H. McRaven, and Adam Segal, "Innovation and National Security:
Keeping Our Edge", *Council on Foreign Relations*, Independent Task Force Report No. 77, https://www.cfr.org/report/keeping-our-edge/

167 E. Richard Gold, "The Fall of the Innovation Empire and its Possible Rise through Open Science", *Research Policy*, 50(5), June 2021, https://www.sciencedirect.com/science/article/pii/S0048733321000305

are European.[168] The region is increasingly distant from the technological frontier and this development has implications going beyond employment and economic growth. It affects Europe's ability to understand and access frontier research and innovation, and its power to establish policies and standards that others want to follow.

New-firm growth is also a problem for the EU. Specifically, European start-ups struggle to expand due to a lack of access to large amounts of patient capital, especially in later-stage growth investments where the US spends about 20 times more than Europe. In spite of the progress made in Europe over the past decade, the region's capital markets are still underdeveloped and too focused on bulk asset management in sovereign and corporate debt. The EU is also overregulated, and becoming even more so. Cross-border investments and company expansion are hampered by the wide variation in laws, guidelines, taxes, and standards throughout the 28 member states.

For the EU to gain more geopolitical clout and be capable of managing threats related to China, it is necessary for it to change its way of thinking. The European tendency for being risk averse is a major contributor to the problems Europe is today facing in geoeconomics. Over the last decades, R&D spending by European firms in industrial sectors have been reallocated to the US and China because European regulations hamper discovery – such as in the case of Genetically Modified Organisms (GMOs). The limited availability and approach to venture capital is indicative of this. Without it, risk-averse financing facilities are the mainstay of European

---

168 Iliyana Tsanova and Roger Havenith, "Europe is no longer an innovation leader. Here's how it can get ahead", March 14, 2019, *World Economic Forum*, https://www.weforum.org/agenda/2019/03/europe-is-no-longer-an-innovation-leader-heres-how-it-can-get-ahead/

entrepreneurs, something that will hamper innovation.[169] This is also one of the reasons that European start-ups move to the US and, increasingly, China.

China's Dominant Position in the Global Rare Earth Minerals Industry

China has a dominant position in the global rare earth minerals industry, a family of 17 elements integral to all forms of 21st-century products – from mobile phones to wind turbines and advanced weapons systems. This is a major challenge to the US, the EU and other democracies. Modern technology relies heavily on rare earth elements, and China - representing two thirds of the global supply – largely controls the global supply. And growth is going to remain strong. The primary driver of the anticipated growth in demand will be electromobility.[170] Recent estimates suggest that more than ninety percent of all-electric vehicles sold worldwide are equipped with electric drives employing NdFeB permanent magnets, making this technology the undisputed leader. In addition, hybrid electric vehicles commonly use nickel-metal hydride (NiMH) batteries containing rare earths to store energy. These metal alloys indicate a further substantial use of rare earths.[171]

---

169 Iliyana Tsanova and Roger Havenith, "Europe is no longer an innovation leader. Here's how it can get ahead", March 14, 2019, *World Economic Forum*, https://www.weforum.org/agenda/2019/03/europe-is-no-longer-an-innovation-leader-heres-how-it-can-get-ahead/

170 Eric Onstad, "China frictions steer electric automakers away from rare earth magnets", *Reuters*, July 19, 2021, https://www.reuters.com/business/autos-transportation/china-frictions-steer-electric-automakers-away-rare-earth-magnets-2021-07-19/.

171 K. Bradsher, "China Tightens Grip on Rare Minerals", *The New York Times*, August 31, 2009, at http://www.nytimes.com/2009/09/01/business/global/01minerals.html.

China entered the rare-earths market in the mid-1980s and now runs a strongly state-supported strategy to dominate the global rare-earths market. For sure, the country has had an advantage over other economies in terms of environmental loads and damages associated with the mining, separation, and processing of rare earths, such as those derived from radioactive uranium and thorium as well as other acids. Adequate environmental protection would have been costly for US and EU rare earth miners. For China it was relatively simple to achieve price competitiveness because its environmental regulations were lax or non-existent.

Figure 15: US' Rare Earth Imports from China

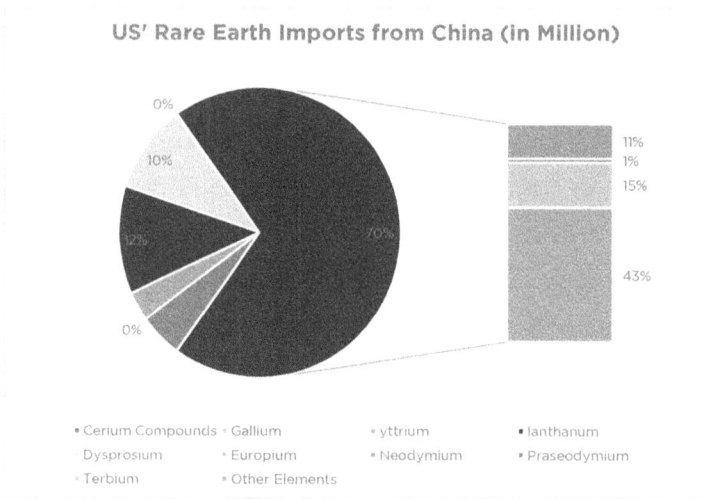

US' Rare Earth Imports from China (in Million)

Source: "Does China Pose a Threat to Global Rare Earth Supply Chains?" in China Power, CSIS[172]

---

172 "Does China Pose a Threat to Global Rare Earth Supply Chains?", *CSIS*, https://chinapower.csis.org/china-rare- earths/

The US imports 80 percent of its rare-earth compounds and metals from China.[173] In a similar vein, China provides as much as 98 percent of the EU's supply of rare earth elements. (Details of the percentage of imports for the particular rare-earth commodity for both the US and EU are provided in the graphs.) In addition, China has become a technological leader in the isolation and processing of rare earths during the past decades. China processes nearly all rare earth ores mined throughout the world. China currently produces approximately 90 percent of all rare earth oxides.[174] Even farther down the value chain, China controls the production of all key rare earth applications, including the fabrication of high-performance magnets. China's share of the global market for NdFeB magnets, to take one example, has surpassed 80 percent.[175] China has only one third of the worlds rare earth reserves, but controls 60 percent of the production, 85 percent of processing capacity and over 90 percent of the production of rare earth permanent magnets.[176] The transformation of China to become the largest producer, but also consumer, of rare earth minerals has been a consistent process, minimizing foreign investments in the process.

With the reliance on China, an emergent debate in the US and the EU on how to decrease dependency on China has focused

---

173 "How to Ease China's Hold on Rare Earths", *Bloomberg*, March 25, 2021, https://www.bloomberg.com/opinion/articles/2021-03-25/how-u-s-should-ease-china-s-rare-earth-dominance.

174 June Teufel Dreyer, "China's Monopoly on Rare Earth Elements", *Foreign Policy Research Institute*, October 7, 2020, https://www.fpri.org/article/2020/10/chinas-monopoly-on-rare-earth-elements-and-why-we-should-care/.

175 X. Du, T.E. Graedel, "Uncovering the end uses of rare earth elements", *Science of the Total Environment*, Vol. 461-462, 2013, pp. 781-784.

176 Xianbin Yao, "China is Moving rapidly up the Rare Earth Value Chain", *Brink News*, Marsh McLennan, August 7, 2002, https://www.brinknews.com/china-is-moving-rapidly-up-the-rare-earth-value-chain/

on reshoring rare-earth minerals by opening new mining processing operations domestically. However, considering the financial and technical challenges, and how China dumps prices to defend its market position,[177] the US and the EU have been unable to address the vulnerabilities that come with this dependency. China's strengthened regulation of the rare-earth mineral industry, as well as the practice of encouraging State-Owned Enterprises to acquire key international competitors, suggests a coordinated effort to control the flow of strategic minerals.

It is urgent for the US and the EU to devise a plan to wean themselves off this mineral dependence on China. This concern has only been exacerbated by China's use of mineral supply for political purposes. For instance, it has played around with export controls for certain buyers and threatened to withhold supply to other governments. European manufacturers of batteries to EVs – competing with Chinese battery manufacturers – have found that Beijing can deny some access to China's minerals. In retaliation for Japan's imprisonment of a Chinese fishing trawler captain, China prohibited exports to Japan of a vital category of minerals used in products such as hybrid cars, wind turbines, and guided missiles.[178] It is an obvious threat that China intends to leverage global dependency on its rare earth minerals even more in the future. China's increasingly aggressive military posture only heightens fears over its use of coercive tactics.

---

177 "China's Dumping Undermines free and fair International Trade?", *Aegis Europe*, February 2016, http://www.aegiseurope.eu/news/chinas-dumping-undermines-free-and-fair-international-trade.

178 Keith Bradsher, "Amid Tension, China Blocks Vital Exports to Japan", *The New York Times*, September 22, 2010, https://www.nytimes.com/2010/09/23/business/global/23rare.html.

Dependency is also strong in other raw materials. China provides the many critical raw materials to the EU that are required for the green transition. China is the primary provider for six of the 30 elements on the EU's list of Critical Raw Materials (CRMs), and one of the primary suppliers for four others.[179] Regardless of the fact that several others are imported from African and Latin American nations, China has gradually increased its investments in mining in these regions and intend to effect stronger control of the global supply. It also has expressed a strategy to dominate the global market of CRMs.

Deng Xiaoping was once quoted of saying that "中东有石油，中国有稀土", which translates into "The Middle East has its oil, China has rare earth". This is partially true. According to the US Geological Survey, China is responsible for 80 percent of the rare earth imports, so the bulk of the minerals is not in China but under Chinese control.[180] The speed of the control and assertiveness in investing in rare earth minerals have increased during Xi Jinping and has resulted in a massive control of ongoing mining operations for CRMs. This is not only the domestic control that Deng was referring to but a much more coordinated approach to develop CRMs all over the world and ensure the control of the processing technology that will increase international dependency on China controlled assets.[181]

---

179 "Study on the EU's list of Critical Raw Materials (2020)", *European Commission*, 2020, https://ec.europa.eu/docsroom/documents/42883/attachments/1/translations/en/renditions/native; Michael Penke, China's dominance of strategic resources, 13 April, 2021, Deutsche Welle, https://www.dw.com/en/how-chinas-mines-rule-the-market-of-critical-raw-materials/a-57148375

180 Samantha Subin, "The new US plan to rival China and end cornering of market in rare earth metals", *CNBC*, April 17, 2021, https://www.cnbc.com/2021/04/17/the-new-us-plan-to-rival-chinas-dominance-in-rare-earth-metals.html

181 Marina Yue Zhang, "Will China Seek to Exploit Its Rare-Earth Dominance?" *The National Interest*, November 26, 2022, https://nationalinterest.org/feature/will-china-seek-exploit-its-rare-earth-dominance-205944

In the final days of the Trump administration, the US Congress authorized a spending package including more than $800 million to support research on rare earths and strategic minerals in an attempt to counter Chinese market dominance. In addition to providing subsidies for research and development on rare earth elements and scarce metals, the bill required the US Geological Survey to forecast metals demand in the same manner as the Energy Department forecasts oil use. Moreover, it instructed the Director of National Intelligence to provide an annual report on China's mining interests abroad, leaving no doubt as to the motivation for this increased attention. It was lauded as a "bipartisan victory and a watershed policy for a US mine-to-magnet supply chain" because of its potential to restore investment in renewable energy.[182] Subsequently, the Biden administration issued an Executive Order requiring the Departments of Commerce, Energy, and Defense to submit reports within 100 days outlining threats to the supply chain for "critical minerals" and "other identified strategic materials," such as rare earth elements.[183]

This massive 100-day report revealed, among other things, that China's net reliance on imports for strategic and critical materials had increased substantially due to rising domestic production of rare earth elements (REEs) and critical metals not keeping pace with the rapid expansion of the Chinese economy. China has stepped up its efforts to dominate the value chain for technologies like permanent magnets, batteries, and semiconductors due to rising demand for

---

182 Ernest Scheyder, "Miners praise US spending bill that funds rare earths programs", *Reuters*, December 30, 2020, https://www.reuters.com/article/us-usa-mining-congress/miners-praise-u-s-spending-bill-that-funds-rare-earths-programs-idUSKBN29424R.

183 "America's Supply Chains", February 24, 2021, https://www.federalregister.gov/documents/2021/03/01/2021-04280/americas-supply-chains

these and other resources, including cobalt, copper, lithium, platinum group metals, and rare earth elements.[184]

Similar concerns were aired in Europe too. In her 2022 State of the Union address, the EU Commission President, Ursula von der Leyen, proposed a new piece of legislation called the Critical Raw Material Act. The primary goal of this act is to reduce reliance on China.[185] While the Commission has worked on concerns over mineral dependencies previously, this was the first time that the EU came up with real policies to achieve its objectives. She said the EU wanted to "prevent becoming dependent again, as we did with oil and gas". Moreover, she said:

> "From mining to processing to recycling, we will find critical projects all along the supply chain. Additionally, we will stockpile in areas where there is a threat to supply. That's why I'm proposing a Critical Raw Materials Act for Europe today."[186]

The Critical Raw Materials Act is not flawless but shows the EU is taking a more assertive stance toward eliminating a core supply chain risk. In order to diversify and expand European CRM output, a partnership involving industry actors, investors, the European Investment Bank, and EU member states is being pursued. The

---

184 "Building Resilient Supply Chains, Revitalizing American Manufacturing, and Fostering Broad-Based Growth", 100-Day Reviews under Executive Order 14017, June 2021, https://www.whitehouse.gov/wp-content/uploads/2021/06/100-day-supply-chain-review-report.pdf.

185 Oliver Noyan, "EU aims to lessen dependency on China with Raw Materials Act", *EURACTIV*, 14 September, 2022, https://www.euractiv.com/section/circular-economy/news/eu-aims-to-lessen-dependency-on-china-with-raw-materials-act/ ; "European Raw Materials Alliance", https://erma.eu/

186 "European Raw Materials Alliance", https://erma.eu/

European Union has also unveiled a comprehensive CRM plan, with the primary goals of expanding mining within the EU, diversifying imports, and promoting sustainable recycling.[187] These European efforts will not be sufficient to ensure a more independent and secure CRM access, but they are important first steps.

While the United States is concerned about the geopolitical consequences of supply chain reliance, the European Union seems more concerned with the geoeconomics. Initiatives inside the EU to increase CRM extraction have not fared well, and there are some obvious reasons for negative reactions: mineral deposits are rarely found in sufficient quantities to make extraction and processing economically viable. Furthermore, explorations for new mineral projects are often met with resistance from green campaigners, who point to the damage done to the environment and the social fallout from processing the ore. The European Union will be forced to look beyond their immediate sources and build networks independently of China to sustain economic predictability and independence.

An example of these challenges is Germany's botched attempt to involve its businesses in the development of CRMs. After several years, it still hasn't managed to raise sizable funding.[188] Most illuminating is the demise of the industry-driven German Raw Material Alliance, which included such behemoths of German industry as Bayer, Daimler, and Thyssenkrupp.[189] It ended in 2015 without

---

187 "Critical Raw Materials Resilience: Charting a Path towards greater Security and Sustainability", *European Commission*, https://ec.europa.eu/docsroom/documents/42849

188 Simon Brook, Sophie Crocoll and Jorn Petring, "The New Resource Monopoly," *Wirtschafts Woche*, April 25, 2019, https://www.wiwo.de/my/politik/ausland/gute-mine-boeses-spiel-das-neue-rohstoff-monopoly/24253302.html?ticket=ST-1088580-ekuethAGcNP6WcalKoRB-cas01.example.org

189 "Rare Earths", *DW*, January 30, 2012, https://www.dw.com/en/german-industry-sets-up-alliance-to-secure-raw-materials/a-15703849

having accomplished anything significant. Europe's business sector has shown a lack of willingness to take the risks associated with controversial projects – especially if the concern sectors where China is strong.[190]

Since societal and environmental regulations are stronger in the EU than in China, it will be difficult to increase supply capacity. So far, companies have had no incentive to challenge China's monopoly on rare earth elements and CRM processing technologies; they have rather relied on imports from a country with lower regulatory requirements and a skewed state-controlled market. As a result, there has been some opposition in the EU to the intentions of the Critical Raw Materials Act. Experts in the field have questioned Von der Leyen's plan, saying it would require significant resources and add new burdens to industries already affected by high energy costs. However, von der Leyen's Act has been approved and will be executed in the next few years.

While the US and the EU are devising new policies, China is also working to strengthen its global leadership in rare earths and metals. For the stated goal of "supporting the high-quality development of the industry, stabilizing the market, and preserving national interests and industrial security," Beijing issued new regulations on the administration of rare earths in 2021.[191] The new legislation was called a "deterrent" and a "bargaining chip," and was presented as a weapon of retribution against the United States, by the state-run

---

190 "Raw materials alliance in a new format", *BDI,* https://bdi.eu/artikel/news/rohstoffallianz-in-neuem-format/

191 Chi Jingyi and Tulei, "China released draft regulation on rare earths, including quota control, investment management", *Global Times*, January 15, 2021, https://www.globaltimes.cn/page/202101/1212941.shtml.

Global Times.[192] Furthermore, Beijing stated later that year that the Aluminum Corporation of China, China Minmetals, and the Ganzhou Rare Earth Group would be merging to form a single entity that would control nearly 70% of the country's output of key metals. While the efficiency gains from the merger are obvious, the Chinese media has referred to the company in a less reassuring way, calling it an "aircraft carrier".[193] The US and the EU should pay attention.

London's Financial Times has reported that Chinese government officials has inquired how badly US and European industries, especially defense contractors, would be hurt if China banned rare earth exports during a bilateral dispute.[194] Would it have problems, for instance, making F-35 fighter jets if China stopped exports? That prompted a response from Hu Xijian, editor of Beijing's Global Times at the time, who said that the FT was "hyping the adversarial climate between China and the United States, which is praised by some Western media sources."[195] That response was not reassuring; after all, his newspaper has been behind naming the largest rare earth company in China an "aircraft carrier". Despite the destructive effects of a "rare-earth war," it is clear that China has been building up power to use against foreign enterprises that violate China's national interests.

---

192 Michael Lelyveld, "China Raises Threat Level Over Rare Earths", *RFA*, January 29, 2021, https://www.rfa.org/english/commentaries/energy_watch/rareearth-01292021101912.html.

193 Shunsuke Tabeta, "China consolidates 3 rare earth miners into 'aircraft carrier'", *Nikkei Asia*, December 24, 2021, https://asia.nikkei.com/Business/Markets/Commodities/China-consolidates-3-rare-earth-miners-into-aircraft-carrier.

194   "China targets rare earth export curbs to hobble US defence industry", *Financial Times*, February 16, 2021, https://www.ft.com/content/d3ed83f4-19bc-4d16-b510-415749c032c1.

195 Hu Xijin, "Whether China plays 'rare-earth card', there will be no winner in China-US decoupling", Global Times, https://www.globaltimes.cn/page/202102/1215748.shtml.

Reshoring and Rebuilding a Domestic Supply Chain

There is a strong case for both the United States and the European Union to change its supply of minerals. Current dependencies on China are a strategic threat. However, neither the United States nor Europe have responded adequately to these threats.[196] True, the Biden administration has been fairly proactive in addressing supply concerns related to specific raw commodities and the EU is moving ahead with its new act. More needs to be done.

The existing reliance of the United States on imports of rare earths and other vital raw materials has been analyzed in recent reports.[197] In 2017, an Executive Order was issued that aimed at creating strategic measures to guarantee a steady supply.[198] In its "Federal Strategy to Ensure Secure and Reliable Supplies of Critical Minerals," the United States Department of Commerce called for the development of recycling methods and substitutes, the establishment of a supply chain for rare earths outside of China, and the utilization of domestic deposits.[199] In light of current events, the US Department of Defense has been actively pursuing financing

196 E. Barteková, R. Kemp, "National strategies for securing a stable supply of rare earths in different world regions", *Resources Policy*, Vol. 49, 2016, pp. 153-164.

197 "Report by the Subcommittee on Critical and Strategic Mineral Supply Chains", February 2018, *Committee on Environment, Natural Resources, and Sustainability*, National Science and Technology Council, https://www.whitehouse.gov/wp-content/uploads/2018/02/Assessment-of-Critical-Minerals-Update-2018.pdf

198 "The White House: Executive Order on a Federal Strategy to Ensure Secure and Reliable Supplies of Critical Minerals", December, 20, 2017, https://www.whitehouse.gov/presidential-actions/presidential-executive-order-federal-strategy-ensure-secure-reliable-supplies-critical-minerals/.

199 "US Department of Commerce: A Federal Strategy to Ensure Secure and Reliable Supplies of Critical Minerals", June 4, 2019, https://www.commerce.gov/news/reports/2019/06/federal-strategy-ensure-secure-and-reliable-supplies-critical-minerals

for domestic rare earth programs.[200] Defense funding for rare earth production and processing facilities is an area of discussion between the United States and Canada.[201] It has also signed an MOU with Greenland to explore the country's rare earth ores and formed a collaboration to process rare earths in Australia.[202]

But it takes a long time and a lot of money to develop a rare earth project. Wyoming, Texas, and California are all making strides toward rare earths extraction, but recent history offers cautionary tales – for instance, Molycorp's reopening of the historic Mountain Pass mine in California in the early 2000s which went bankrupt in 2015.[203] The mine was purchased by MP Materials in 2017, and production began again that year. The Las Vegas-based firm is especially exploring neodymium-praseodymium in a bid to become the lowest-cost producer and rebuild the domestic rare earths supply chain from mine to magnet. The company has been the recipient of numerous contracts and grants from the US Department of Defense and Department of Energy in recent years.[204] However, Shenghe Resources, a Chinese firm engaged in processing, distribution, and

200 P. Stewart and A. Shalal, "Pentagon seeks funds to reduce US reliance on China's rare earth metals", *Reuters*, May 29, 2019, https://www.reuters.com/article/us-china-usa-rareearth-pentagon/pentagon-seeks-funds-to-reduce-u-s-reliance-on-chinas-rare-earth-metals-idUSKCN1SZ2C6

201 "US and Canada discuss supply of rare earths as China dominates?", *Bloomberg*, https://www.bloomberg.com/news/articles/2019-09-30/u-s-and-canada-discuss-supply-of-rare-earths-as-china-dominates?leadSource=uverify%20wall.

202 Laura Milan Lombrana and Theophilos Argitis, "US and Canada Discuss Supply of Rare earths as China Dominates", *Bloomberg*, September 30, 2019, https://www.mining-technology.com/analysis/australia-and-the-us-a-rare-rare-earth-partnership/

203 Peg Brickly, "California's Mountain Pass Mine to be Auctioned in Bankruptcy", *The Wall Street Journal*, February 1, 2017, https://www.wsj.com/articles/californias-mountain-pass-mine-to-be-auctioned-in-bankruptcy-1485955874.

204 Ernest Scheyder, "American quandary: How to secure weapons-grade minerals without China", *Reuters*, April 22, 2020, https://www.reuters.com/article/us-usa-rareearths-insight/american-quandary-how-to-secure-weapons-grade-minerals-without-china-idUSKCN2241KF.

refining, is both a major client of the firm and a partial owner. Even if scientists at the Department of Energy have been alarmed by the link, government financing for the rare earth minerals separation facility has been maintained.[205]

Lynas Corporation plays a major role as well, being one of the largest rare earth minerals processors outside of China. The Australian mining company, which already has a separation facility in Malaysia, was awarded $30.4 million by the Pentagon to construct a light rare earths processing facility in Texas. It has also won a contract to construct a heavy rare earths separation facility in Texas, this time in conjunction with Blue Line Corp.[206] The reality is that even if EU and the US would increase their outtake of minerals, the smelting and refining facilities are in concerningly short supply in both EU and the US. It is only in Finland that there is a major mineral processing plant, for cobalt processing specifically. The EU accounts for 20 percent of the global cobalt processing but it is one of the few smelting and processing plants in the region.[207]

Developing the smelting and processing facilities in the EU and the US will also take time and resources. Better supply security in both minerals and processing capabilities are central important but is difficult to reach anytime soon. A mix of strategies will have to be employed in the meanwhile. Domestic investments in especially processing capacity should take priority and policymakers can help

205 Ernest Scheyder, "Pentagon resumes rare earths funding program after review", *Reuters*, July 21, 2020, https://www.reuters.com/article/us-usa-rareearths/pentagon-resumes-rare-earths-funding-program-after-review-idUSKCN24M2Z4

206 "Pentagon awards $30 million in rare earths funding Australia's Lynas", *Reuters*, February 1, 2021, https://www.reuters.com/article/us-usa-rareearths/pentagon-awards-30-million-in-rare-earths-funding-to-australias-lynas-idUSKBN2A135Y.

207 Rodrigo Castillo & Cailin Purdy, *China's Role in Supplying Critical Minerals for the Global Energy Transition, Brooking Institute*, 2022, https://www.brookings.edu/wp-content/uploads/2022/08/LTRC_ChinaSupplyChain.pdf

by providing tax credits and subsidies. Better use of current stocks and imports of rare earth metals can also help to reduce dependency risks. Pressing and sintering, a procedure involving compression and heat treatment without melting, is now used to shape magnets into basic geometries. Offcuts and waste occur when these shapes are shaved down to get the desired form.[208] Innovation can also help, for instance by developing downstream technology that are less dependent on the rare earths controlled by China. Moreover, supply can be diversified by deepening trade and partnership relations with alternative supply countries – some of which are located in or near the European region.

208 David Matthews, "Researchers scramble to cut European dependence on Chinese rare earth magnets", *Science Business*, June 30, 2022, https://sciencebusiness.net/news/researchers-scramble-cut-european-dependence-chinese-rare-earth-magnets

SIX

*Building a Green and Sustainable
Supply Chain Network: Can the US and EU
Emerge as Drivers for Change?*

Climate change forces new demands in the EU and the US to support technology and innovation, not least in the energy sector. In light of Europe's project to wean itself off its reliance on energy from Russia, projects like the wind farms in Italy and Croatia have taken on new significance and urgency. In this process, Europe is unfortunately moving from one worrying dependence to another, because many parts of renewable energy sector are dominated or heavily influenced by Chinese companies that are under the influence of Beijing. For example, MingYang turbines began powering Italy's first offshore wind farm at the port of Taranto in 2022.[209] Similarly, Chinese firm Norinco International opened Croatia's biggest wind farm in the

---

209 Michelle Lewis, "The Mediterranean's first offshore wind farm, off Italy, is now up and running", *Electrek*, April 22, 2022, https://electrek.co/2022/04/22/the-mediterraneans-first-offshore-wind-farm-off-italy-is-nearly-halfway-complete/.

coastal town of Senj only a few months earlier.[210] Shanghai Electric, another of China's leaders in the wind business and one of the top-10 companies in the world, manufactured these turbines.[211]

A similar situation was witnessed in the US, and to counter this in February 2022, the Department of Energy released the first comprehensive US government strategy to construct an Energy Sector Industrial Base.[212] In light of the Executive Order on America's Supply Chains,[213] this strategy looked at technologies and interdisciplinary topics for analysis as part of a government-wide effort to determine how best to secure the nation's most important supply chains in order to revitalize the economy and domestic manufacturing. Raw material availability, manufacturing capacity, reliance on foreign supplies, worker training, global trade practices, cyber security, and the research and data analysis required to create a clean energy economy were all cited as examples of the enormous challenges facing the United States.

Additional tax incentives for more robust solar business growth were included in the comprehensive Inflation Reduction Act signed

---

210 "Norinco completes Senj wind farm, Croatia's biggest so far", *Balkan Green Energy News,* November 21, 2023, https://balkangreenenergynews.com/norinco-completes-senj-wind-farm-croatia-biggest-so-far/.

211 Agatha Kratz, Charlie Vest, and Janka Oertel, "Circuit Breakers: Securing Europe's Green Energy Supply Chains", *Rhodium Group,* May 12, 2022, https://rhg.com/research/circuit-breakers-securing-europes-green-energy-supply-chains/.

212 "America's Strategy to Secure the Supply Chain for a Robust Clean Energy Transition", *US Department of Energy,* February 24, 2022, https://www.energy.gov/sites/default/files/2022-02/America%E2%80%99s%20Strategy%20to%20Secure%20the%20Supply%20Chain%20for%20a%20Robust%20Clean%20Energy%20Transition%20FINAL.docx_0.pdf.

213 "Executive Order on America's Supply Chains", *The White House,* February 24, 2022, https://www.whitehouse.gov/briefing-room/presidential-actions/2021/02/24/executive-order-on-americas-supply-chains/.

into law in 2022 by US President Joe Biden.[214] The Obama administration had set a goal of tripling US solar production by 2024. Some in the solar business had been calling for US action to increase local manufacturing and to level the playing field between the US and China for some time, and this law was finally delivered. American businesses have long griped that Chinese manufacturers may undercut them on the price of solar panels and other hardware. However, according to a report from the International Energy Agency (IEA) published in July, China's rising solar panel production and innovative techniques have contributed to a worldwide decrease in manufacturing prices.[215] The National Renewable Energy Laboratory, another observer in the industry, reported a substantial decline in prices beginning in 2010 and continuing for the next decade.[216] This could strengthen the Chinese dominance in innovation and development of new technologies and create a dependency similar to the current European on Russian fossil fuels.

Besides, the United States has historically been the most significant contributor to climate change, accounting for about 22 percent of historic greenhouse gas (GHG) emissions, equal to the past emissions of 181 countries combined.[217] The United States

214 "President Biden Signs Inflation Reduction Act Into Law", *Sherrod Brown*, August 16, 2022, https://www.brown.senate.gov/newsroom/press/release/ sherrod-brown-president-biden-signs-inflation-reduction-act-into- law#:~:text=WASHINGTON%2C%20D.C.%20E2%80%93%20Today%2C%20 President,roughly%2040%20percent%20by%202030.

215 Yvonne Lau, "There's a huge problem for the clean energy shift and it comes from China, unprecedented IEA report says", *Fortune*, July 7, 2022, https:// fortune.com/2022/07/07/iea-report-clean-energy-solar-transition-china- dominance/.

216 "Documenting a Decade of Cost Declines for PV Systems", *The National Renewable Energy Laboratory*, February 10, 2021, https://www.nrel.gov/news/ program/2021/documenting-a-decade-of-cost-declines-for-pv-systems.html.

217 "Climate Watch (CAIT): Country Greenhouse Gas Emissions Data", *World Resources Institute*, April 10, 2014, https://www.wri.org/data/climate-watch-cait- country-greenhouse-gas-emissions-data.

disproportionately affects global climate, yet its leadership on this issue has been patchy. Unfortunately, the United States' previous landmark climate legislation, the American Clean Energy Security Act (also known as the Waxman-Markey bill), was soundly defeated in Congress in 2009. This followed the country's refusal to ratify the Kyoto Protocol in 2001 and its withdrawal from the Paris Agreement in 2020. Intergovernmental Panel on Climate Change (IPCC) warned that the world is on track to exceed the Paris Agreement's goal of not exceeding 1.5 degrees Celsius of global warming within the next decade, with every fraction of a degree resulting in a disproportionate increase in the severity and frequency of devastating climate impacts.[218] This came as the United States swung from being a climate leader to a climate pariah in the eyes of many, but this is also something that Beijing has used in their disinformation strategy against the US. Recognizing climate change or not, this has severely impacted the US role as a leader of the international community, particularly the Western world, which puts a great deal of emphasis on climate change.

While primarily directed at domestic matters and containing certain contentious provisions related to drilling, which underscore the continued influence of the oil and gas sector, this legislation marks the largest-ever commitment to climate action in the history of the United States and is poised to bring about significant changes on the global stage. The Inflation Reduction Act will likely bring the United States closer to fulfilling its obligation under the Paris Agreement. President Biden announced an improved Nationally Determined Contribution (NDC) at the 2021 Leaders' Summit on

---

218 Solomon Hsiang, Robert Kopp, and Trevor Houser, "Estimating economic damage from climate change in the United States", *Science*, June 30, 2017, https://www.science.org/doi/10.1126/science.aal4369.

Climate, committing the United States to "achieving a 50-52 percent reduction from 2005 levels in economy-wide net greenhouse gas pollution in 2030."[219] Independent estimates predict that the Inflation Reduction Act will reduce GHG emissions by around 31–44 percent, or 37–41 percent below 2005 levels by 2030, compared to what was predicted under the present policy.[220] Both models agree that these expenditures, together with state and federal regulatory action, will make it possible to achieve the entire target of a 50% decrease in emissions by the end of the decade.[221]

The Inflation Reduction Act is also said to improve the United States' standing in international commerce thanks to more than $70 billion in clean domestic manufacturing investments. These expenditures, along with domestic content credits and the robust "Made in America" program[222] of the Biden administration, will equip the United States with the tools it needs to incorporate climate and economic objectives into global trade debates and hopefully take a more explicit leadership role. The Inflation Reduction Act will also

---

219 "FACT SHEET: President Biden Sets 2030 Greenhouse Gas Pollution Reduction Target Aimed at Creating Good-Paying Union Jobs and Securing US Leadership on Clean Energy Technologies", *The White House*, April 22, 2021, https://www.whitehouse.gov/briefing-room/statements-releases/2021/04/22/fact-sheet-president-biden-sets-2030-greenhouse-gas-pollution-reduction-target-aimed-at-creating-good-paying-union-jobs-and-securing-u-s-leadership-on-clean-energy-technologies/.

220 Ben King, John Larsen, and Hannah Kolus, "A Congressional Climate Breakthrough", *Rhodium Group*, July 28, 2022, https://rhg.com/research/inflation-reduction-act/.

221 Megan Mahajan, Olivia Ashmoore, Jeffrey Rissman, Robbie Orvis, Anand Gopal, "Modeling The Inflation Reduction Act Using The Energy Policy Simulator", *Energy Innovation*, August 2022, https://energyinnovation.org/wp-content/uploads/2022/08/Modeling-the-Inflation-Reduction-Act-with-the-US-Energy-Policy-Simulator_August.pdf.

222 "Made in America", *The White House*, https://www.whitehouse.gov/omb/management/made-in-america/.

strengthen the safety of the US economy and its energy supply.[223] Extreme weather and other climate impacts can destabilize governments and governance institutions, which can have cascading geopolitical and geostrategic effects, as the United States Department of Defense acknowledges.

The United States is also likely to be less reliant on a global economy dominated by fossil fuels and primarily dictated by countries that do not share American ideals thanks to the Inflation Reduction Act's investments in clean energy. Specifically, the Inflation Reduction Act will reduce US oil demand by over twice as much as the country has ever imported from Russia.[224] For reference, the US imported about 672,000 barrels per day of crude oil and petroleum products from Russia in 2021, according to data from the Energy Information Agency.[225] As a result, the Inflation Reduction Act, in conjunction with other federal executive actions, will significantly lessen the vulnerability of the US economy to fluctuations in the prices of foreign fossil fuels, thereby preventing future summers like the one in 2022, when Americans were forced to pay exorbitant gas prices while oil and gas companies reap record profits.[226]

Finally, the Inflation Reduction Act might improve ties with the

---

223 Bernd Heid, Martin Linder, and Mark Patel, "Delivering the climate technologies needed for net zero", *McKinsey*, April 18, 2022, https://www.mckinsey.com/capabilities/sustainability/our-insights/delivering-the-climate-technologies-needed-for-net-zero.

224 Robbie Orbis, "Energy Security Benefits Of Congressional Climate And Clean Energy Policy", *Energy Innovation*, March 2022, https://energyinnovation.org/wp-content/uploads/2022/03/Congressional-Proposals-and-U.S.-Energy-Security-EPS-Modeling.pdf.

225 "The United States imports more petroleum products than crude oil from Russia", *US Energy Information Administration*, March 22, 2022, https://www.eia.gov/todayinenergy/detail.php?id=51758.

226 Sally Hardin and Jenny Rowland-Shea, "These Top 5 Oil Companies Just Raked In $35 Billion While Americans Pay More at the Pump", *American Progress*, May 17, 2022, https://www.americanprogress.org/article/these-top-5-oil-companies-just-raked-in-35-billion-while-americans-pay-more-at-the-pump/.

European Union, a crucial ally, to lessen the Union's energy reliance on Russia. The Inflation Reduction Act provides $500 million to encourage the development of heat pumps and spur essential mineral processing projects in light of the US-EU Task Force on European Energy Security's increased deployment of energy efficiency technologies like heat pumps and smart thermostats. Provisions like the methane reduction fee, which mandates that oil and gas producers who vent, flare, or leak methane pay a price that could reach $1,500 per ton for some operators by 2026, and a provision mandating that companies pay a 16 percent royalty on vented, flared, or leaked methane on public lands are consistent with EU priorities on methane emissions. The Inflation Reduction Act enhances US-EU cooperation on decreasing methane emissions, while issues like reporting methodology and accounting for supply chains must be handled.

However, as the pandemic progressed, the risks of a world depending on China were made more apparent than ever, and even now, after the pandemic and in the midst of the Russian invasion of Ukraine, the consequences continue to linger on. Price increases can be attributed to the high shipping cost from China and other exporters overseas. For example, the price of polysilicon, a vital ingredient in solar cells, has quadrupled in the past year as an oversupply has caused manufacturers to halt production, leading to a subsequent shortage as demand has increased. Forty percent of the world's polysilicon is manufactured in China's Xinjiang region, a region also fiercely debated due to its human rights violations and connection to forced manufacturing by detained minority populations and due to Xinjiang's fragile environmental situation.

Manufacturing and green supply chains

Traditional manufacturing has been, as earlier noted, associated with a negative impact on the environment, but to some degree, the manufacturing industries have been leading some of the innovations in green supply chains, not least in recycling and waste management. Leading sports brands could be one example where they have been at the forefront of greening their products[227], to some extent due to their consumers' environmental concerns and awareness but also due to legislation and increased competition. This is not to neglect the impact that the consumers would have to select green products themselves and refuse products that fail to meet an international set standard. The challenge is that consumers have a microscopic overview of the entire supply chain, and this process is not only a question of green manufacturing but also deals with the more extensive method of distribution, design, marketing, material, and energy consumption.[228] In addition to the green manufacturing process, there is a growing concern about the environmental impact of products during or after their usage, such as recycling and waste management.[229]

This is an area in the green supply chain where the US and, particularly, the EU, due to their commitment and legislation, could have a significant positive impact and lead the change by

---

227 Rajiv Banker, Inder Khosla and Kingshuk Sinha, "Quality and Competition", *Management Science*, September 1, 1998, https://pubsonline.informs.org/doi/10.1287/mnsc.44.9.1179

228 Syed Abdul Rehman Khan, Introductory Chapter: Introduction of Green Supply Chain Management in Syed Abdul Rehman Khan (ed.), *Green Practices and Strategies in Supply Chain Management*, IntechOpen, September 11, 2019. https://www.intechopen.com/chapters/63678

229 Deyan Yang, Dongping Song and Cunfang Li, "Environmental responsibility decisions of a supply chain under different channel leaderships", *Environmental Technology & Innovation*, Vol. 26, May 2022, https://www.sciencedirect.com/science/article/pii/S2352186421007951

standardization of compliance and sustainability targets. Unfortunately, few states have institutions that could guarantee transparency and legal stability to develop international norms that could drive change, and the EU and the US are two of the very few. Such a chain would not only focus on the greening of the supply chain but also the sustainability in terms of human rights and ethical behavior in all nods of the chain. Green and clean supply chains are valuable targets, but very few companies live up to the expectations. What is needed is the enforcement of a sound due diligence process that could enforce expectations and legal norms, even if it is unlikely that China and Russia, as two examples, would agree to a mandatory process and much less realistic that it would actively work for such a change internationally.[230] This would also be a positive change for many down-stream states that are negatively affected by environmental degradation and social instability due to the placement of dangerous production in such conditions.

Where does China Position in the Energy Supply Chains?

The concentration of clean technology manufacturing facilities is astounding, even if challenges and neglect are still present in all industries, especially energy and minerals extraction. Some of the most exciting developments have been in the energy sector, not only due to the war in Ukraine but also due to the high costs and finite fossil fuels. During the past two decades, China has become the undisputed leader in battery and solar equipment production, much

---

230 Rodrigo Castillo and Caitlin Purdy, "China's role in supplying critical minerals for the global energy transition: What could the future hold?", August 1, 2022, *Brookings*, https://www.brookings.edu/wp-content/uploads/2022/08/LTRC_ChinaSupplyChain.pdf

due to the increased costs related to fossil fuels but also to the reality that China imports the bulk of its energy resources, and it has been hell-bent on reducing this dependency. China is home to 70 percent of the world's production capacity in 11 different forms of sustainable energy. China's efficient, integrated production hubs that dominate renewable energy manufacturing were designed with a combination of top-down incentives, cheap costs, growing demand, rules that favor local enterprises, and fierce domestic rivalry. No other country has done as much to improve the economics of the energy transition by making use of economies of scale to lower the price of solar and batteries. But political currents are shifting. Policymakers are beginning to see the same focus that boosts efficiency as a massive weakness, but the reality is that the transatlantic powers and its allies are currently far behind China.

On the one hand, the impressive development that China has accomplished should be saluted, on the other hand, the reality is that China has surpassed the transatlantic partners regarding research and development in this and related areas. The future challenges for the US and EU do not point to what China has done or controlled, but maybe more in the direction of what it has failed to do in the West. Again, the question how to decrease the dependency could be more in the West than related directly to China There is no doubt that the dependency on Chinese technology or even the export of energy could be a new challenge, but once more, the failure points to the slow reaction towards new technology, in this case particularly from the US. Regardless, if you believe in climate change or not, the Chinese state has successfully developed technology that will not only reduce climate change and energy costs, but also leapfrog China in many related technologies. The US and the EU need to invest heavily in research and development in this area to decrease the technology gap with China and to simplify regulations and investment in the area to make it more attractive.

Localizing Clean Energy: The Extent of the Challenges

The rising tensions in the Taiwan Strait, the ongoing conflict in Europe, and the geopolitical polarization resulting in make a compelling case for increasing supply diversification. In addition to geopolitical hazards, modern renewable energy supply chains face various threats. The United States and the European Union, in particular, have been eager to bring manufacturing of sustainable energy technologies back home, even if they are far from as successful as they would like to be. Due to the enormous expenses involved and a short-sighted view, it has been difficult for Western politicians to set up domestic manufacturers in a streamlined fashion.

An analysis by Bloomberg New Energy Finance estimated that it would cost $149 billion in Europe and $113 billion in the United States to construct factories to produce enough solar panels, batteries, and electrolyzers to meet domestic demand in 2030. These preliminary expenditures make supply chains more resilient to future geopolitical and natural disaster risks. Still, China is home to "the bleeding edge knowledge" in P.V., battery, and electrolyzer production.[231] If Chinese corporations met less resistance when establishing factories in the United States and the European Union,

---

231 Bleeding edge knowledge refers to services or technologies that are in operation, but it so new and experimental that it has not been fully tested and made effective so it can be unreliable over time, both in an operational sense as well as financially.

they could more quickly transfer some of this knowledge outside of the country[232], but this would be creating a further dependency on Chinese technology and know-how. The solution should instead be to invest in and develop domestic technologies and cooperate with like-minded nations, such as Japan and South Korea, rather than exchange one dependency against another. Unilateral measures are not feasible as it seems impossible for one single actor to bridge the gap to China, but an extended partnership would be able to reduce the gap to China and potentially create greener and more independent supply chains.

For example, it would cost billions to construct the factories required to supply local demand for battery components, battery metals, solar, lithium-ion batteries, and electrolyzers by, say, 2030. Roughly $149 billion in Europe and $113 billion in the United States, according to current estimated and 62% of that is allocated in Europe to the battery supply chain.[233] The total cost of building a battery factory would exceed that of any other battery manufacturing facility, including metal refineries.[234] Swedish Northvolt is Europe's largest battery producer and its first homegrown battery producer, a producer struggling to find economically sustainable areas to create more factories despite a $350 million loan agreement from the

---

232 "Localizing Clean Energy Value Chains Will Come at a Cost", *Bloomberg New Energy Finance,* November 7, 2022, https://about.bnef.com/blog/localizing-clean-energy-value-chains-will-come-at-a-cost/.

233 Jackie Northam, "Sweden's Northvolt wants to rival China's battery dominance to power electric cars", *NPR,* July 1, 2023, https://www.npr.org/2023/07/01/1184867278/sweden-northvolt-electric-car-lithium-battery.

234 "Localizing Clean Energy Value Chains Will Come at a Cost", *Bloomberg New Energy Finance,* November 7, 2022, https://about.bnef.com/blog/localizing-clean-energy-value-chains-will-come-at-a-cost/.

European Investment Bank.[235] There is a need to further increase investment in such initiatives, or Northvolt will be forced to move outside of the EU Due to delays in the expansion into Germany, Northvolt have been opting to move to the US, but also other states outside of the trans-Atlantic structure could be relevant for producers to consisder. In the case of the move of Germany, it is the increased energy costs that are behind the reluctance, and this is something that has been a greater issue after the Russian invasion of Ukraine and the hike in energy prices. Still, there is a need to realize the strategic necessity of such companies further and further simplify investments and innovation in such areas. It is very much the Inflation Reduction Act and the new climate laws that give Northvolt the opportunity to invest in battery production to reduce reliance on China, in this particular case, the loss of EU could be the gain of the US but in another scenario, it could as likely be the gain of Beijing.

In most cases, the price of implementing environmentally friendly technology in the supply chain is much greater than the price of constructing the accompanying manufacturing facilities. For example, to meet the growing demand for low-carbon hydrogen in Europe, the price tag for the electrolyzer factories required to do so is a mere $2.8 billion, about a tenth of the $27 billion needed to install low-carbon electrolyzers, excluding the accompanying renewables capacity.[236] These implementation costs would grow if clean technology were developed in the West. In addition, many have held that challenging China's dominance in the solar and battery

---

235 "European backing for Northvolt's battery Gigafactory in Sweden", *European Commission*, 29 July, 2020, Press release, https://ec.europa.eu/commission/presscorner/detail/sv/IP_20_1422

236 "Hydrogen: Commission supports industry commitment to boost by tenfold electrolyser manufacturing capacities in the EU", *European Commission,* May 5, 2022, https://ec.europa.eu/commission/presscorner/detail/en/ip_22_2829.

area was an impossibility for a very long time. August 12, 2022, can be remembered as the turning point. The Inflation Reduction Act was Joe Biden's crowning achievement, and its enactment gave the United States its first legitimate national climate policy in decades. As a result of its provisions, manufacturers have access to a veritable subsidy buffet, most notably in the form of tax credits that may be claimed not only for the deployment of clean technology but, more importantly, for the output of manufacturing facilities. Those tax breaks are crucial. All American wind, solar, and battery manufacturers can get subsidies based on their production volumes. As a result, they pay for a sizable portion of production expenditures until 2032. Trade obstacles (many of which were carried over from the Trump administration) and local content provisions for the components and refined metals used in subsidized electric vehicles are sticks to complement the subsidies' carrots. Europe preceded with its REPowerEU to decrease its dependency on Russian fossil fuels, which has forced severe investments into the EU economic area and should be expanded into a broader focus on dependence on fossil fuels.[237] As a forerunner to the Green Deal Industrial Plan, this was instrumental in setting the agenda and forcing the EU to act more long-term and reduce its dependency on possibly hostile nations.

Drawbacks of Local Policies

Both projects mentioned earlier highlight the European Union's difficulties in achieving a sustainable and reliable energy future. Because of delays in product delivery, a Chinese turbine manufacturer was

---

237 "RepowerEU: A plan to rapidly reduce dependency on Russian fossil fuels and fast forward the green transition", *European Commission,* 19 May, 2002, https://ec.europa.eu/commission/presscorner/detail/en/ip_22_3131

able to seize an opportunity in the Taranto project. Norinco International is investing heavily in Senj and supplying essential gear, it is a massive Chinese state-owned industrial behemoth and a significant defense business and supplier of weapons and equipment to the Chinese People's Liberation Army.[238] If anything, this was a reiteration of China utilizing its economic might to gain strategic advantages. It further restated that though Europe's dependency on Russian oil and gas is a more pressing issue, the continent's growing reliance on China for renewable energy technologies is just as problematic in the long run. China has emerged as a major player in numerous green technology sectors, making it crucial to the EU's green transition. The same hazards of becoming too reliant on an authoritarian power exist here as they do in Russia. On the other hand, China's non-market economy is significantly more extensive and exerts far more influence on international technology markets than Russia.

But what's even more unexpected is that the cost of these subsidies will never end. The Biden administration predicts the IRA will devote $370 billion to sustainable energy, but the accurate price might be far higher depending on participation. It's important to note that Europe is also awake and alert. Several grants are funding new battery and electrolyzer plants. In contrast to the IRA's coordinated effort, the European Union's backing appears piecemeal and depends on contributions from individual member states to be effective. Even though the European Union is the largest free-trade bloc in the world, its members are naturally reluctant to local content regulations. However, on October 26, the French president called for a "Buy European Act" to mirror Washington's approach to

---

238 Jack Lau, "Strong sales growth for China's top defence firms as demand rises at home", *South China Morning Post,* December 5, 2022, https://www.scmp.com/news/china/military/article/3202167/strong-sales-growth-chinas-top-defence-firms-demand-rises-home.

encouraging green technology. According to EU plans, battery sales in the European Union will be subject to mandated carbon footprint limitations beginning in 2027.[239]

To get through this, policymakers both in the US and Europe would need to make tough decisions, such as reevaluating the geopolitical risks vis-à-vis Russia and China that affect supply chain resilience, deliberately right-sizing exposure to dependence on China and Russia to eliminate complete decoupling, prioritizing business-friendly policies, upholding high quality environmental and ethical standards to achieve long-term sustainability, and working with allies, primarily the United States, and other partners.

How Can the US and EU Work Together Towards Resilient Green Supply Chains?

In the contemporary global landscape, a critical imperative emerges for the US and the EU to jointly address the exigency of establishing environmentally sustainable practices and resilient green supply chains. The multifaceted challenges of climate change, geopolitical uncertainties, and the persistent global pandemic necessitate a paradigm shift in the way we approach supply chains. In this context, both the US and the EU acknowledge the urgency of transitioning towards green technology and sustainable supply chains, not merely as a matter of environmental responsibility but as a strategic imperative. In light of the ongoing transformation in energy and technology sectors towards sustainability, these policy recommendations aim to

---

239 Michael Nienaber, "Germany's Scholz Urges EU to Move Past Subsidy Spat With US", *Bloomberg*, December 14, 2022, https://www.bloomberg.com/news/articles/2022-12-14/germany-s-scholz-urges-europe-to-move-past-subsidy-spat-with-us#xj4y7vzkg.

delineate a cohesive strategy for the US and the EU to collaborate in strengthening green supply chains. This partnership is pivotal for promoting sustainability and maintaining a competitive edge in the ever-evolving global marketplace.

Shifting Global Dynamics

The world is undergoing a rapid transformation catalyzed by the Russian invasion of Ukraine and the persistent COVID-19 pandemic. These events have acted as accelerants, compelling nations to reevaluate their energy and technology choices and increasingly ensuring a shorter supply chain that increases supply chain security. The transition towards green energy and technology is no longer confined to the peripheries of environmental advocacy, but has extended its reach to encompass critical industries that intersect with national security, innovation, and public health. Concurrently, the decisions to invest in new nuclear energy initiatives in Europe and embark on oil exploration in Alaska underscore the inevitability of moving towards green and near-shored technology. This transition, characterized by sustainability and renewable energy sources, offers a diversified and geographically resilient alternative that can ensure the US and EU's future vitality.

Reinforcing Supply Chain Control and Diligence

To forge resilient green supply chains, it is imperative to lay a robust foundation built upon the bedrock of liberal economic values that are implemented on a level playing field. Transparency, accountability, and sustainability are the cardinal principles in constructing this edifice. It is paramount for both the US and the EU to collectively champion, and enforce, these principles as they embark on the transformation of their supply chains. This liberal economic fundament serves as the ethical underpinning of supply chain practices and positions both regions as vanguards of responsible global commerce. Realizing that many states outside of the liberal economies do not have the institutions or the political willingness to enforce these three principles there will be necessary to limit import from such states, but also to assist and reinforce such economies.

- **Transparency:** A core element of this approach is the imposition of stringent transparency standards on businesses operating within these regions. These standards should include the disclosure of raw materials' origin, energy sources, and the results of environmental impact assessments. Harmonization of these reporting standards is vital to streamline global trade and reduce information asymmetry.[240] Failure to disclose this should result in limitation, or exclusion, from markets within the transatlantic community.

- **Accountability:** Enforcing accountability for sustainable practices is imperative. This accountability must extend to businesses and their responsibility for the environmental impact of their supply chains. Implementing environmental audits and certifications can serve as instrumental tools to

---

240 "Enhancing market transparency in green and transition finance", *Network for Greening the Financial System*-Technical document, April 2022, https://www.ngfs.net/sites/default/files/medias/documents/enhancing_market_transparency_in_green_and_transition_finance.pdf

ensure that companies uphold their commitments to green supply chains.[241]

- **Sustainability:** The concept of sustainability must be imprinted on every facet of supply chain management. This includes adopting circular economy practices, optimizing transportation to minimize emissions, and inculcating an organizational culture that champions environmental responsibility.

It is essential to note that the growth of Environmental, Social, and Governance (ESG) investments is set to reach $50 trillion by 2025. However, the impact of these investments on the climate transition remains uncertain due to a lack of standardized classification. Recent regulatory changes in the US and the EU indicate a shift toward formalized sustainability disclosure. The EU's Corporate Sustainability Reporting Directive (CSRD) mandates rigorous standards for sustainability reporting, while the US Securities and Exchange Commission (SEC) proposed rules on climate-related disclosures to enhance transparency. Nonetheless, differences in the scope, principles, rigor, standards, and assurances between the US and EU disclosure rules may lead to challenges in trade and investment flows. The emerging International Sustainability Standards Board (ISSB) could serve as a global standard to bridge this gap.[242]

241 Kasia Klaczynska Lewis, "Four actions for law departments to address supply chain ESG risk", *Ernst and Young*, December 1, 2022, https://www.ey.com/en_us/law/four-actions-for-law-departments-to-address-supply-chain-esg-risk.

242 Addisu Lashitew, "The coming of age of sustainability disclosure: How do rules differ between the US and the EU?", *Brookings*, June 6, 2022, https://www.brookings.edu/articles/the-coming-of-age-of-sustainability-disclosure-how-do-rules-differ-between-the-us-and-the-eu/ .

The common institutions among liberal economies serves to assist in resolving, or managing the differences, but there should be a realization that many issues will not be easy to resolve without common institutions that regulates the internal differences. That said, it is evident that the institutions will mitigate much of the challenges that could be faced.

Human Rights and Fair Pay

As the trajectory towards green supply chains unfolds, protecting human rights and guaranteeing fair pay should be non-negotiable principles.[243] Historically, European and American companies have been culpable of outsourcing "dirty" industries to less affluent nations in need of investments and with weak institutions and regulations,[244] a practice that China perpetuates. To reverse this trend, it is imperative for the US and EU to ensure the application of green and sustainable goals at every tier of the supply chain, regardless of geographical location. This necessitates heightened transparency, responsibility, and accountability.[245]

- **Fair Labor Practices:** Central to the green supply chain policies should be the assurance of fair pay, safe working conditions, and the safeguarding of labor rights. Collaborative efforts between governments and businesses

---

243 Jerry Haar, Rebeca B. Sánchez-Flores & Pierre Courtemanche, "The Status, Policies and Outlook for Green Supply Chains in North America", *Wilson Center*, May 18, 2023, https://www.wilsoncenter.org/article/status-policies-and-outlook-green-supply-chains-north-america.

244 Joseph Winters, "Rich Countries Are Illegally Exporting Plastic Trash To Poor Countries, Data Suggests", *Investigate West*, April 18, 2022, https://www.invw.org/2022/04/18/rich-countries-are-illegally-exporting-plastic-trash-to-poor-countries-data-suggests/.

245 "Sustainable Global Supply Chains: G7 Leadership on UNGP Implementation", *United Nations High Commissioner for Human Rights*, January 2022, https://www.ohchr.org/sites/default/files/2022-05/report-sustainable-global-supply-chains-g7.pdf.

should yield global standards that preempt exploitation and reinforce labor rights.[246]

- **Human Rights Due Diligence:** Companies must embark on thorough human rights due diligence, encompassing the rigorous assessment of risks and the conduct of audits to ensure that their supply chains remain free from human rights abuses. Mechanisms must exist within legal frameworks to hold businesses accountable for any transgressions.[247]

- **Inclusive Supply Chains:** A fundamental facet of green and sustainable supply chains is the promotion of inclusivity. These supply chains should not perpetuate social and economic inequalities. Encouraging the participation of minority-owned businesses and those located in underrepresented regions becomes a mandate in this paradigm.

The EU's proposed Corporate Sustainability Due Diligence Directive (CSDD) aims to enforce corporate responsibility for social and environmental impacts along the entire supply chain, including their own operations, products, and services. It covers companies with 250+ employees and over €40 million in annual turnover globally, introducing transition periods based on company size. This EU law is expected to become effective upon agreement between the European

---

246 "U.S.-EU Joint Statement of the Trade and Technology Council", *Office of the United States Trade Representative*, May 31, 2023, https://ustr.gov/about-us/policy-offices/press-office/press-releases/2023/may/us-eu-joint-statement-trade-and-technology-council

247 ibid

Parliament and the Council of Ministers. Its application includes companies operating in the EU with more than €150 million turnover and €40 millions of it in the EU, while SMEs will be indirectly affected as suppliers. The law obliges companies to identify, prevent, mitigate, and remedy human rights and environmental impacts and encourages transparent, public reporting and control of measures' effectiveness. It further requires companies with an annual turnover exceeding €150 million to outline their contribution to the Paris Climate Agreement's emission reduction targets. The law's liability clause allows civil action against companies if human rights or environmental violations occur in their supply chain, with the possibility of exemption through code of conduct compliance.

The EU's CSDD establishes stricter regulations on supply chain management, environmental protection, and human rights than currently exist in the US by adopting similar legislation, the US can enhance corporate responsibility and ensure the ethical treatment of workers and sustainable environmental practices, promoting a fair and sustainable global economy. It would also benefit American companies operating in the EU and those collaborating with European firms, streamlining their compliance with international supply chain standards. Furthermore, a consistent global approach to supply chain regulation would foster international trade and investment by reducing conflicts between different national regulations, ultimately advancing the global effort for responsible corporate governance and sustainability.[248] This would also strengthen the role of democratic and responsible practices internationally, if they are to do business with the transatlantic partners.

---

248 Kai Leisering, "EU Supply Chain Law Obliges Companies to Operate in a Fair and Sustainable Manner", *EQS Group*, June 14, 2023, https://www.eqs.com/compliance-blog/eu-supply-chain-law/.

Multinational Corporations (MNCs) and Government Accountability

The pivotal role of multinational corporations (MNCs) in driving supply chain sustainability necessitates comprehensive accountability. MNCs needs to shoulder the responsibility for the entire production process, including downstream phases like smelting and fossil fuel extraction. In cases where governments play a role in the supply chain, it is imperative that they, too, be held accountable through international agreements and regulations, ensuring adherence to sustainability standards but also to Human Rights and democratic development.

- **MNC Responsibility:** Multinational corporations, often spanning multiple countries and regions, must proactively spearhead green and sustainable practices. These corporations should formulate internal sustainability policies and invest in research and development to foster the creation of more sustainable products.[249]

- **Government Regulations:** Governments should promulgate regulations mandating that MNCs adhere to specified environmental and sustainability standards within their supply chains. These regulations should apply

249 Peer Schouten, "The EU should make corporations accountable for their impacts in the global south", *Danish Institute for International Studies*, November 25, 2021, https://www.diis.dk/en/research/the-eu-should-make-corporations-accountable-their-impacts-in-the-global-south; Verónica H. Villena and Dennis A. Gioia, "A More Sustainable Supply Chain", *Harvard Business Review*, March-April 2020, https://hbr.org/2020/03/a-more-sustainable-supply-chain.

to both domestic and international operations, making no distinction between the two.[250]

• **International Agreements:** The establishment of international agreements is crucial to achieving harmonized green supply chain standards. These agreements should ensure that MNCs operating globally are subject to a unified set of rules, thereby invoking consequences for non-compliance.[251]

Bridging the Innovation Gap through Investment in Green and Sustainable Technology

Both the US and the EU find themselves in a relative technological lag behind China in various aspects of green and sustainable technology[252], even if not in the area of government responsibility and human rights. To regain their primacy, a profound change in policy becomes imperative. Collaborative investments in research and development, innovation, and education emerge as the cornerstone for bridging this gap and surmounting global competitors. Governments should incentivize businesses and research institutions to

250 Marlis Afridah and Nazalea Kusuma, "How MNCs Can Thrive Towards Sustainable Supply Chain", *Green Network*, March 14, 2022, https://greennetwork.asia/featured/how-mncs-can-enforce-policies-and-thrive-towards-sustainable-supply-chain/.

251 "Promoting Sustainable Global Supply Chains: International Standards, Due Diligence And Grievance Mechanisms", *OECD*, February 15-17, 2017, https://www.ilo.org/wcmsp5/groups/public/---dgreports/---inst/documents/publication/wcms_559146.pdf.

252 Anna Holzmann and Nis Grünberg, "Greening" China: An analysis of Beijing's sustainable development strategies", *MERICS Report*, January 7, 2021, https://merics.org/sites/default/files/2021-03/MERICSChinaMonitor%20GreeningChina%202.pdf.

undertake pioneering work in green technologies, thereby securing a competitive advantage for both regions.[253]

- **Research and Development (R&D) Investment:** Governments should significantly amplify investments in R&D for green and sustainable technologies. Public-private partnerships should be cultivated to expedite the development of innovative solutions for sustainable supply chains.[254] Currently Europe and the US are lagging behind investments and research in the area of green and sustainable technologies, not least in solar energy. This is something that could create dependencies on China in the future, in regard to modern and clean energy and technology.

- **Innovation Hubs:** The establishment of innovation hubs and technology parks should be actively encouraged, fostering collaboration between academia, industry, and government. These hubs should concentrate their efforts on the development of green technology, serving as the cradles

253 "Securing Europe's competitiveness", *McKinsey Global Institute*, September 2022, https://www.mckinsey.com/~/media/mckinsey/business%20functions/strategy%20and%20corporate%20finance/our%20insights/securing%20europes%20competitiveness%20addressing%20its%20technology%20gap/securing-europes-competitiveness-addressing-its-technology-gap-september-2022.pdf.

254 "Sustainable Manufacturing and Eco-Innovation: Framework, Practices and Measurement", *OECD*, 2009, https://www.oecd.org/innovation/inno/43423689.pdf; "Enhancing financing for the research, development and demonstration of climate technologies", *Technology Executive Committee Working Paper - UNFCCC*, 2017, https://unfccc.int/ttclear/docs/TEC_RDD%20finance_FINAL.pdf

of innovative solutions.[255] Additional to the investments there is also a need for deregulation and more effective frameworks to create such innovation hubs, arguably the EU is drifting further back in this regard due to its lack of deregulation in the area.

- **Education and Workforce Development:** Nurturing a skilled workforce, instrumental in propelling green technology innovations, must stand at the forefront of this agenda. Investments in education and vocational training programs should be marshaled to ensure that the US and EU are equipped with the necessary talent to lead the charge in green technology development.

Propagating a Network of Liberal Economies is crucial to ensure a sustainable green supply chains. The trajectory toward green and sustainable supply chains warrants the creation of a network of liberal economies collectively dedicated to environmental betterment. This network, constituting likeminded nations and regions, must collaborate to establish standards and regulations that accentuate sustainability, transparency, and fairness throughout the supply chain. The foundation of this network should rest upon liberal

---

255 "America's Strategy to Secure the Supply Chain for a Robust Clean Energy Transition", *USDepartment of Energy Response to Executive Order 14017*, "America's Supply Chains", February 24, 2022, https://www.energy.gov/policy/articles/americas-strategy-secure-supply-chain-robust-clean-energy-transition; "European Digital Innovation Hubs", *European Commission*, https://digital-strategy.ec.europa.eu/en/activities/edihs.

institutions that ensure individual freedoms, democratic values, and market-driven principles.[256]

- **Collaborative Initiatives:** The US and EU must proactively engage with like-minded nations and regions to initiate joint programs that advocate for sustainable supply chains. Establishing forums for discussion, information sharing, and policy development should be the crux of this endeavor.

- **Standardization of Best Practices:** International collaboration should culminate in the standardization of best practices pertaining to green supply chain management. Shared guidelines, certifications, and standards should be formulated to simplify compliance and augment transparency.

- **Legal and Regulatory Frameworks:** Governments should work in conjunction to develop legal and regulatory frameworks that proactively champion environmentally responsible supply chains. These frameworks should encompass mechanisms for dispute resolution and the enforcement of sustainability standards.[257]

---

256 "Financing the Future: Incentivizing Inclusive and Sustainable Supply Chains", *World Bank*, April 14, 2023, https://live.worldbank.org/events/spring-meetings-2023-supply-chains.

257 Kristy Balsanek Teresa Hitchcock Jonathan Exten-Wright Brooke Goodlett Sonakshi Kapoor Amanda Swenson Joanna Kass, "EU's Proposed Directive on Corporate Sustainability Due Diligence: What US companies need to know", *DLA Piper*, September 25, 2023, https://www.dlapiper.com/en/insights/publications/global-esg-alert/2023/eus-proposed-directive-on-corporate-sustainability-due-diligence-what-us-companies-need-to-know

A Gradual Transition Spanning Decades

It is vital to acknowledge that the transition towards green and sustainable supply chains is a long-term endeavor, potentially spanning several decades. Despite promising developments arising from the Russian invasion of Ukraine and the transition away from oil and gas, it is imperative to recognize that change will be incremental. As such, the US and EU must embrace policies that effectively balance the exigency of environmental concerns with the need for a measured transition, enabling industries and economies to adapt at a sustainable pace. The implementation of policies should be phased to allow businesses and industries to adapt progressively. This phased approach minimizes disruptions and supports a smoother transition.

Further, governments should proactively extend incentives, such as deregulation, tax breaks and subsidies, to businesses that wholeheartedly embrace green supply chain practices. These incentives can help offset the initial costs of transition and encourage swift adoption. Inculcating public awareness and education campaigns becomes instrumental in informing citizens about the importance of green supply chains. Informed consumers possess the power to steer demand towards sustainable products and practices, thereby driving change.

While striving for an inclusive transition, it is imperative to maintain a clear demarcation between liberal economies and state-controlled economies. The US and EU must ensure that their unwavering commitment to liberal economic values remains resolute. State-controlled economies often exhibit differing priorities and interests, which can result in disparities in their environmental responsibilities. Consequently, the US and EU must steadfastly uphold their principles during negotiations. Transparent and diplomatic dialogues must be initiated by the US and EU with state-controlled economies. The aim is to encourage the adoption of sustainable practices and emphasize the importance of global cooperation on environmental issues. The economic influence wielded by the US and EU should be harnessed to advocate market-based approaches and trade policies that reward sustainable practices. This may include imposing tariffs or restrictions on products originating from regions with lax environmental standards. The US and EU should actively seek alliances with other nations that share their values and commitment to sustainability. These alliances can collectively present a united front during negotiations with state-controlled economies.

Collaboration with Like-Minded Nations

In addition to reinforcing the partnership between the US and the EU, both regions should actively collaborate with like-minded nations and organizations to spearhead a global movement towards green supply chains. International platforms, such as the G7, G20, and other similar initiatives, offer diplomatic engagement and cooperation opportunities to achieve shared environmental objectives even if there are challenges with all these bodies as well. The US and EU should leverage these platforms to foster global consensus and galvanize change and to decrease dependency and trade with non-democratic and totalitarian states over time. This is not least visible after the Russian invasion of Ukraine and the need to act. As prominent leaders of the G7 and G20, the US and the EU must utilize their positions to champion sustainable supply chain practices and encourage member nations to adopt them. The US and the EU should engage in negotiations to forge bilateral agreements with other nations, furthering the cause of green supply chains and fostering cooperation in technological innovation. Aid and development programs can be strategically tailored to support sustainability efforts in developing nations. Such programs can be instrumental in building green supply chain management capacity in these regions.

The transition towards resilient green supply chains represents a defining challenge of our time that demands unwavering commitment and determined action. Collaboration between the United States and the European Union could spearhead this transformation, if political support in the different capitals could be mustered, a requirement that is not a given. A liberal economic fundament, reinforced control over supply chains, investments in green technology, and an inclusive approach constitute the cornerstones of this ambitious endeavor, both to decrease unfair trade, invest in a greener future and to secure the long-term supply chains for democracies. By establishing a network of liberal economies dedicated to environmental betterment and strengthening their collective efforts, the US and the EU can lead in creating sustainable, resilient, and green supply chains. In doing so, they secure their future prosperity and set a compelling example for the world to emulate, igniting a global movement towards sustainability and environmental responsibility.

SEVEN

Diverging Transatlantic Approaches in Digital Technology: A Growing Threat to Security

Both the United States and European Union have been paying close attention to China because of the country's meteoric climb to challenge their position as the world's technological leaders. According to many observers, the technical arena has emerged as the "primary battleground for competitiveness and rivalry with China."[258] China has overtaken the United States as the leading high-tech producer in certain sectors, with a production of 250 million computers, 25 million vehicles, and 1.5 billion cell phones in 2020.[259] China has emerged not only as a manufacturing giant but also as a significant

---

258 Graham Allison Kevin Klyman Karina Barbesino Hugo Yen, "The Great Tech Rivalry: China vs the U.S.", Harvard Kennedy School, Belfer Center, December 2021, https://www.belfercenter.org/sites/default/files/GreatTechRivalry_ ChinavsUS_211207.pdf.

259 Graham Allison Kevin Klyman Karina Barbesino Hugo Yen, "The Great Tech Rivalry: China vs the U.S.", *Harvard Kennedy School*, Belfer Center, December 2021, https://www.belfercenter.org/sites/default/files/GreatTechRivalry_ ChinavsUS_211207.pdf.

player in cutting-edge fields like artificial intelligence, 5G networks, quantum information science (QIS), semiconductors, biotechnology, and renewable energy. In some segments of the high-tech industry, it can be argued that China has already surpassed its Western competitors. If the country continues on its current path, it may overtake the United States overall in the technology sector within the next decade. This development is not only a result of Chinese innovativeness and China's IP theft but also the failure to sustain the European and American innovativeness over time. The EU and the US, in particular, have taken their technological superiority for granted for so long that they did not realize that they were challenged. Even today, many political leaders still refuse to acknowledge the significance of the problem and the importance to take new action.

Concerns have been voiced in the United States, the European Union, and elsewhere about the effects of China's rapid technological development on the country's economy and national security. With a stronger role for China in global knowledge creation, there is also risks for the global spread of liberal ideals and sound government. Moreover, worries have been raised regarding the fragmentation of the global technology sector, particularly the establishment of divergent standards and norms, as China aspires to be the new power for setting new standards.

Thus, this chapter will delve into debates on China's significant position in the tech value chains and its ability to undermine the security of critical networks, but also the failure of the transatlantic partners to meet the challenges and how they could turn the tide. A strategy to address these concerns cannot only rest on defensive measures against China's aggressive behavior. More importantly, the transatlantic economies need to spend much more resources on knowledge and technology creation to improve their position. The reality is that the EU and the US can only do so much regarding the defensive measures, but there is much more control over the proactive measures that could strengthen the technological base and innovation capacities. Both the proactive and defensive measures are best managed in as broad coalitions as possible, even if some sectors need more direct national action. In this vein, the chapter will explore the possibilities of greater cooperation between the US and EU in the fields of 5G technology, Information communication technologies, cybersecurity, artificial intelligence, robotics, research collaboration, and tech cooperation to combat China's growing dominance in innovation and remain in the forefront of tech innovation. Most importantly, it would explore the possibilities of having "A High Technology Alliance for a New Era" with the US and EU in a focal position of the tech value chains, characterized by deregulations and investments in future technologies.

China's crucial position in the tech value chain

China's position in the ICT market has consistently strengthened during the past few decades. While Western technology companies continue to control the most cutting-edge parts of determining the future of the internet, the bulk of the manufacture and assembly of the main products and gadgets has been outsourced to Asia, with China having a central position in these supply chains. Additionally, China has also made significant improvements in their cutting-edge technology, not least in AI and surveillance technology. Chinas growing domestic market, centralized and politicized because of the increasing control by the Communist Party, has enabled China to shape an industrial policy by engaging an all-society approach to an extent that is not possible in a democratic state.[260]

Moreover, China continues to pursue a policy of "technology for markets access" requirements where foreign companies have been forced to surrender technology or excluded from the Chinese market. One example is the 2017 regulation that demanded that the Chinese partner would master all core technologies in new energy vehicles to allow production licenses in China.[261] Beijing has claimed to improve the legislation in favor of foreign companies, but these changes did not amount to more than decorative improvements.[262] The issue of IP theft remains rampant. Despite all the negative aspects of Chinas technological rise it should be noted that Beijing has been successful in its focus on innovation and improving its position in technology markets.

China is now considered a "full-spectrum peer competitor" in artificial intelligence, the cutting-edge technology with the potential to have the largest influence on economy and security in the coming decade. The Pentagon's Defense Innovation Board predicts that "China is on course to duplicate in 5G what happened with the United States in 4G." [263] The United States and Europe may have

---

260 Nai Bahar Sharif, "Dream of Reality", HKUST IEMS Thought Leadership Brief No. 11, 2016 https://iems.ust.hk/publications/thought-leadership-briefs/china-as-the-worlds-technology-leader-in-the-21st-century-dream-or-reality

261 Dan Prud'homme, Reform of China's "forced" Technology Transfer Police's, July 22, 2019, Faculty of Law Blogs, University of Oxford, https://blogs.law.ox.ac.uk/business-law-blog/blog/2019/07/reform-chinas-forced-technology-transfer-policies

262 Shi Jiangtao & Vanessa Cai, "Will Beijing's new 'umbrella law' deepen uncertainty for foreign companies in China?", *South China Morning Post*, June 29, 2023, https://www.scmp.com/news/china/diplomacy/article/3225802/will-beijings-new-umbrella-law-deepen-uncertainty-foreign-companies-china

263 Eric Schmidt and Graham Allison, "Is China Winning the AI Race?", *Project Syndicate*, August 4, 2020, https://www.project-syndicate.org/commentary/china-versus-america-ai-race-pandemic-by-eric-schmidt-and-graham-allison-2020-08.

the upper hand when it comes to 5G standards and chip design, but they are years behind China when it comes to rolling out 5G infrastructure, giving China a significant head-start in creating the foundations for the 5G era. It is estimated that 87 percent of the world's 5G market in 2020 was in China. As the world is moving into future technology, China is already filing 35% of the world's patents on 6G.[264] China is also making a strong bid to set the technology and market norms for what will come after 5G.

China's national push provides a strong challenge to America's long-held position as the leader in quantum information science. In quantum communication, China has already exceeded the United States and the European Union, and in quantum computing, China is fast closing the gap with the United States and has already bypassed the EU.[265] By 2018, after launching a breakthrough project on quantum information science, China accounted for 52 percent of all quantum patents globally. With 1157 patents in one year coming from China, the US represented 363 patents and none of the EU members were among the top five patent filers.[266] The challenge is not only that China is competing with – and sometimes surpassing – liberal democracies, but that China also puts more resources into taking these technologies to the market and allowing its firms to experiment and innovate in ways that Western technology regulations do not allow for.

---

264 Zeyi Yang, "China holds 35% of Global 6G patents, Government Report says", *Protocol*, April 26, 2021 https://www.protocol.com/china/china-6g-patents

265 "China Fast Closing Gap With US in Advanced Tech – SCMP", *Asia Financial*, June 8, 2022, https://www.asiafinancial.com/china-fast-closing-gap-with-us-in-advanced-tech-scmp; Graham Allison, Kevin Klyman, Karina Barbesino, and Hugo Yen, "The Great Tech Rivalry: China vs the U.S.", Harvard Kennedy School, Belfer Center, Paper December 2021.

266 Graham Allison, Kevin Klyman, Karina Barbesino, and Hugo Yen, "The Great Tech Rivalry: China vs the U.S.", Harvard Kennedy School, Belfer Center, Paper December 2021, p. 15.

Taiwan, and to lesser degree South Korea, has a leading position in the global semiconductor manufacturing sector, a position the US held before Asia took over, with TSMC (Taiwan Semiconductor Manufacturing Company) and Samsung Electronics accounting for 54 and 17 percent of the worlds advanced chip production respectively.[267] Despite this, the US, still hold a central position in the semiconductor sector through its input in the ensign and overall input in the semiconductor supply chain, and despite Chinese efforts they are still lagging behind. China has been working hard for decades to catch up as a leading semiconductor producer and designer with high investments but with small returns due to its constraints in innovations and development, despite importing some 25 percent of the worlds production[268] Part of the challenge is that China has, despite major investments, been unable to develop all technological capacity, such as the lithographic technology that is pivotal in developing micro-chips, an industry that ASML from Netherlands are leading with Nikon and Canon. Maybe this lack of success is one of the few reasons why China has not further weaponized its down-stream control of the supply chain, such as rare earth minerals?

Though the United States is home to seven of the ten most valued life sciences companies, China is proving to be a strong competitor in the field of biotech R&D. Both the United States and Europe have been eclipsed by Chinese researchers in CAR T-cell

267 Chris Miller, *Chip War*, Scribner, New York, 2022; Heather Hall, "The 10 Largest Chip Manufacturers in the World and What They Do", November 30, 2022, https://history-computer.com/the-10-largest-chip-manufacturers-in-the-world-and-what-they-do/

268 Elliot Ji, "Great Leap Nowhere: The Challenges of China's Semiconductor Industry", *War on the Rocks*, February 24, 2023, https://warontherocks.com/2023/02/great-leap-nowhere-the-challenges-of-chinas-semiconductor-industry/

therapy and the Clustered Regularly Interspaced Short Palindromic Repeats (CRISPR) gene editing methods.[269] Subsequently, China has become the world's largest manufacturer, user, and exporter of such technologies, giving it a strong position supported by favorable regulation and easy access to capital. To be sure, China has its problems in these sectors, and lack the innovative market capacity that many US firms have in biotechnology, but the country's life science sector is growing at an extraordinary pace and will continue to get closer to global frontier positions in more and more niches.

The US and the EU are increasingly aware of the threat to national and economic security coming from China's technology development. Worryingly, it is also beginning to dawn on some policymakers that Western economies are increasingly reliant on China as a technology superpower. The United States and Europe has discovered that their chief long-term rival is technologically intertwined with them. This realization has hit Washington and Brussels hard. Over the course of many years and for many reasons, especially America built those technological ties. There are many ways in which US and European companies, academic institutions, and consumers benefit from China's booming tech industry. However, China's military expansion, unfair trade practices, and oppressive social control are all part of China's booming tech industry, something that is strictly regulated in Chinese legislation making each company an important cog in the strategy of the Chinese Communist Party. This has brought to the fore a discussion about whether there should

---

269 Jeffrey Algazy, Franck Le Deu, Sydnie Li, Fangning Zhang, and Josie Zhou, "Vision 2028: How China could impact the global biopharma industry", McKinsey & Company, August 2022, https://www.mckinsey.com/~/media/mckinsey/industries/life%20sciences/our%20insights/vision%202028%20how%20china%20could%20impact%20the%20global%20biopharma%20industry/vision-2028-how-china-could-impact-the-global-biopharma-industry.pdf.

be technological decoupling from China. The reality is that China has come much further in decoupling than the West so it would be more a question of reciprocity than initiating a new change, and a total decoupling is no longer realistic even if it is necessary in critical sectors.

The United States Department of Commerce has issued new rules that severely restrict the export of high-tech microchips and chip-making equipment by American companies and individuals, as well as by foreign entities that use US equipment or technology in their manufacturing operations.[270] The new rule, reported *The New York Times*, "appeared to impose the broadest export curbs enacted in a decade," and "takes a comprehensive approach" to restricting China's access to sophisticated semiconductor technologies.[271] Measures included in the rule will require enterprises to get a special license to provide advanced chips, chip-making equipment, and associated items to China. And when deciding whether to provide licenses, the Department of Commerce will use a "presumption of refusal" policy.[272] The measure would also prohibit the sale or transfer of a variety of products utilizing US technology to the 28 PRC entities included on the US Entity List. Finally, it would prevent nationals of the United States from contributing to China's advanced semiconductor manufacturing, integrated circuit production, or advanced integrated circuit development.

In a similar vein, new foreign direct investment screening and

---

270 "Implementation of Additional Export Controls: Certain Advanced Computing and Semiconductor Manufacturing Items; Supercomputer and Semiconductor End Use; Entity List Modification", *Bureau of Industry and Security*, October 7, 2022, https://public-inspection.federalregister.gov/2022-21658.pdf.

271 Anna Swanson, "Biden Administration Clamps Down on China's Chip Technology", *The New York Times*, October 7, 2022, https://www.nytimes.com/2022/10/07/business/economy/biden-chip-technology.html

272 Bureau of Industry and Security, no. 5

export control policies in the European Union have been detailed by the European Commission. While the EU did not have a unified FDI screening framework prior to 2019, 25 out of the 27 member states have since implemented their own FDI screening processes.[273] In the first two years with the new screening instrument, member states evaluated 740 projects, but only a handful of transactions were blocked. There was no "impact on security or public order" (i.e. national security) in approximately 71% of applications that "did not require formal [FDI] screening" in 2021. Only 1% of cases that were decided in 2021 had their transactions blocked by national authorities, and only 3% of transactions were reversed. Over 66% of all the deals that were examined were in the manufacturing and ITC sectors.[274]

The EU implemented a new Export Control Regulation in May 2021, and cooperation between the US and EU has been strengthened through the US-EU Trade and Technology Council (TTC).[275] Since its inception in June 2021, the TTC has amassed a total of ten groups, one of which is focused solely on export regulations.[276] The Surveillance Technology Expert Group is developing due diligence methods related to the additional provisions added to the Export Control Regulation to include risks linked with "internal

273 "EU investment screening and export control rules effectively safeguard EU security", *European Commission*, September 2, 2022, https://ec.europa.eu/commission/presscorner/detail/en/IP_22_5286.

274 "Second Annual Report on the screening of foreign direct investments into the Union", *European Commission*, January 09, 2022, https://ec.europa.eu/transparency/documents-register/detail?ref=COM(2022)433&lang=en

275 "U.S.-EU Trade and Technology Council (TTC)", *US Department of State*, June 2021, https://www.state.gov/u-s-eu-trade-and-technology-council-ttc/.

276 "Regulation (EU) 2021/821 of the European Parliament and of the Council", EUR-Lex, May 20, 2021, https://eur-lex.europa.eu/eli/reg/2021/821.

repression or serious abuses of human rights and/or international humanitarian law.[277]

In recent times, the TTC has been the most promising platform for interdisciplinary collaboration on technological and innovative projects. It aims to "lead worldwide, like-minded [democratic] partners in supporting an open, interoperable, secure, and reliable digital realm and to remain pioneers in developing and defending tomorrow's technology." Agricultural subsidies, the Boeing-Airbus dispute, and the Trump administration's steel and aluminum tariffs are not on the Council's agenda because they have been the source of long-standing disagreement and friction between the United States and Europe. However, the ambition is that tighter collaboration on technology matters between the EU and the US will also help to resolve old problems.

The TTC has also advanced collaboration on future technology issues. New areas of collaboration include establishing an early warning system for disruptions in the semiconductor supply chain and cyber risks; coordinating information, communication and security projects with third countries, beginning with Kenya and Jamaica; cooperating on emerging technologies, especially through a newly agreed joint AI roadmap that will inform approaches to risk management and trustworthy AI. Despite their many joint efforts, the two partners continue to disagree on some key issues, including export restrictions on technology and ways to counter China and this has been utilized in Beijing's counternarrative in both EU and the US.

Further, as a result of global semiconductor shortages and diminishing local chip manufacture, the United States and Europe have also invested heavily in the semiconductor business to further

---

277 European Commission, no. 8

secure the supply chain. The United States CHIPs and Science Act of 2022 provides funding of $52 billion for semiconductor research, manufacturing, and education. In the beginning of 2023, the Commerce Department started awarded access to these funds. Even if the geopolitical impact is unclear, businesses have signaled their intention to expand expenditure on semiconductor production.[278] Intel, Samsung Micron and TSMC are all expanding production in the US, but this all happened before the CHIPs act, with the exception of Micron, and is much more due to the geopolitical instability surrounding Taiwan that controls the majority of the chips. Even though EU has lagged behind the United States in the legislative process, the European Union's proposed Chips Act will boost European competitiveness and resilience in the semiconductors industry. New production capacity is now being built. Many scholars and industry leaders, however, are skeptical that the €43 billion the EU says it has mobilized in funds to support semiconductor competitiveness will be sufficient to achieve the goal of controlling 20 percent of the global chips market by 2030

The EU and the US also struggle with Chinee competition in Artificial Intelligence. The competition is not just about the technological development but also the uses, rules and ethics of AI. The United States and the European Union have both policies to [279] pursue ethical and responsible AI, making sure that the technology is applied in a manner consistent with democratic principles and

278 Julia Trehu, "The GMF Digital Semiconductor Investment Tracker", *German Marshall Fund*, https://www.gmfus.org/gmf-digital-semiconductor-investment-tracker.

279 Dan Robinson, "EU still getting its act together on European Chips Act funding", *The Register*, November 24, 2022, https://www.theregister.com/2022/11/24/eu_chips_act_funding/.

human rights.[280] The European Union has a new Artificial Intelligence Act on its books,[281] which is the first comprehensive law governing artificial intelligence use and development worldwide. While no equivalent bill is making its way through Congress in the United States, the White House and US authorities have issued guidelines and established norms for responsible AI.

China, on the other hand, has less interest in such principles, which is a serious problem in itself. On the contrary, technology in China is widely used to control and monitor the population in respective states (and across borders), and AI also forms a strong part of how Beijing intends to fight wars in the future. China is also taking a lead with voice recognition application such as the Chinese iFlytek with 700 million users, doubling the amount that uses Siri's. 90 percent of the Chinese population uses mobile payments, while the US and Europe are still in the credit card age: with 900 million people use WeChat pay, compared to 44 million using Apple Pay.[282] This is not only an indication that Europe and the US has been bypassed, but the sheer amount of data that comes out of the Chinese tech experiment enables them to reach new levels of excellence also in AI.

It has become apparent that China has developed a talent pool in technology, not least in AI, that surpasses the transatlantic economies. This calls for a much more integrated and cooperative research and development strategy, not only between the transatlantic partners,

---

280 Alex Engler, "The EU and US are starting to align on AI regulation", *Brookings*, February 1, 2022, https://www.brookings.edu/blog/techtank/2022/02/01/the-eu-and-u-s-are-starting-to-align-on-ai-regulation/.

281 "What is the EU AI Act?", *The AI Act*, https://artificialintelligenceact.eu/.

282 Graham Allison, Kevin Klyman, Karina Barbesino, and Hugo Yen, "The Great Tech Rivalry: China vs the U.S.", Harvard Kennedy School, Belfer Center, Paper December 2021, p. 5.

but also with like-minded nations such as Japan, India, South Korea, and others. The EU and the US are still more attractive as a base than China, much due to the national restrictions in China and the social control, but the pool of talents in China has been rapidly increasing, and Chinese capital for innovative companies are available and plenty, even outside of the Chinese population. Research initiatives and grants in the EU and the US needs to be reinforced and should enable joint research and collaboration in high tech research over the borders of like-minded nations to counter the Chinese excellence and dominance in the field.

US-EU Tech Dis-alignment.

The China threat has caused hopes and ambitions that Europe and the United States would collaborate deeper – especially in areas of technology development and policy. But the two sides are not as aligned as needed and there are clear signs of divergence between the partners. Digital and tech regulations are causing new frictions between the EU and the US, not least as Europe seems more interested in distancing itself from US tech than creating better bases for innovation. Policies on ICT standards in Europe are creating a wedge too, and gradually leads to China and Chinese bodies and courts taking a greater role in determining prices and market norms for global technology markets.

There are also more bumps in technology cooperation of more direct application in national security policy, and they have poisoned the climate for broader technology collaboration. The United States, United Kingdom, and Australia signed a new defense technology pact known as AUKUS in September 2021, a mere week before the first meeting of the TTC between US and EU diplomats were scheduled to take place. The French foreign minister, Jean-Yves Le Drian, called the agreement a "stab in the back" because it ended a partnership between France and Australia and snubbed France. As a result of this disagreement, France has become a leading opponent to future talks on technological cooperation, and despite the need there has not been as much coordinated efforts as would be needed.

Additionally, cooperation has also been hampered by divergent views regarding the concerns over data privacy. The European Union's attitude toward major technology firms has hardened in recent years. To ensure the secure transfer of European data across the Atlantic, it has pushed the United States to adopt digital privacy practices in line with European standards. Addressing many of these challenges in an interview with the Atlantic Council in 2021, the EU Commissioner for the Internal Market, Thierry Breton expressed that "there is, indeed, growing feeling in Europe ... that something is broken in our transatlantic relations." The same feeling is shared by many US policymakers, but it should be noted that despite the differences in views between the transatlantic partners there is a broad common ground, something that is lacking in relation to China and Russia.

The gap between Washington and Brussels in digital regulations is significant for EU-US technological cooperation, especially as the EU aspires toward digital and technological sovereignty from the US. This is a pipe dream that is fueled more by protectionism than national security concerns, but it also draws on adversarial actions by the US. For instance, the Trump administration abandoned the United States' traditional role as a global leader in digital regulation. Chaotic policies on digital and technology regulation have since then undermined the reliability of the US as partner and regulators, prompting other countries to go down a unilateral route. US withdrawal from leadership in international bodies and agreements where digital and economic issues are managed are causing the EU and others to distance themselves from the US.

The opportunities for US-EU collaboration on semiconductors are good. Both sides have demonstrated an acute awareness of the immediate threat, and preliminary arrangements for cooperation have been made. The microelectronics industry in the United States and Europe has established a mutually beneficial ecosystem based on mutual investments, collaborative research, knowledge transfers, and supply arrangements. Companies from Europe have collaborated on research projects aimed at improving chip manufacturing in the United States (Sematech, the University at Albany's College of Nanoscale Science & Engineering, the extreme ultraviolet, or EUV, consortia of the United States' national labs), and companies from the United States have joined European research organizations like IMEC in Belgium, Fraunhofer in Germany, and CNET-Leti in France. Infineon, X-Fab, and BAE Systems are just some of the European companies that have set up chip manufacturing operations in the States (Intel, GlobalFoundries, ON Semiconductor, IXYS, Analog Devices).[283] Big chip design centres are run by companies from both regions in the other. With the backing of governments in both the United States and Europe, Intel, a major US semiconductor producer, is launching a massive investment programme in advanced semiconductor manufacturing in both regions.

While this level of integration is certainly a good starting point, any joint US-EU endeavor to build a more robust semiconductor

---

283 "US-EU Trade Relations", *Congressional Research Service*, June 3, 2022, https://crsreports.congress.gov/product/pdf/R/R47095.

value chain will undoubtedly face significant obstacles.[284] A look back at previous attempts at EU-US government cooperation shows little cause for optimism. Significant differences over regulatory policy and heated industry battles, especially in agriculture, doomed projects like the New Transatlantic Agenda (1995), the Transatlantic Economic Partnership (1998), and the Transatlantic Trade and Investment Partnership (TTIP).

More importantly, with its continued reliance on the United States and China for technical advancements, Europe finds itself in the midst of a struggle that threatens to explode. Europe is up against not one but two forms of dependencies. The first is how much it is reliant on China. The European Union has extensive ties to the Chinese technology industry, and Chinese software and hardware are widely used across the EU's network infrastructure. China's low-priced technology and financial pledges aren't without strings and sacrifices, which Europe is aware of but is having trouble negotiating as a unified bloc. One such example is the European Union's indecision and lack of a unified policy among its member states over the deployment of Huawei's 5G equipment. Unlike nations like Italy,[285] which has banned national operators from pursuing deals with Huawei, Germany and others appear eager to continue some form of partnership with China, albeit with some constraints.[286]

---

284 Please see, Sarah Kreps and Paul Timmers, "Bringing economics back into EU and US chips policy", Brookings, December 20, 2022, https://www.brookings.edu/techstream/bringing-economics-back-into-the-politics-of-the-eu-and-u-s-chips-acts-china-semiconductor-competition/.

285 Giuseppe Fonte, Elvira Pollina, "Italy vetoes 5G deal between Fastweb and China's Huawei: sources", *Reuters*, October 23, 2020, https://www.reuters.com/article/us-huawei-italy-5g-idUSKBN2782A5.

286 William Boston and Stu Woo, "Huawei Gets Conditional Green Light in Germany as Government Approves Security Bill", *The Wall Street Journal*, December 16, 2020, https://www.wsj.com/articles/huawei-gets-conditional-green-light-in-germany-as-government-approves-security-bill-11608117504.

The United States represents the second dependency. European officials realize they must maintain some form of cooperation with American tech firms in the digital sphere but also want to build their own companies. Therefore, the EU is much focused on limiting the role of US corporations within its borders in a vain attempt to come up with rivals in for instance cloud services. While the EU is right in its ambition for commercial success, it needs to focus its efforts on creating better opportunities for future technology innovation in the EU rather than litigating missed opportunities in the past. This is also an issue with strong national security dimensions, and so far, the EU has failed to see the strategic importance of offering a better innovation climate and a policy that makes the US more interested in and dependent on the EU.

EIGHT
Rethinking Supply Chains

Decoupling from China, or de-risking trade relations with the country, now have increased political importance for the United States, the European Union, and a great number of other states. Russia's full-scale invasion of Ukraine added additional political motivation for this project of de-risking, and in the case of Russia complete decoupling. While it is evident that it is not an easy task to have a better security management of trade relations (and broader economic dependencies) with China, it has grown more important over time – and not just for direct geopolitical reasons such as the risk of military aggressions by Beijing but for a wider array of reasons. China is increasingly using economic and commercial policy in a way that is distortive and threatening to the economic security of many nations. Beijing's unilateral measures and the rising number of assertive and aggressive actions – globally and in Asia – underline the urgency of diversifying away from important global supply chains that are overly dependent on China.

Europe has now started to take action as well, actions that has been long overdue. Despite obvious and legitimate reservations about a "tariff war" with China, which does not achieve much new security, the European Union has been moving forward with measures designed to counter China's unfair trade and market practices, political influence campaigns, and intellectual property theft. Public procurement is one area where the European Commission has proposed new policies to respond to countries restricting trade with Europe more effectively. It has proposed a Foreign Subsidy Instrument to prevent foreign companies receiving subsidies from their home governments from accessing the EU's single market, and it has also agreed on an Anti-Coercion Instrument to be used against foreign governments that use economic instruments to coerce other countries into submission.[287] These are just a few recent proposals that expand on current efforts to pinpoint product categories, service sectors, technological domains, and industrial ecologies where European countries are overly reliant on nations with divergent perspectives on liberal democracy and the norms of open trade. There is a need to diversify the hubs and spokes of a new supply chain, but it is important to ensure that these measures are not negatively affecting like-minded states, such as the US, but rather increases trade and cooperation. The same goes for the US.

In the diversification of the transatlantic economies, particular attention should be paid to Asia, Africa, and the Pacific region because of the opportunities they present for multinational corporations seeking to expand their operations abroad and diversify

---

287 "Foreign subsidies distorting the internal market: the provisional political agreement between the Council and the European Parliament", *Council of the European Union*, July, 15, 2022, https://www.consilium.europa.eu/en/press/press-releases/2022/06/30/foreign-subsidies-regulation-political-agreement/.

their sources of supply. These areas feature either in newly emerging markets, favorable and inexpensive labor forces, locations rich in resources, a geographically advantageous economic position, or regions gradually experiencing rising geopolitical gravity. Countries like Australia, India, and Japan, which are strategic partners and allies of the United States and maintain strategic partnerships with the European Union, can play a significant role in the trans-Atlantic supply chain management because they are "likeminded" and have been working to strengthen their supply chain resilience against disruptions. Likewise, countries like Thailand, Malaysia, and Vietnam have reaffirmed their potential as investment alternatives. An uptick in FDI has been seen in these countries, and some, like Vietnam, are already considered integral to the "China plus one" strategy.[288] Many Asian economies, for instance, are expected to become global leaders in apparel production over the next decade.[289]

This does not indicate that it will be an easy transition from China to other Asian economies, as many countries lack China's advanced infrastructure and have less competitive producers. However, there are competitive alternatives to China in the medium-to-long term, especially for assembly operations and basic manufacturing output, as they improve and as China is losing some of its competitive edge. Many Western firms have already made this transition and deepened capital and investment in non-China Asia and Pacific regions – gradually helping to improve the quality of their industrial sectors.

---

288 Sara Hsu, "Which Asian Nations Can Benefit from the 'China Plus One' Strategy?", *The Diplomat*, June 11, 2021, https://thediplomat.com/2021/06/which-asian-nations-can-benefit-from-the-china-plus-one-strategy/

289 "Asia to remain dominant player in garment manufacturing in coming decade: Report", *The Economic Times*, July 14, 2020, https://economictimes.indiatimes.com/industry/cons-products/garments-/-textiles/asia-to-remain-dominant-player-in-garment-manufacturing-in-coming-decade-shows-report/articleshow/76963643.cms?from=mdr

Some are also doing for reasons to reduce their exposure in China because of deteriorating business conditions. As China's economic climate has worsened and an increasing number of firms are facing increasing political pressures from Beijing, they have taken actions to lower business risks.

Transatlantic policymakers also need to take additional measures to support diversification in sectors that are of strategic importance and where China has central roles to play over the supply chain. Health, energy, defense, infrastructure, critical digital technologies, and related raw materials are all examples of sectors that require government action to strengthen supply-chain resilience. In the first place, keeping a good tab of the evolution of supply chains and how dependencies change when products, technologies, and markets change is a necessity. But then there are two more specific priorities: first, cutting the economic dependence on China in strategic and important sectors, and second, helping diversification of sources of supply and generally more diversified supply chains by pro-active measures. Some progress has already been made on both accounts. Now, however, more concerted action is needed.

This chapter will look closer at both these action points and outline a deep Transatlantic agenda for new policies that impact on dependencies and vulnerable supply chains. The impetus for this chapter is the necessity of cooperation between the EU and the US, as well as other like-minded countries or geopolitical allies, to reduce reliance on China's economic coercion and security pressure. In fact, cooperation with like-minded partners in the Americas, Africa, and Asia are central for both the EU and the US achieving its objectives of reducing their exposure to supply from China.

In this chapter we will consider two examples of strategies

aiming at reducing risks related to China. The first case is semi-conductors. China is not a power in the global market for chips but it is racing to take up a significant position, and with much of the global supply coming from countries like Taiwan, the West has felt compelled to use government subsidies to support "home sourcing" or investment in new chips manufacturing capacity. The other example is rare earths – products where there is significant dependence on China (and, for some minerals, Russia). While there are mining opportunities in both American and Europe, the cost of rare earth extraction and the long time it will take to obtain necessary approvals suggest that import diversification is a faster route to less dependence on China. To achieve such an outcome, building and deepening trade and other partnerships with other countries and regions are of critical importance.

Working with Regional and Global Partners

As we have discussed previously in the book, supply-chain resilience could be improved through increased cooperation between the United States and Europe and collaboration between the transatlantic partners and other like-minded countries. Such cooperation will also aid in fostering greater policy coherence and addressing shared worries about China's behavior and power over production and trade in some strategic areas. However, boosting cross-border collaboration on supply-chain resilience calls for a great deal of shared ambition on the part of all supply-chain partners. It touches on sensitive topics like trust, solidarity, and collective decision-making.

More collaboration is required to assess supply chain vulnerabilities, especially considering the reliance on China in technology-intensive sectors and for some sectors where China is the dominant actor throughout the entire supply chain. Gathering and disseminating data on supply chain vulnerabilities and bottlenecks is an essential part of this process, as is mapping the key players involved in these chains and how these partners could be more effectively integrated into a blue supply chain. Particularly for vital supply chains, stress testing can play an important role.

The US and the EU would do well to plan for shared strategic reserves of necessities to establish safety nets, in addition to building new networks to secure strategic resources. The European Union has already proposed stockpiling of essential medical equipment as an area for increased transatlantic cooperation, and this is a natural place to start.[290] It becomes crucial not to exchange one dependency towards one other, the question of limiting the impact of too long and fragile supple chains towards shorter and more efficient ones are a top priority. This also calls for research and development to ensure that resources that are critical, and lacking, in today's supply chain, are exchanged for materials and processes more suited for the needs of the EU and the US.

Greater transatlantic cooperation in the area of crucial raw materials will be required in the future. To meet their demand, the United States and Europe must ensure a steady supply and collaborate with friendly countries, especially Australia and Canada, which have extensive rare-earth mineral reserves and resources, but also Indonesia and several African partners. Strategically significant products like semiconductors and electric vehicle batteries rely on

---

290 European Commission (2020), "A new EU-US agenda for global change", Joint Communication to the European Parliament, the European Council and the Council, JOIN(2020) 22 final, 2 December 2020, https://ec.europa.eu/info/sites/info/files/joint-communication-eu-us-agenda_en.pdf.

rare-earth elements, and Japan, South Korea, and especially Taiwan are essential partners in securing these supply chains and falls into the category of like-minded nations, for diverse reasons.

The intelligence alliance known as 'Five Eyes' includes the United States, Canada, UK, New Zealand, and Australia, and could serve as a springboard for improving supply-chain resilience,[291] and function as a model for "minilaterals" in the supply chain discussion. Considering China's dominance in the area of rare earths, the group could serve as a foundation for the development of a strategic economic relationship for critical raw materials like rare earths. The Five Eyes alliance could be used to establish "trusted supply chains," as announced by the former Australian Prime Minister Scott Morrison.[292] Other countries with similar values can, and should, join the structure, not least the EU. There has already been leaks that there has been both a nine and 14 eyes network involving close allies to the US such as Denmark, Norway, Germany, and Sweden.[293] There have been calls for Japan to join a more comprehensive Five Eyes-style alliance.[294] Adding the United States to the supply chain resilience

291 Rogers, J., Foxall, A., Henderson, M. and Armstrong, S., "Breaking the China Supply Chain: How the 'Five Eyes' can Decouple from Strategic Dependency", Henry Jackson Society, 14 May 2020, https://henryjacksonsociety.org/publications/breaking-the-china-supply-chain-how-the-five-eyes-can-decouplefrom-strategic-dependency.

292 Whyte, S., "Coronavirus exposes weaknesses in global supply chains, Five Eyes alliance to help", Canberra Times, 10 June 2020, https://www.canberratimes.com.au/story/6786721/five-eyes-to-be-used-forsupply-chains-as-virus-exposes-weaknesses

293 Alan Weedon, "Why Japan wants to join the Five Eyes intelligence network", *ABC NEWS*, 18, September 2020, https://www.abc.net.au/news/2020-09-19/five-eyes-intelligence-japan-bid-yoshihide-suga-shinzo-abe/12665248

294 Armitage, R. L. and Nye, J. S., Jr, "The U.S.-Japan Alliance in 2020: An Equal Alliance with a Global Agenda'", Center for Strategic and International Studies, 7 December 2020, https://www.csis.org/ analysis/us-japan-alliance-2020; Wintour, P., "Five Eyes alliance could expand in scope to counteract China", Guardian, 29 July 2020, https://www.theguardian.com/uk-news/2020/jul/29/ five-eyes-alliance-could-expand-in-scope-to-counteract-china.

initiative (SCRI) established in April 2021 by Australia, India, and Japan would be a good idea for several reasons.[295]

Expanding trade agreements with third countries could help the United States and Europe, especially the European Union and the United Kingdom, to diversify their markets and reduce their dependencies. Trade in necessary goods may be facilitated by eliminating tariff and non-tariff barriers and enhanced cooperation on standards and regulations. Given their mutual importance as trading partners, the United States, the European Union, and the United Kingdom should all reexamine and redouble their efforts toward negotiating bilateral trade agreements. Although there is continuing support for working to strengthen transatlantic trade ties, now is not the time for more comprehensive agreements.

When it comes to trade and technology, enhancing the safety of digital supply chains could be another area of concentrated effort between the two regions. Specifically, sharing data and coordinating efforts around risk assessments are important tasks, allowing for better risk management and a clearer delineation of what the Transatlantic partnership need to develop in order to reduce risks. Under the Trade and Technology Council (TTC), which was established in April 2021, the United States and the European Union have identified "key policies on technology, digital issues, and supply chains" as an area for increased cooperation.[296] In addition, the TTC has the potential to evolve into a transatlantic mechanism for reviewing and developing a joint initiative that would establish global standards

---

295 "Executive Order on America's Supply Chains", *The White House*, February 24, 2021, https://www.whitehouse.gov/briefing-room/presidential-actions/2021/02/24/executive-order-on-americas-supply-chains/.

296 European Commission, "EU-US launch Trade and Technology Council to lead values-based global digital transformation", 15 June 2021, https://ec.europa.eu/commission/presscorner/detail/en/IP_21_2990

for the regulation of the essential technologies and industries at the forefront of the Fourth Industrial Revolution (also known as Industry 4.0), such as artificial intelligence, machine learning, advanced robotics, quantum computing, and synthetic biology. Such a council would be able to structure the backbone of a larger, potentially global, framework.

In order to influence discussions at the highest levels of government on the topic of supply-chain resilience, existing mechanisms (such as the G7 or G20) could be improved in addition to diversifying supply chains toward regional partners.[297] There may be a clear opportunity to fortify supply chains among allies by participating in emerging platforms among like-minded democracies, such as the UK's D10 initiative (which would add Australia, India, and South Korea to the existing G7 format, creating a club of 10 democratic partners).[298] More generally, developing an framework for international governance for emerging technologies that improve supply chain visibility and traceability (like blockchain) or assist businesses in rapidly adjusting production (such as 3D printing) is important.

Collaborating with Asia

The wider Asia region is going to be central for reducing the dependence on China for critical supply and China-dominated sectoral supply chains. Lower costs, a good supply of workers, and an already-established manufacturing base make Asia an attractive

---

297 "G7 to vow diversifying of supply chains, filling bank regulatory gaps -draft", *Reuters*, March 12, 2023, https://www.reuters.com/markets/g7-finance-chiefs-agree-scheme-diversify-global-supply-chain-draft-communique-2023-05-12/.

298 Erik Brattberg and Ben Judah, "Forget the G-7, Build the D-10", *Foreign Policy*, June 10, 2020, https://foreignpolicy.com/2020/06/10/g7-d10-democracy-trump-europe/.

alternative for businesses as global trade dynamics and the pandemic continue to force the relocation of international supply chains. Manufacturers had been drawn to Southeast Asia for several years prior to the pandemic because of the region's growing consumer base, advanced infrastructure, and highly trained workforce, but also its abundance of minerals and mining opportunities.

The investor-friendly reforms in the region have been highlighted in a KPMG review, which also projects that the ASEAN will have the world's fourth-largest economy by 2030, with a consumer market worth US$4 trillion.[299] Companies from a wide range of industries have recently announced plans to set up businesses in developing nations like Vietnam, Thailand, and India. The Eastern Economic Corridor, which runs parallel to the country's eastern coast and features industrial estates home to electric vehicle assembly lines, biotech, and aviation firms, is Thailand's largest infrastructure investment to date.

Meanwhile, a US $90 million factory will soon open in northern Thailand, run by Murata, the world's largest manufacturer of capacitors for phones and power supplies.[300] To mitigate supply chain risks in an era of geopolitical uncertainty over China, the company plans to expand the facility to the size of its facility in Wuxi, near Shanghai. Malaysia is also benefiting from foreign investment for high-value products as foreign investment in China is reduced and directed elsewhere in the Asian region. In 2022, electronics

---

299 "Rethinking supply chains in Asia Pacific", *KPMG*, https://kpmg.com/xx/en/home/insights/2021/10/rethinking-supply-chains-in-asia-pacific.html.

300 Biman Mukherjiand Ralph Jennings, "China's loss is Southeast Asia's gain as supply chains shift away to cheaper climes", *South China Morning Post*, January 7, 2023, https://www.scmp.com/week-asia/economics/article/3205858/chain-reaction-chinas-loss-southeast-asias-gain-supply-chains-shift-away-cheaper-climes?module=perpetual_scroll_0&pgtype=article&campaign=3205858

production in Malaysia increased by 32 percent year-over-year as the country jumped to fill China's supply gap. An all-time high of about 209 billion ringgit (US$46.6 billion) was reached in FDI in 2021, with electronics and electricals making up 81.5 percent of the total. The semiconductor industry has flocked to the country, with Intel constructing a US$7 billion semiconductor packaging plant in Penang and Infineon Technologies constructing a US$1.9 billion fabrication unit in Kulim.

Vietnam, where Apple produces AirPods and other iPhone components, has been trying to compete with China in several low-value product categories by emphasizing its cost advantage. In 2021, the country saw an annual increase in FDI by 9 percent, to a total of US$31.15 billion.[301] Manufacturing of shoes, electronics, and appliances, such as Apple's AirPods and other iPhone accessories, were common themes among the proposals. At a groundbreaking ceremony in Binh Duong, a province in Vietnam's south, the Danish toymaker Lego officially broke ground on a $1 billion factory in November.[302] This will be Lego's second Asia facility and sixth overall. Vietnam's export market share for textiles and garments in 2021 was second only to China's.[303] As part of an industry-wide trend away from China, popular shoemakers like Nike and Adidas have settled on Vietnam as their new primary manufacturing hub.

301 "Seaport enterprises set for promising year in 2022", *Viet Nam News*, February 10, 2022, https://vietnamnews.vn/economy/1153328/seaport-enterprises-set-for-promising-year-in-2022.html.

302 "The Lego Group Breaks Ground On New USD 1 Billion Vietnam Factory", *LEGO*, November 3, 2022, https://www.lego.com/es-es/aboutus/news/2022/november/the-lego-group-breaks-ground-on-new-usd-1-billion-vietnam-factory?locale=es-es.

303 Thu Nguyen and Kyssha Mah, "An Introduction to Vietnam's Import and Export Industries", *Vietnam Briefing*, March 18, 022, https://www.vietnam-briefing.com/news/introduction-vietnams-export-import-industries.html/.

Naturally, resource-rich Indonesia plans to cash in on the expected rise in demand for electric vehicles. The government has made it easier for businesses to purchase land in special economic zones since 2014. These zones provide tax breaks to companies that are located there. Japanese electronics giant Panasonic and South Korean industrial behemoth L.G. have both set up shop in Southeast Asia's most populous country, Indonesia. There has been no doubt that with the diversification away from China, its neighbors have been benefitting extensively.

Governments of several nations in the region are also actively pursuing the opportunity to attract manufacturers by offering land, tax benefits, and other incentives. Countries in the region have also entered into several free trade agreements (FTA) and partnerships, thereby enabling manufacturers to consider these countries as viable hubs for export. The region is also host to some of the busiest ports in the world, facilitating seamless trade flow for manufacturers. With a projected population of over 661 million by 2020,[304] the ASEAN region will contribute over \$3.1 trillion to the global economy, providing a significant demographic dividend.[305] The region's manufacturing sector is being propelled by several factors, including an expanding labor force, an expanding industrial base, and a burgeoning economy.

---

304 "Vietnam is an investment destination in post-pandemic period: Bangkok Post", *Vietnam Bond Market*, October 20, 2021, https://mof.gov.vn/webcenter/portal/tttpen/pages_r/l/detail?dDocName=MOFUCM212334.

305 Ibid.

Factors Making ASEAN Economies Important for Western Sourcing

Large Consumer Markets

As a result of its dynamic economy, expanding middle class, and young population, the Asia-Pacific region is home to a sizable consumer market. The ASEAN region is projected to have a $4 trillion consumer market and a 70 percent middle class by the year 2030, making it the world's fourth-largest economy.[306] Increases in disposable income are expected to lead to a doubling of regional consumption. India's large population means there are a lot of potential buyers, and the country's increasing wealth should help boost consumer spending.[307] If businesses decide to set up shop in the area, they will have access to a large domestic consumer base and will be able to set up export-oriented units to serve the globl market

Competitive Labor

As a result of their low production costs and abundant skilled and semiskilled labor force, many Asian countries have become manufacturing powerhouses over the years. The cost of labor in emerging markets like Vietnam, Thailand, India, and the rest of Asia and the ASEAN region is much lower than in more developed economies like those of Europe and North America.

---

306 "Future of Consumption in Fast-Growth Consumer Markets: ASEAN", *World Economic Forum*, June 2020, https://www3.weforum.org/docs/WEF_Future_of_Consumption_in_Fast_Growth_Consumer_Markets_ASEAN_2020.pdf.

307 "India's Impending Economic Boom", *Morgan Stanley*, November 8, 2022, https://www.morganstanley.com/ideas/investment-opportunities-in-india.

With lower labor costs, businesses can make their wares more affordably. However, the minimum wages in these areas are increasing, which may drive up labor costs in the future.

Availability of skilled talent pool

A large pool of skilled and semiskilled workers is available in Asia to meet the manufacturing sector's needs. In addition to utilizing universities to supply skilled graduates, governments in various countries are launching skill development programs tailored to manufacturing sub-segments like electronics, life sciences, and others to continuously upskill and upgrade the workforce to equip them with the technological skills necessary to meet the growing needs of the industry.

Robust infrastructure development

One of the main reasons why businesses choose to move to Asia is because of the region's rapidly improving infrastructure. The US and the EU businesses should take advantage of the region's robust manufacturing ecosystem, which includes access to industrial parks and dedicated manufacturing zones catering to different segments of the manufacturing industry.[308] The region's attractiveness to manufacturers as an export hub is boosted by the presence of major seaports and airports, which provide access to most of the world. The governments of the countries in the area are investing more money to improve the region's already robust road and rail networks.

---

308 "Skills Development Pathways in Asia", *OECD*, https://www.oecd.org/cfe/leed/ Skills%20Development%20Pathways%20in%20Asia_FINAL%20VERSION.pdf

Investor-friendly climate

Considering the current trade dynamic and the pandemic, companies are evaluating alternative manufacturing locations, prompting governments in Asia and the ASEAN region to announce several subsidies and incentives designed to entice companies to establish manufacturing operations in the region. The Japanese government, for instance, made it clear early on that it would subsidize Japanese manufacturers who relocated production from China to other South Asian or ASEAN countries in order to diversify Japanese supply chains. Accordingly, the government of Vietnam issued a decree exempting from taxation any company engaged in R&D in the fields of science and technology.[309] Some of the benefits included lower corporate tax rates, lower lease fees for land and water, and tax credits. To encourage international investment in research and development and new product development, Taiwan has established the Global R&D Innovation Partner Program.[310] This program offers subsidies of up to 50 percent of the total R&D spend, with a particular emphasis on technologies that are either still in their infancy in Taiwan or could help Taiwan develop into a global leader in technology.[311] The Indian government implemented production-linked incentive (PLI) schemes to entice foreign businesses to set

309 Charles Ormiston, "Southeast Asia's Pursuit of the Emerging Markets Growth Crown", *Bain and Company*, November 14, 2022, https://www.bain.com/insights/southeast-asias-pursuit-of-the-emerging-markets-growth-crown/.

310 "Attracting major international firms to set up R&D centers", *Executive Yuan*, https://english.ey.gov.tw/News3/9E5540D592A5FECD/bb6ffff2-f923-4b0a-b5dc-66437be2df41.

311 "Production Linked Incentive Scheme (PLI) for Large Scale Electronics", *Ministry of Electronics and Information Technology, India*, https://www.meity.gov.in/esdm/pli.

up shop in the country and encourage domestic businesses to establish or expand their factories. Businesses can earn incentives through the program if they increase their sales of goods produced in India.[312] The PLI scheme currently helps 13 industries, including the automotive and auto parts industries, the pharmaceutical and medical device manufacturing, and the electronic sector. Investments of at least $1.1 billion (5 billion Ringgits) made by Fortune 500 companies in high-end technology, manufacturing, or value-added industries in Malaysia over a period of five years are eligible for incentives totaling $238 million (1 billion Ringgits).[313] In addition, it paved the way for investors and businesses eager

New Asia-Pacific Manufacturing Hubs for non-China Supply – The Case of Semiconductors

Because of their trade-friendly policies, government support, large consumer base, growing middle class, and availability of labor, many countries in the Asia-Pacific region are among the most attractive locations for foreign direct investment. Major investors in the region come from countries like Japan, China, the United States, South Korea, and European countries like the Netherlands.

Manufacturing is at the center of the new investment and sourcing boom in non-China countries in the wider Asian region.

312 Radhika Gaggar, Abhishek Kalra, Abhay Singh and Chandni Ochani, "India: Foreign direct investment regulations", *Global Competition Review*, December 06, 2022, https://globalcompetitionreview.com/guide/foreign-direct-investment-regulation-guide/second-edition/article/india.

313 Bernama, "Over 150 Indian companies invest US$3 billion in Malaysia", New Straits Times, January 29, 2022, https://www.nst.com.my/news/nation/2022/01/767262/over-150-indian-companies-invest-us3-billion-malaysia.

Integrated circuits are "printed" in fabrication facilities (fabs) by layer-by-layer depositing of transistor elements (at the atomic scale) onto raw silicon wafers. Semiconductor fabs are the most exacting of all manufacturing industries because they must exercise extreme control over the process using highly specialized and sensitive equipment. Sustainable semiconductor production requires high-priced, technically complex SMEs that meet stringent standards for accuracy, throughput, cleanliness, and reliability. Given this fact, production is largely limited to a few major corporations and geographical areas. Semiconductor manufacturing equipment (SME) entails both front- and back-end wafer fabrication equipment, as well as test and packaging equipment for semiconductors.[314]

The Indo-Pacific has a sizable market for semiconductor manufacturing equipment enterprises. While the United States and this region account for the bulk of the world's fabs, the Indo-Pacific region earns 77% of the global SME market share.[315] When it comes to purchasing wafer fabrication, assembly, and test equipment in 2021, the region's businesses spent more than $104 billion. Spending on high-tech packaging equipment is not included in the $104 billion total. TechInsights data is heavily relied upon in this report's semiconductor manufacturing equipment supply chain analysis.

The United States is home to more than 40 percent of the world's SMEs, while Japan's SME sector accounts for 29 percent. Along with the Netherlands, these three countries are major generators of SME enterprises. The availability of trustworthy domestic SMEs is an issue in both Taiwan and China. Among the major manufacturing

---

314 "Semiconductor Equipment Database", *TechInsights*, 2023, https://www.techinsights.com/blog/techinsights-semiconductor-equipment-report.

315 Ibid.

countries in the Indo-Pacific region, Taiwan has the smallest SME industry despite being leading in high end semiconductor production, while China produces less than 2% of the world supply. South Korea's thriving SME sector generates significant output and boasts a cutting-edge technological infrastructure.[316]

Japan is the undisputed SME assembly and test equipment leader, while the United States dominates the wafer fab and advanced packaging equipment markets. More than 70 percent of the world's wafer fab equipment comes from the United States and Japan. Despite being significantly under-represented in comparison to other major markets, South Korea's 4.2% share of the global market is still quite sizeable. Japan's manufacturing sector is second only to Europe's in terms of assembly equipment, and the country holds roughly 43% of the global market share in test equipment. The United States provides 35.3%, and South Korea provides 10.8% of the market for test equipment, both of which are sizable contributions.[317]

Manufacturers' relationships with fab managers continue beyond the sale of equipment. Continuous post-sale support in the form of operational troubleshooting, software updates, spare parts, and maintenance is required for semiconductor manufacturing equipment, such as wafer fabrication tools. In addition to selling their products, equipment manufacturers also make money through service and support. In 2021, LAM Research, a major US equipment supplier, earned over $2 billion in revenue from its servicing division alone[318]

---

316 Sam Kim, "South Korea to Surpass China in Chip Machine Spending Next Year", *Bloomberg*, March 27, 2023, https://www.bloomberg.com/news/articles/2023-03-27/south-korea-to-surpass-china-in-chip-machine-spending-next-year

317 Ko Fujioka, "Japan to subsidize domestic chipmaking beyond the cutting edge", *Nikkei Asia*, February 7, 2023

318 Ibid.

Ninety percent of sales of SMEs in the United States and Japan come from the Indo-Pacific region. In the meantime, Chinese and South Korean equipment producers mainly sell within their own countries. Despite their relatively modest sales, nearly all of China's SME's sell their products domestically. About 73% of the products produced by South Korean SMEs are exported (some of which have production facilities outside of South Korea). Companies like SEMES, Wonik IPS, PSK, and Eugene Tech are at the forefront of South Korean manufacturing among SMEs.[319]

In recent years, China has been the largest market for SMEs in the Indo-Pacific, purchasing more than $28 billion of equipment in 2021. Notably, 30 percent, 29 percent, and 20 percent of all US, Japanese, and South Korean SME sales, respectively, go to customers in China. Conversely, China buys 45 percent of its total SME stock from the United States and 28 percent from Japan. In 2023, South Korea is expected to overtake China as the top market for SMEs.

Numerous national and international initiatives have been launched by various governments—including the United States and China – to strengthen and restructure the semiconductor supply chain in order to achieve national security and geopolitical goals. In order to increase domestic semiconductor production capacity, the United States CHIPS and Science Act of 2022 authorized nearly $50 billion in investments.[320] The "K-Chips Act," a new South Korean law, significantly reduces taxes for the semiconductor

319 "FACT SHEET: Engaging with US Partners and Allies", *CHIPS for America Fact Sheet*, February 28, 2023, https://www.nist.gov/system/files/documents/2023/02/28/CHIPS_NOFO-1_International_Engagement_Fact_Sheet.pdf.

320 Sankalp Phartiyal, "India Expands Incentives for Chip, Display Units in Renewed Push", Bloomberg, September 21, 2022, https://www.bloomberg.com/news/articles/2022-09-21/india-expands-incentives-for-chip-display-units-in-renewed-push#xj4y7vzkg.

industry.[321] Japan, India, and the European Union have also announced similar measures.[322] These shifts highlight the growing significance of policy alongside market forces in shaping the future of the global semiconductor industry. In addition to economics, national security and technological sovereignty are driving forces behind existing and planned policies (and related subsidies). In light of these revolutionary shifts, it is imperative that policymakers evaluate the significance of the Indo-Pacific region to semiconductor supply chains.

As it stands, technological and economic constraints have spawned a highly specialized and intricate semiconductor supply chain. No nation has yet succeeded in becoming fully self-sufficient in semiconductor manufacturing despite persistent efforts on their part. US policy should seek to develop a robust semiconductor eco-system in which allies and partners play a crucial role in successfully fortifying the United States' supply chain position and mitigating risk. The CHIPS Act relies heavily on this very mechanism, and the Department of Commerce has already acknowledged as much. Implementation of the CHIPS Act is led by the Department of Commerce's CHIPS office, with primary goals including the coordination of investment and incentive programs, the promotion of knowledge exchanges and collaboration, and the facilitation of cross-border commerce.[323] To avoid making the same investments twice, build on each nation's domestic industry's comparative strengths, and reduce the risk associated with critical dependencies,

---

321 Ibid.

322 "European Chips Act", *European Commission*, https://commission.europa.eu/strategy-and-policy/priorities-2019-2024/europe-fit-digital-age/european-chips-act_en.

323 Ibid.

it is crucial to keep the lines of communication open with key allies, especially in the Indo-Pacific.

Simply put, almost no consumer electronics would exist without the semiconductor industry. The economies of the United States and the European Union, the technological competitiveness of American and European businesses, and the quality of life for ordinary citizens would all be severely impacted by disruptions in the semiconductor industry's supply chain. Damage to the semiconductor supply chain could have far-reaching effects on the national security and critical infrastructure of the United States and the European Union. Advanced semiconductor technologies are crucial to the military's ability to defend itself and wage war, but they are hard to come by without financial backing from the government. As of right now, only Taiwan and South Korea have the installed capacity to produce semiconductors at technologies smaller than 7 nanometers (nm), putting at risk the supply of high-end semiconductors to the military forces of the United States and the European Union.[324] The United States' critical national infrastructure, which includes the country's communications networks and transportation systems, relies heavily on semiconductors.

These essential parts of the technology on which modern society has come to rely are supplied by dispersed networks that span the globe. The United States works with partners all over the globe,

---

324 In its current form, the semiconductor supply chain is extremely vulnerable to disruption. This holds true regardless of the cause of the disruption, be it a natural calamity like an earthquake or typhoon, a global shock to the trading system like the COVID-19 pandemic, or a disruption caused by political considerations like an armed conflict. Because of its complicated political situation and the challenges posed by China, Taiwan's semiconductor supply chain is especially vulnerable to potential disruptions. Earthquakes and typhoons are regular occurrences in Taiwan, making the country vulnerable to natural disasters. "World Fab Forecast (WFF)," *SEMI*, December 14, 2021, https://www.semi.org/en/products-services/market-data/world-fab-forecast.

but Taiwan could be a game changer for international technological cooperation. Two of the world's three largest IDMs are headquartered in the United States. IDMs are essential to the semiconductor industry as they both design and produce the components. Contract semiconductor manufacturers (sometimes referred to as "foundries") based in Taiwan are another vital link in the US and European supply chain. Many of the United States and Europe's closest allies also rely heavily on Taiwan as a source of technology. This includes companies like Apple, Texas Instruments, and Qualcomm.[325]

Given its current structure, the risks for disruption in the semiconductor supply chain are significant. That is true whether the source of the disruption is a natural disaster like an earthquake or typhoon, a global shock to the trading system like the COVID-19 pandemic, a disturbance caused by political considerations such as an armed conflict, or other factors. Potential risks to the semiconductor supply chain are especially acute in Taiwan, given its complex political situation and the challenges posed to it by China. Taiwan is also at risk for natural disasters, as earthquakes and typhoons are common occurrences.

Given its significance, the United States and Europe must do more to advance its semiconductor industry. Investments in future cutting-edge technology for the US market, incentivized with government funding, could help bend the curve moderately. A positive result is possible, but it will probably take a long time and a lot of money to get there. Once fully funded, the CHIPS for America Act will be a positive step toward bolstering the US semiconductor industry by encouraging companies like TSMC, Samsung, and Intel

---

325 "Revenue of leading outsourced semiconductor assembly and test (OSAT) companies from 2019 to 2021, by quarter," *statista.com*, https://www.statista.com/statistics/1120619/leading-global-osat-companies-revenues/.

to construct state-of-the-art semiconductor fabrication facilities in the United States.[326] To further strengthen the United States' position in the vital semiconductor sector, it has been recommended that tax credits for manufacturing and design be added to the proposed FABS Act.

Among the world's top semiconductor producers, Taiwan has emerged as a major center of cutting-edge manufacturing. Along with Taiwan's rising prominence, foreign investment in the country's semiconductor industry has also increased. Not only have companies like Qualcomm and semiconductor material producer Entegris recently increased their presence on the island, but Micron Technology, a major and long-term investor that has acquired and operates several memory fabs there, is another example. Taiwan has become the largest semiconductor equipment market in the world.[327] The high level of equipment spending in Taiwan has been maintained as local businesses there expand their production capacities and modernize their technologies. Since semiconductor equipment has a long lead time, Taiwan is positioned to dominate the industry for the next few years.

TSMC is essential to the development of the semiconductor industry on the island. As the world's largest foundry chipmaker, the company can produce around 13 million 12-inch equivalent wafers annually.[328] TSMC is at the forefront of technological innovation and uses a wide variety of technologies, from the more traditional

---

326 "Global Semiconductor Equipment Billings Jump 38% Year-Over-Year in Q3 2021, Log Fifth Straight Quarterly Record, SEMI Reports," *SEMI Worldwide Semiconductor Equipment Market Statistics (WWSEMS) Report,* December 1, 2021, https://www.semi.org/en/news-mediapress/semi-press-releases/global-semiconductor-equipment-billings-jump-38%25-year-over-year-in-Q3-2021-log-fifth-straight-quarterlyrecord-semi-reports.

327 Ibid.

328 "About TSMC," *TSMC,* https://www.tsmc.com/english/aboutTSMC.

2 microns to the most advanced 3 nm.[329] Broadcom, Qualcomm, NVIDIA, AMD, Apple, Xilinx, etc., are just some of the top fabless companies in the United States that use TSMC's foundry services.

A new state-of-the-art TSMC fab is being built in the United States, and in May 2020, TSMC made a historic announcement that they would be investing heavily in their manufacturing operations. TSMC announced that a new fab would be constructed in Arizona and would have the capacity to produce over 20,000 wafers per month using the company's 5 nm process. The fab's construction began in 2021, and production there is anticipated to start in 2024. This only represents a small portion of TSMC's global footprint, as its primary operations are still based in Taiwan. The TSMC fab will be one of the most advanced facilities in the US, and at an estimated cost of US$12 billion in 2020, it will be a significant foreign investment for the US.

More diversification also emerges in the semiconductor supply chain. Sunlit Chemical, a leading Taiwanese chemical supplier to the semiconductor industry, has broken ground on a new facility in the greater Phoenix area.[330] Following TSMC, Samsung and Intel have recently announced massive investments in the United States too, with Samsung planning to spend US$17 billion in Texas and Intel planning to spend US$20 billion on two new plants in Arizona. Intel announced initial funding of more than US$20 billion in 2022 to construct two cutting-edge chip factories in Ohio. China imports advanced chips, especially from Taiwan, despite the country's best

---

329 Ibid.

330 Arizona Commerce Authority, "Sunlit Breaks Ground on Phoenix Facility," *SignalsAZ.com*, January 23, 2022, https://www.signalsaz.com/articles/sunlit-breaks-ground-on-phoenix-facility/.

efforts to foster a domestic semiconductor industry. Even China's most cutting-edge semiconductor firms are technological relics compared to TSMC. This disparity means that most Chinese consumer technology products use semiconductors made in Taiwan, putting Chinese companies at high risk of damage if the supply chain is disrupted. The semiconductor industry in Taiwan has significantly benefited from China's demand, and the two countries' economies are intertwined across the Taiwan Strait. For example, Huawei, the Chinese tech giant, was TSMC's second-largest customer before 2020, and China received a sizable portion of TSMC's exports.[331] The United States, however, announced sanctions in May of 2020, compelling TSMC to make adjustments. Orders from other major clients have made up for the revenue lost due to the United States restrictions.[332] Total revenue for the company in 2021 increased by 18.5% from the previous year.[333]

Policy discussions regarding Japan's economic security have heated up ever since Fumio Kishida was elected prime minister in 2021. Kishida appointed Takayuki Kobayashi to the newly created Minister of Economic Security position soon after taking office. After much debate, the Japanese Diet finally passed the Economic Security Promotion Law on May 11, 2022. This law is meant to facilitate the implementation of economic policies that strengthen national security in a thorough and efficient manner.

331 Ryan Hass, "This US-China downturn may be difficult for Taiwan," *Brookings Institution*, February 24, 2020, https://www.brookings.edu/blog/order-from-chaos/2020/02/24/this-us-china-downturn-may-be-difficult-for-taiwan/.

332 Cheng, Ting-Fang and Lauly Li, "TSMC says 2020 revenue to jump 30% despite losing Huawei orders," *Nikkei Asian Review*, October 15, 2020, https://asia.nikkei.com/Business/Technology/TSMC-says-2020-revenue-to-jump-30-despite-losing-Huawei-orders

333 "Financial Results -2021 Monthly Revenue," *TSMC*, March 15, 2022, https://investor.tsmc.com/english/monthly-revenue/2021.

In the case of Japan, the Ministry of Economy, Trade and Industry (METI) has examined critical materials in supply chains to determine the degree of import dependence and substitutability.[334] When it comes to manufactured goods, Japan relies on foreign suppliers the most for computers (63.4% of all imports) and smartphones (94% of all imports). [335] According to research analyzed by the Cabinet Office, in value terms, 1,133 of some 5,000 imported items, accounting for 23 percent of the total, were found to have more than a 50 percent dependency on China, a much higher rate compared to the US at 18 percent[336] and Germany at 8.5 percent.[337] Due to the interconnected nature of global value chains, finding suitable alternatives to China's shipments is challenging in the event of a disruption. Therefore, METI is eager to ensure a reliable domestic supply. METI has recently introduced subsidy programs to encourage Japanese businesses to broaden and consolidate their supply bases. There are two goals for the program. The first is encouraging domestic investment through the relocation of overseas manufacturing facilities to Japan. The second is to build solid supply chains involving ASEAN member countries to entice Japanese firms to relocate or set up shop in these areas. The program

334 Farrell, Henry & Abraham L. Newman, "Weaponized Interdependence: How Global Economic Networks Shape State Coercion," International Security, 44 (1), 2019, pp. 42-79.

335 "World Economic Trends II", Cabinet Office, Government of Japan, February 2023, https://www5.cao.go.jp/keizai3/world_economic_trends-e/22-2-e.pdf.

336 "Outline of the Projects under the FY 2020 Supplementary Budget," Japanese Government Ministry of Economy, Trade and Industry, April 2020.

337 Ibid.

has been characterized as an attempt to wean Japanese businesses off China as a production hub.[338]

In particular, after Russia's full invasion of Ukraine, the Japanese government implemented several measures to guarantee a constant supply of vital materials. For instance, the Japanese government has prioritized budgeting for sizeable subsidies to guarantee access to semiconductors and other crucial materials that could disrupt the supply chain. The Japanese government also launched a program to encourage investment in Japan to further strengthen supply chains and promote the diversification of overseas supply networks. Japan's supplementary budget for 2021 included an extra 617 billion yen, or about $4.5 billion, to establish domestic production sites for advanced semiconductors.[339] In addition, 250 billion yen was earmarked for a program meant to nurture key technologies and promote rapid research development and commercialization of critical technologies in advanced fields, such as quantum technology and artificial intelligence.

In this light, the Diet passed the Economic Security Promotion Law on May 11, 2022. It sets up four pillars: 1) a system to guarantee constant supplies of critical materials like semiconductors; 2) a system to guarantee constant service delivery via critical infrastructure; 3) a system to foster the growth of crucial technologies; and 4) a secret patent system. On July 19th, the government drafted basic guidelines to ensure a steady supply of critical materials like semiconductors in order to effectively implement the law. According

---

338 Isabel Reynolds and Emi Urabe, "Japan to Fund Firms to Shift Production Out of China", Bloomberg, April 8, 2020, https://www.bloomberg.com/news/articles/2020-04-08/japan-to-fund-firms-to-shift-production-out-of-china?in_source=embedded-checkout-banner.

339 Asia Pacific Initiative, "100 Japanese Companies Survey on Economic Security," Dec. 24, 2021.

to reports, the drafted guidelines for the law's central component, funding for the development of cutting-edge technologies, prioritize 20 technology fields like semiconductors, pharmaceuticals, and rare earth metals. The 20 areas largely align with the 14 US technologies designated as emerging or fundamental under the Export Control Reform Act. The government will back the manufacturer of a critical material if deemed necessary. According to the proposed framework, the government will assist companies that deal with critical materials if those materials are 1) necessary for the survival of the people, 2) highly dependent on external sources, with supply bias toward specific countries, 3) likely to be disrupted due to the suspension of exports, or 4) have a history of supply disruption. Companies providing critical materials are subject to investigation by the government and could face consequences if they refuse to cooperate with inquiries.[340]

Businesses in Japan are struggling to adapt to the government's policies meant to strengthen the country's economy. Seventy-five percent of Japanese companies cited "uncertainty in the US-China relationship" as an issue affecting economic security in a survey on financial security conducted by the Asia Pacific Initiative in 2021, and 60.8% said their businesses were "affected" by the US-China rivalry. Furthermore, 98 percent reported being aware of economic security issues, and 86.9 percent reported taking action. 33.3 percent "have a goal of increasing" their sales in China, while 41.9 percent "have a goal of increasing" their sales in the United States.[341]

Although Japanese companies know China's influence on

---

340 "Significance and Issues of the Economic Security Promotion Law", *Japan Institute for International Affairs*, May 31, 2022, https://www.jiia.or.jp/en/column/2022/05/economy-security-linkages-fy2022-01.html.

341 "US-China Tech Rivalry and Japan's Policies for Economic Security", *Global Asia*, Accessed February 28, 2024. https://www.globalasia.org/v17no4/cover/us-china-tech-rivalry-and-japans-policies-for-economic-security_hideyuki-miura

economic security, this awareness may not be reflected in corporate behavior. According to a survey by the Development Bank of Japan, although companies are restructuring their supply chains by diversifying and decentralizing procurement sources, standardizing products and parts, and strengthening mutual aid systems with other companies, Japanese companies continue to invest actively in China.[342] The number of company withdrawals from China over the past 10 years has been around 3 percent, just slightly higher than in other regions. In the past, Japan, as a development-oriented nation, promoted strong industrial policies and guided private companies; however, as Japanese companies became internationally competitive, they have been able to ignore or defy state regulations.[343] The Japanese government is using subsidies and other means to encourage Japanese firms to review their supply chains and withdraw from China, but firms may not act accordingly. Further onshoring could increase the vulnerability of supply chains to shocks.

To protect its national interests from weaponized interdependence, Japan, like other developed nations, is trying to enhance its economic security by developing robust supply chains. To accurately identify which technologies are important to Japan's national interests and protect them from interference by China, the government is promoting partial decoupling, which involves relocating production to Japan or to ASEAN countries and closely examining critical and highly vulnerable products that have a large impact on economic activity and people's lives.

In the meantime, China's position as a major export hub is

342 "Japan makers to reduce reliance on China suppliers: Nikkei survey", *Asia Nikkei*, December 1, 2022, https://asia.nikkei.com/Spotlight/Supply-Chain/Japan-makers-to-reduce-reliance-on-China-suppliers-Nikkei-survey.

343 Ibid.

changing. China has a large domestic market, great potential, and years of experience in industrial production, but it is no longer a top export destination. As a result, businesses are not likely to move their supply chains away from China if they deal with non-essential goods and industries that threaten economic security less. Therefore, it's implausible that decoupling will take place. Also, moving all mission-critical industries, like semiconductor production, to Japan is hard due to the high costs involved.

New Policy Frameworks for China Diversification

Consequently, the idea of friend-shoring, or creating a safe supply chain through cooperation with friendly countries, have riser in prominence. In this regard, the May 23, 2022, introduction of the Indo-Pacific Economic Framework (IPEF) was significant. IPEF brought together the 14 countries to discuss creating a resilient economic framework. However, Excluding China from producing all critical materials is difficult and unreasonable. So, while Japan follows the United States' lead and beefs up economic security policies, it must also maintain communication with China and lobby for a shift in Beijing's approach to trade and international finance.

The Biden Administration has launched a new dialogue forum with Japan and South Korea on friend-shoring semiconductors, inviting companies to compete for a share of the $50 billion already approved to revitalize the US chip industry in an effort to outcompete China in technological terms. The United States, Japan, and South Korea held their first annual Economic Security Dialogue meeting in Honolulu. The semiconductor industries in Japan and South Korea are two of the most advanced in the world. Therefore, this forum would focus on topics like data transparency amid the US-China trade war and the resilience of the supply chains for semiconductors, batteries, and critical minerals.[344]

In addition, the government released the first CHIPS for America funding opportunity, inviting businesses to compete for a portion of the resources set aside to finance the development of new and expanded domestic manufacturing semiconductor facilities.[345] Companies like Taiwan Semiconductor Manufacturing Company, Samsung Electronics, and Micron Technology, which are already producing some of the world's most advanced chips, will use the money to expand their operations in the United States.[346] The Biden administration's efforts to rein in China's semiconductor industry face challenges such as getting Seoul to join the United States in banning the export of sophisticated chip-making equipment to the country. Japan and the Netherlands have already supported this move. Both are home to corporations at the forefront of the worldwide semiconductor industry.

However, it has been feared that Washington's efforts to reshape the global semiconductor ecosystem will have a negative impact on Taiwan's semiconductor industry, which is seen as one of the island's most robust defenses against an invasion from Beijing. With new investments allocated in the US, some in Taiwan are concerned that moving its production to the US and elsewhere may weaken one of

---

344 "Readout of the Trilateral United States – Japan – Republic of Korea Economic Security Dialogue", *The White House*, February 28, 2023, https://www.whitehouse.gov/briefing-room/statements-releases/2023/02/28/readout-of-the-trilateral-united-states-japan-republic-of-korea-economic-security-dialogue/.

345 "Biden-Harris Administration Launches First CHIPS for America Funding Opportunity", *US Department of Commerce*, February 28, 2023, https://www.commerce.gov/news/press-releases/2023/02/biden-harris-administration-launches-first-chips-america-funding.

346 Ibid.

the island's most important geopolitical assets known as the "silicon shield." This is a concern that should be taken seriously and arguably Taiwan's dominance in the advanced semiconductor segment is a security defense.

Theoretically, the silicon shield protects Taiwan from a Chinese military invasion in two ways. First, China depends on TSMC to produce the bulk of the chips it needs for its consumer electronics industry, linking Beijing's bottom line to Taiwan's stability, which may push China toward military restraint. Second, the dependence on major economies, including the US and the European Union, motivates those countries to stand up for Taipei's sovereignty.

Recently, senior officials from the US, South Korea, Japan, and Taiwan held a virtual preliminary meeting for the proposed Chip 4 initiative designed to stabilize semiconductor supply chains, including by setting up an early warning system to prevent disruptions, potentially including chipmaking raw materials and manufacturing equipment.[347] Meanwhile, China is ramping up its own domestic chip capacity. It reportedly plans on a massive $140 billion package to bolster self-sufficiency and counter US moves.[348] In this context, the Chinese Foreign Ministry spokesperson Mao Ning stated that Washington has "overstretched the concept of national security, abused export control measures, disrupted normal economic and trade activities, and destabilized global industrial and supply chains" to maintain economic and technological supremacy.[349] An argument

---

347 "Taiwan says 'Fab 4' chip group held first senior officials meeting", *Reuters*, February 25, 2023, https://www.reuters.com/technology/taiwan-says-fab-4-chip-group-held-first-senior-officials-meeting-2023-02-25/.

348 Julie Zhu, "Exclusive: China readying $143 billion package for its chip firms in face of US curbs", *Reuters*, December 13, 2022, https://www.reuters.com/technology/china-plans-over-143-bln-push-boost-domestic-chips-compete-with-us-sources-2022-12-13/.

349 Ibid.

that rings hollow considering the weaponization of the Chinese economy and its restrictions on both trade and export of rare earth minerals as well as their own decoupling in sensitive areas from the US economy.

Commerce Secretary Gina Raimondo spoke in 2023 about the administration's plans to "build a reliable and resilient semiconductor industry that protects America's technological leadership for the coming decades". She promised that more funding opportunities for supply chain companies and R&D investments would be announced. Raimondo stated that, in 1990, the United States produced 37% of the world's semiconductors and that the country is down to 12 precent now.[350] The pandemic-induced semiconductor shortage caused trouble in numerous industries, from automobiles to consumer electronics. The US Department of Commerce estimated that the chip shortage significantly dented the country's 2021 economic growth.[351]

Policy frameworks for deeper trade and supply-chain cooperation between America and the EU, one the one hand, and the wider non-China Asia-Pacific region could improve significantly. While semiconductors have become a much-discussed topic and attracted the embrace of government subsidies, the reality is that diversification should emerge in other sectors too and that it is too expensive for the US, European or Asian governments to pay companies significant sums to establish new factories in their home countries. There is a limit to how much governments can allocate to industrial support, and such support is no panacea and can easily

---

350 Gina M. Raimondo, "Remarks by US Secretary of Commerce Gina Raimondo: The CHIPS Act and a Long-term Vision for America's Technological Leadership", *US Department of Commerce*, https://www.commerce.gov/news/speeches/2023/02/remarks-us-secretary-commerce-gina-raimondo-chips-act-and-long-term-vision.

351 Ibid.

be manipulated by firms that are getting free money. It is important to harness the power of the market and create institutions that will prompt businesses to make new investments and reorient themselves away from Chinese supply.

Both America and Europe lack a trade strategy for deeper engagement with the Asia-Pacific region. After America pulled out of the Transpacific Partnership, that then became the Comprehensive and Progressive Agreement for Trans-Pacific Partnership (CPTPP), the White House has not had a credible idea for how it wants to engage with non-China countries in the region – leading to many missed opportunities to guide policy in a direction that reduces the economic significance of China. The EU, like the US, has a series of Free Trade Agreements with Asian and Pacific countries on the books but have shied away from greater trade leadership in the region, something that China in particular has been utilizing in developing its trade strategy in the region.

Countries in the region are moving ahead by their own volition but absent America and Europe there is the risk that China will eventually come back to set the main direction also of such initiatives. China has already applied to join the CPTPP, and if it does it will have a significant impact on how trade and supply chains in the region will develop over time. Now, China may not be allowed to join, and many CPTPP countries have express concerns over such a development. However, if the EU and the US keep neglecting trade policies in the region, the risk is that the gravitational pull of China's economy in the region will also lead to wider trade agreements with Beijing at the center.

The EU and the US could apply to join the CPTPP. For the US, this would largely mean the recovery of the old trade strategy for the

Asia-Pacific region. The EU has claimed that it can achieve better market access by negotiating country-by-country with the CPTPP countries it does not already have a trade agreement with, but this argument has not aged well as the EU has failed to achieve these new agreements. Moreover, it misses the point. The CPTPP remains manufacturing-oriented and is one of the best vehicles available to shape an agreement between broadly like-minded partners that al have capacity to contribute to important industrial supply chains and effect a diversification of supply away from China. In strategic and geopolitical terms, it is a non-brainer. It would also boost economic growth in both the EU and the US.

Collaborating outside of Asia

The global mineral supply chain is already narrow, and China has an overwhelming lead with respect to rare earth metal extraction and processing. This market dominance enables Beijing to manipulate access seemingly at will. Beyond minerals, China's status as the world's top manufacturer also makes raw material building blocks like plastics, chemicals, and agriculture products vulnerable to Beijing's geopolitical ambitions.

This vulnerability for the US industry dependent upon reliable supply chains underscores the need to pursue a pivot. Decoupling is unrealistic, but diversifying supply is a necessary long-term strategy. Africa, as an obvious example, represents a key opportunity for American interests seeking new, secure supply chains. Gaining attention, the African market affords a spectrum of trade, investment, and sourcing opportunities across fifty distinct markets. African economies can become major participants in global supply chains by harnessing their vast resources of materials needed by high-technology sectors and their growing consumer markets, the United Nations Conference on Trade and Development (UNCTAD) outlined in its Economic Development in Africa Report 2023.[352] Supply chains encompass the systems and resources needed to develop, produce, and transport goods and services from suppliers to customers. "This is Africa's moment to bolster its position in global supply chains as diversification efforts continue. It's also an opportunity for the continent to strengthen its emerging industries, foster economic growth, and create jobs for millions of its people," UNCTAD Secretary-General Rebeca Grynspan said.

Despite Africa's 11.7 million square miles across 54 countries, vast agricultural scope, and abundant raw materials, its supply chain is often neglected, even if Russia and China have been more opportune that the West and invested in the supply chain, but also in its political capital. In the World Bank's "Ease of doing business" rankings, just two African countries showed up in the top 50: Mauritius (13) and Rwanda (38). This is not necessarily something that limits China's and Russia's reach in Africa, but most surely European and American influence.

According to the United Nations, "it (Africa) holds 65% of the world's total arable land, 30% of the world's mineral reserves, 8% of the world's natural gas, and 12% of the world's oil reserves." That includes "40% of the world's gold" and the "largest reserves of diamonds, cobalt, platinum and uranium" on the planet. Compound that with a population of 1.4 billion people, with many people soon entering the workforce (the median age is 19), and it seems like

---

352 "Economic Development In Africa Report 2023", *UNCTAD*, https://unctad.org/publication/economic-development-africa-report-2023

Africa should be a significant part of the global supply chain. But that's still a work in progress.

Africa's abundance of critical minerals and metals, including aluminum, cobalt, copper, lithium, and manganese, vital components in technology-intensive industries, positions the continent as an attractive destination for manufacturing, as recent upheavals caused by trade turbulence, geopolitical events, and economic uncertainty compel manufacturers to diversify their production locations. Africa also offers advantages such as shorter and simpler access to primary inputs, a younger, technology-aware, and adaptable labor force, and a burgeoning middle class known for its growing demand for more sophisticated goods and services. The report highlights that creating an environment conducive to technology-intensive industries would help raise wages on the continent.

Deeper integration into global supply chains would also diversify African economies, boosting their resilience to future shocks. Expanding energy supply chains into Africa is also an opportunity to accelerate climate action. The continent's vast renewable energy potential, particularly in solar power, can help reduce production costs and decrease reliance on fossil fuel-based energy sources. Africa needs more investment in renewable energy to help bridge the significant investment gap and tackle other obstacles to manufacturing solar panels on the continent. Only about 2% of global investments in renewable energy go to Africa. The growth of investment in renewable energy, as shown by UNCTAD, could promote the manufacturing of solar panels on the continent. For example, in 2022, the Democratic Republic of the Congo was the largest producer of copper in Africa, at 1.8 million metric tons – and beyond exploration and extraction, the country is a potential destination for refining metal products for the electric vehicles industry.[353]

Rare Earth Minerals

Africa's full potential in rare earths is largely untapped, given low levels of exploration. In 2021, the mining exploration budget in sub-Saharan Africa was the second lowest in the world—roughly half that of Latin America, Australia, and Canada—despite having triple the surface area of Canada and Australia. In 2021, Canada's exploration budget rose by 62 percent yearly, followed by 39 percent in Australia, 37 percent in the US, and 29 percent in Latin America. The budget for Africa grew only 12 percent, and the vast majority of exploration continues to be concentrated in gold rather than rare earths or green metals critical to the clean energy transition.[354]

Scaling up exploration is critical for enabling Africa to identify and extract rare earth elements. Already, several rich deposits have been found. In 2022, Mkango Resources, a Canadian exploration firm, announced that its Songwe Hill rare earths mine in Malawi is expected to commence production in 2025.[355] Bannerman Energy, an Australian firm, announced that it had acquired a 41.8% stake in Namibia Critical Metals, which owns 95% of the Lofdal heavy rare earths operation. The mine produces 2,000 tons of rare earth oxides per year and has rich deposits of two of the most valuable

---

353 "Africa's rise as a global supply chain force: UNCTAD report", *UNCTAD*, August 16, 2023, https://unctad.org/news/africas-rise-global-supply-chain-force-unctad-report#:~:text=As%20an%20example%2C%20in%202022,for%20the%20electric%20vehicles%20industry.

354 Gracelin Baskaran, "Could Africa replace China as the world's source of rare earth elements?", *Brookings*, December 29, 2022

355 "Songwe Hill Rare Earths Project, Malawi, East Africa", *Mining Technology*, July 2022, https://www.mining-technology.com/projects/songwe-hill-rare-earths-project-malawi-east-africa/.

heavy rare earth metals—dysprosium and terbium. South Africa's Steenkampskraal Mine has one of the world's highest grades of rare earth elements.[356] It contains 15 pieces and 86,900 tons of rare earth oxides, with large deposits of neodymium and praseodymium. In 2020, the Angolan subsidiary of Pensana Rare Earths, a British firm, received exclusive mining rights for the Longonjo Mine, a rare earth operation, for a 35-year period. These deposits are not insignificant considering Africa's small share of global exploration.[357]

Recent policy announcements from the European Union and the United States show increasing interest from the major players in Africa's supply of raw materials. Both the EU and the US have emphasized the need to mitigate commodity supply chain risks and develop strategic agreements with countries that are able to supply responsibly sourced critical minerals.

In March 2023, the European Commission proposed its Critical Raw Materials Act, which aims to secure the EU's access to minerals and metals critical for net-zero technologies by strengthening international engagement and facilitating extraction, processing, and recycling. The intention is to prevent the dilution or offset of EU's carbon reduction efforts by increasing emissions outside its borders through the relocation of production to countries that have less ambitious policies to fight climate change. The EU also recently announced it was negotiating to source critical minerals from the Democratic Republic of Congo (home to much of the world's cobalt) and intended to do the same with other African countries such as

---

356 "Bannerman Energy Acquires 41.8% stake in Namibia Critical Metals", May 23, 2022, https://africanminingmarket.com/bannerman-energy-acquires-over-41-percent-stake-in-namibia-critical-metals/13263/.

357 "Pensana's Longonjo Rare Earths Project in Angola gets mining title approval", *NS Energy*, April 28, 2020, https://www.nsenergybusiness.com/news/company-news/pensana-longonjo-rare-earths-project/.

Rwanda, Gambia, and Zambia. The EU already has an agreement in place with Namibia in this respect.[358]

Similarly, the United States signed the Inflation Reduction Act 1 (IRA) into law in August 2022. Among other things, the law only permits subsidies for electric vehicles if 40 percent of their critical minerals were mined or processed in the US or a country with which the US has a free trade agreement.[359] Other clean energy technologies, such as wind and solar, do not need domestically sourced critical minerals to qualify for the subsidies. Still, the Act includes a 10% bonus credit to incentivize companies to use locally sourced essential minerals of their clean energy components. The IRA names 50 applicable vital and rare earth minerals for the energy transition, including cobalt, lithium, chromium, and neodymium (used in turbine magnets), all abundant in Africa.[360]

At present, the majority of Africa's critical minerals are exported in the form of ores or concentrates. Certain countries in Africa, including Namibia and Zimbabwe, have imposed export restrictions on some of their unprocessed critical minerals, such as lithium, noting that they are losing income by exporting the minerals as raw materials and that they are planning to develop the capacity to process these minerals locally. The African Continental Free-Trade Area (AfCFTA), implemented in 2021, has also acted as a strong impetus for African governments to address their infrastructure

---

358 Nelson Banya, "EU seeks critical minerals deals with more African countries", *Reuters*, May 31, 2023, https://www.reuters.com/markets/commodities/eu-seeks-critical-minerals-deals-with-more-african-countries-2023-05-31/.

359 "The Inflation Reduction Act: Here's what's in it", *McKinsey and Company*, October 24, 2022, https://www.mckinsey.com/industries/public-sector/our-insights/the-inflation-reduction-act-heres-whats-in-it.

360 Baker McKensie, "Africa: Increasing demand for the continent's critical mineral reserves to boost energy transition", *Lexology*, June 20, 2023, https://www.lexology.com/library/detail.aspx?g=a7bdde4e-b974-49d5-a287-1c2fda080d10.

gaps, enhance and streamline supply chains, improve climate policies that fulfill net zero commitments, boost manufacturing capacity and overhaul regulation relating to trade, cross-border initiatives, investment-friendly policies, and capital flows. It is expected that the work in mineral commodities in Africa will benefit from these reforms, and (among other factors) this will result in African countries undertaking a more active role in the sustainable processing of metals and minerals, better capitalizing on the continent's vast mineral resource base.

For Africa, the focus now is firmly on how the global demand for critical minerals can be translated into the sustainable growth of its mineral mining operations and production facilities and how it can be ensured that this growth will benefit the African continent and its people, not just in terms of the demand for critical minerals, but in how the continent can make use of its resources to ramp up its energy transition and provide the continent with much-needed access to clean power. Consideration also needs to be given to the development and the implementation, in the near future, of new policies in the EU and the US dealing with decarbonization across the full commodity supply chain, which is intended to preserve current off-take markets for commodities in these regions.

This can also be a good deal for mining exporters in Africa. Beyond increasing exploration, there are several ways African countries can maximize the benefits of rare earths for their economies. First, because there has been a shift from labor-intensive to capital-intensive mining, the primary benefit of these resources is the revenue they bring in rather than job creation. Governments strengthening tax policy to increase revenue collection, while keeping stable fiscal policy to prevent volatilities that deter investments, can benefit substantially from mining.

Second, mining can help to build larger regional value chains involving more than just one exporter. Expanding value on the basis of raw material extractions is of central importance for prosperity creation in many African countries, and a new mining boom can help build better foundations for regional prosperity. For instance, it could help leverage the African Continental Free Trade Area (AfCFTA) to boost regional trade. The extraction and value addition process are difficult to do within a single country due to the high cost of rare earths separation facilities. The US set aside $156 million for a single facility to extract and separate rare earths – a sum out of reach for most African countries. Yet without continental separation facilities, African countries will export ores and miss out on local processing and manufacturing benefits.[361] If implemented effectively, the AfCFTA would enable countries to enhance value addition within the bloc before exporting. We have already seen the power of cooperation – Zambia and the Democratic Republic of Congo signed an agreement to build a regional value chain by manufacturing electric batteries using the minerals found in both countries. Such efforts could multiply and also help importing countries ensuring a diversified supply chain with less concentration to one single country.[362]

Third, Africa should use resources strategically to build strong

361 "Biden-Harris Administration Announces $156 Million for America's First-of-a-Kind Critical Minerals Refinery", *Energy.gov*, September 9, 2022, https://www.energy.gov/articles/biden-harris-administration-announces-156-million-americas-first-kind-critical-minerals

362 Theo Acheampong, "Zambian mineral royalties increase", January 11, 2019, https://www.spglobal.com/marketintelligence/en/mi/research-analysis/zambian-mineral-royalties-increase.html; "Zambia and DRC Sign Cooperation Agreement to manufacture electric batteries", ECA, April 29, 2022, https://www.uneca.org/stories/zambia-and-drc-sign-cooperation-agreement-to-manufacture-electric-batteries.

trade partnerships and strengthen its presence in global value chains, particularly with the US, EU, and Australia. US Treasury Secretary Janet Yellen has called for "friend-shoring," or building supply chain networks with allies and friendly countries, to reduce exposure to political disruptions. Canada recently invested $162 million to help position Quebec as a center of excellence for critical minerals processing, specifically building global solid supply chains and strengthening trade relationships with allies. African countries can, as a bloc, forge long-term trade partnerships with these countries who are seeking to build more resilient rare earths value chains.

A Variety of Diversification Strategies

There is no single bullet that can help the EU and the US to wean themselves off dependence on China in all sectors: a variety of measures are already being applied. Industrial subsidies have been the preferred strategy for semiconductors, partly because of the consequences emerging from the chip shortage during the Covid-19 pandemic when supply chains were distorted. There are also other motivations at play, even if the actual dependence currently is not related primarily to China. However, the risk of Chinese aggressions across the Straits have fueled European and American determination to have better domestic capacities for semiconductor manufacturing and ensure that necessary investments are made in R&D. Obviously, there is also competition between the EU and the US here.

There are also direct measures taken to reduce China's market access. The new arsenal built up by the EU to deter commercial aggressions and unfair trade practices by China are likely to have some effect on the composition of trade between the EU and China, leading to reductions in some imports. However, it is unlikely that these measures will have an impact on areas where the real vulnerabilities manifest themselves. Europe's measures will not impact on the imports from China of rare earths. Nor will they lead to better management of the full supply chains where China is dominant across the entire chain – from start to finish. A case in point is EV batteries. The EU has recently signalled it is planning to put contingent measures in place to reduce this exposure, and other – and more targeted – measures are likely to come as well. Through the Inflation Reduction Act, the US has attempted a different approach – to support, in the first place, investment in auto plants in America and reduce market access for EVs with significant value represented by China.

In some areas there is a healthy relation between America and Europe – built on policy cooperation allowing for market competition – but the general trend in the past twenty years have disjointed the two partners. Both sides could benefit substantially by deepening policy coordination on economic security and advance specific and targeted agreements (e.g. on standards) that have substantial impacts on their import profiles. As outlined in a previous chapter, an extension of the current Mutual Recognition Agreement to include some more manufacturing sectors would reduce imports from China substantially.

Finally, it is obvious that neither the EU nor the US will achieve its objectives on economic security unless they deepen their trade partners with like-minded and friendly countries that pose no geopolitical or economic security risk. If the preferred attitude is one of economic isolation and gradual withdrawal from global economic leadership, China will grow more powerful and influential – and an increasing number of countries will look to Beijing rather than Brussels and Washington, DC for partnerships. Nor is it possible for Europe and America to substitute imports by domestic production (there is not enough labor and capital for it) without seriously hurting themselves. The notion that more industrial support will pave the way for industrial renewal, let alone economic security, does not stand up to scrutiny. Governments are already cash strapped and the amounts needed to achieve state-supported re-shoring would literally break the bank.

Deepening trade relations with the wider Asia-Pacific region and with Africa and using the Transatlantic trade power for global economic leadership, is a cost-effective way to achieve less dependence on China and a lesser role for China in global trade and commercial policy. Beijing's situation is a lot easier when the US and the EU hibernate on global economic policy. That can change. New initiatives for trade in the Asia-Pacific and more assured trade leadership with African countries will yield economic security improvements.

NINE

Going Forward – A Transatlantic Agenda for Economic Security

In the modern era, characterized by rapid technological change and shifting global power dynamics, the relationship between geopolitics and economics has become increasingly intertwined and complex. In this book, we have attempted to put light on some of these issues and highlight the need for the US and the EU to be more alert to threats to strategic economic interests and economic security. Moreover, we have argued that there are several ways to reduce dependence on countries with hostile ambitions towards the West, and that the EU and the US should invest far more time and energy to ensure that measures taken can reach the objective in a manner that is effective, sensitive to time, and that preserves a competitive market economy.

After Russia's full-scale invasion of Ukraine, especially Europe got a crash course in the huge problems that arise when deep trade relations with a hostile country need to be cut. Many observers (including the authors of this book) had made the point over a long period of time: deepening trade in strategic sectors (for example, energy and minerals) with Russia will expose countries in Europe to strategic vulnerabilities that are dangerous and that will cost them a lot to manage. These calls were not heeded in all European capitals and countries like Germany actually doubled down on their energy dependence on Russia, despite the Kremlin and the Russian President broadcasting their strategic view of Ukraine and the region openly. Naivety, but also intended disregard, of the risky combination of geopolitics and economic security ruled in many capitals in the world, but not in Beijing and Moscow that have deliberately utilized this toolbox.

Economic dependence on China is a much bigger and more complex problem than the economic dependence on Russia. China is a much bigger economy and it is systemically important for the health of the global economy. Dependence also spans across many products and sectors, and is not just concentrated to a few products – as was the case with Western dependence on Russia. Moreover, China's contribution to the world economy also contains new technology and innovation, and Chinese firms compete with Western firms across the globe. With the country's massive expansion in higher education and R&D, China is generating innovations that Western buyers want and cannot find elsewhere. Finally, China is also exerting power over maritime trade routes that are absolutely essential for Western supply chains. This should not have been news for anyone, as it has steadily developed over decades and has been an openly stated aim from the communist party in China.

It is apparent that while China, Russia, and other authoritarian states pose risks that must be managed, the transatlantic partners have failed to respond adequately. Managing the economic dependency and the supply chain challenges require actions domestically and internationally. Both the US and the EU have started to act, but the actions have often been improvisations rather the results to rational and structural thinking about problems and solutions. The US "tariff war" against China has hurt the US more than China, and it is costing the US economy a lot because it also takes aim of products that are neither strategic nor important. EU actions are more targeted but lacks potency. It is obvious that both sides are not collaborating sufficiently in designing an approach that would stand a chance to be effective to the objective. In fact, the transatlantic relations are at times more strained than between China and Europe, to take the most glaring example, despite the obvious overlapping transatlantic interests.

The importance of reducing dependence on China and diversifying key import supply has not just been underlined by Russia's aggressions, but also by threats from China against European states, such as Lithuania that has been sanctioned by China economically. Additionally, there is increasing geopolitical turbulence in the world, threatening the stability of supply chains in addition to causing risks to peace and freedom. The Covid-19 pandemic also revealed dependencies that hurt economic and societal capacities to respond flexibly and effectively to different chocks. These events have not only disrupted economic activities across borders but have also raised pressing questions about the security and sustainability of long supply chains and critical supply networks. Additionally, it has made it apparent that the "West" has ended up in a precarious situation, much by its own doing, by allowing strategic products and much of their up-stream supply chain to be controlled by authoritarian states, exposing themselves to insecurity and pressure from countries that have hostile intentions.

The book has explored these themes and their different shades. It has covered the geopolitical strategies of major global actors, the evolving nature of international trade, and the impact of technological change on supply chain management. Each chapter have focused at building a deeper understanding of how the US and the EU should navigate these complex dynamics and how they can increase their national security unilaterally, bilaterally as well as multilaterally. The role of the United States and the European Union in shaping global economic policies, the political economy of international trade, and the specific case studies have illustrated the shifting geopolitical landscape and the domestic vulnerabilities that have emerged over time. The insights gleaned from these chapters offer valuable perspectives on the strategic considerations that nations must grapple with in an increasingly interconnected world.

As we ponder the insights from each chapter, we are presented with a multi-dimensional view of the challenges and opportunities in managing international supply chains. These insights are crucial for understanding the delicate balance that nations must strike between the ideals of economic efficiency and multilateral openness, on the one hand, and national security and geopolitical clarity, on the other hand. The over-reliance on major economies like China and Russia for critical sourcing and supply chains has raised critical questions about the sustainability and resilience of these networks, and how to ensure greater national security for the US and the EU. This book has addressed these questions by providing a nuanced analysis of the economic and geopolitical factors influencing supply chain decisions, and the need for greater international cooperation among like-minded and friendly nations, and not isolation from the international economy.

The significance of the book's exploration has been to extend it beyond academic discourse. The intentions have been to offer practical insights for policymakers, business leaders, and others grappling with the realities of global trade in an era of uncertainty. The book provides a framework for understanding the complexities of supply chain management and the strategic considerations that underpin these networks.

Navigating Geopolitical and Economic Tides

The US and the EU are in the midst of a shifting world order that presents both short-term and long-term dangers. China, Russia and other hostile powers like Iran suffer from their own internal problems, and even if they continue to grow richer and more powerful, they are still far away from the scale, depth and innovativeness of Western economies. Russia's invasion of Ukraine leads to enormous economic costs of the war, and the Russian economy has been forced to reallocate economic resources and substitute imported technology in a way that severely hurts its long-term economic prospects. Likewise, China's economic slowdown will continue regardless of economic policy actions in the West; the country's period of unprecedented catch-up growth is over. The shrill economic power grab under President Xi has exacerbated the Chinese economy's structural problems, with increasing reliance on large and inflexible state-owned companies and more political control over the private sector. Entrepreneurs and private capital are increasingly looking for ways to establish outside of China and escape the long arm of the state – a sure sign as any that something is fundamentally wrong in the economy.

Still, shrinking economic prospects for China and Russia may have deteriorating effect on their desire for geopolitical stability, and they have become resourceful enough to mount a formidable challenge to the West, the rules-based world order, and the economic security of American and Europe. The relative economic decline of the United States and, especially, the European Union will continue, and as a result they will become more dependent on accessing ideas, human capital, technology, patents, goods and services generated outside their own countries and regions. In this way, they will grow more dependent on others just as firms and labor in a sophisticated economy become more dependent on the collaboration with other firms and labor.

There is a need to scrutinize how the transatlantic powers navigate new global challenges, such as the rise of other economic powerhouses and shifting trade alliances, and to change its current policy approaches. Significant changes will need to be implemented in relation to the strategic realignment of trade policies, emphasizing the need to diversify supply chains and reduce over-reliance on specific countries, notably China and Russia. This approach aims to bolster supply chain resilience and security against the backdrop of economic and political instabilities. It includes several core themes.

Energy Security in New Light

The process of changing policies in the contemporary geopolitical and economic landscape brings us to a pivotal intersection: the necessity of integrating strategic imperatives focused on sustainability and energy security. The transition towards carbon neutrality and the emphasis on energy security are not merely environmental or policy objectives but are central to the strategic reorientation of technology dependence.

The European Union's ambitious journey towards carbon neutrality by shifting from fossil fuels to renewable energy sources has exposed the region to new vulnerabilities – both the reliance on Russian gas for the energy transition and Chinese suppliers of renewables technology. Both countries are critical suppliers of rare earths and other minerals necessary for this technological shift.

The global reliance on China for rare earth elements, crucial for the manufacture of high-tech products, renewable energy technologies, and military equipment, presents a strategic challenge. The potential for export restrictions or manipulation of supply for geopolitical gains poses a significant risk to industries dependent on these materials, underscoring the need for diversified sources and increased investment in domestic mining and processing capabilities.

Balancing Economic and Strategic Benefits

The US and the EU need to grasp both economic and strategic benefits and costs. While there are some conflicts between economic efficiency and national security, the new approach in the West need to leverage the economic and innovative power of the market and deepen collaboration between like-minded and friendly countries. Balancing between these ideals and objectives is a complex project and it requires much better insight and also long-term political leadership.

This does not present a binary choice but rather underscores the need for a nuanced strategy that balances the benefits of economic engagement with the imperatives of national security. This "middle path" approach advocates for a selective decoupling in critical areas while pursuing engagement that is strategic, conditional, and aligned with broader geopolitical objectives.

Strategic autonomy, in this context, involves developing domestic capabilities in key sectors and diversifying supply chains to mitigate risks of coercion and supply disruptions. It also calls for international cooperation with allies and partners to create resilient economic blocs that can leverage collective bargaining power against coercive tactics.

The Need for Strategic Planning and Collaborative Effort

Understanding and managing complex and sophisticated supply chains in an increasingly difficult geopolitical situation requires much more strategic planning and collaboration. Many Western governments, stuck in complacent and overly bureaucratic silo structures, need to find better structures for economic policy coordination – internally within governments and between governments in international partnerships. Military institutions and processes have worked a lot better and more efficiently than economic institutions, and it is especially the latter that need to find ways to better manage economic security issues and avoid them getting infected by irrational thought and behavior.

The geopolitical debate surrounding global supply chains is evolving, driven by the rapid advancements in technology, shifts in global power dynamics, and the imperative for economic resilience in the face of pandemics and climate change. A comprehensive strategy that addresses these multifaceted challenges requires a deep dive into the nuances of economic coercion, the strategic calculus of engagement versus decoupling, and the transformative potential of alliances.

This strategy must be adaptive, leveraging diplomatic, economic, and technological tools to safeguard interests while fostering a stable, prosperous global economic order. It calls for a reimagined approach to international cooperation, one that prioritizes the development of norms and standards for digital trade, cybersecurity, and the ethical use of emerging technologies.

Public-Private Partnerships for Economic Intelligence

Developing a comprehensive economic intelligence framework through public-private partnerships can provide early warnings of geopolitical risks. By leveraging the analytical capabilities of the private sector and the intelligence resources of governmental agencies, nations can better anticipate and mitigate risks before they escalate into economic disruptions.

Interconnectivity and Strategic Economic Adaptation

A central theme for Western governments is having the wherewithal of technology and general interconnectivity, and the political and institutional flexibility to adapt to new economic situations. The structures and networks of important supplies and supply chains are often complex and non-transparent, and vulnerable dependencies often arise as a result of omission rather than commission. It is an easy but lazy remark to say that Western countries have been naïve in letting authoritarian states like China and Russia having strategic economic influence over them. The fact is that the free market economy is based on decentralized decision making, and preserving that foundation is central for having a dynamic and innovative economy. Now there has to be a new layer of public supervision of key supplies and supply chains, and a policy framework to steer decentralized economic actors in a direction that reduced strategic vulnerabilities and risks.

Fundamentally, strategic economic adaptation is concerned with fortifying the resilience and agility of supply chain operations to withstand and rapidly recover from perturbations. This necessitates a holistic strategy encompassing the diversification of supply sources, the integration of technological advancements to augment visibility and responsiveness, and the fostering of international collaboration to engender a stable global trade ecosystem.

Enhancement of Domestic Production Capacities

Part of a policy to improve the capability for strategic economic adaptation is to build stronger domestic capabilities. Importantly, this is a policy that should focus on the scale and effectiveness of R&D and investments that governments and others make in higher education. The supply of new technology and relevant human capital is a formidable challenge for the West, especially as they grapple with declining birth rates and global competition for human talent. Education and education results need to improve. Moreover, these capacities encompass infrastructure and transportation, and being capable of supplying what the economy needs to main interconnectivity within nations and across like-minded and friendly countries. There are also sectors where current dependencies have to cut and supplies substituted by domestic firms or firms from cooperation partners.

Fostering International Cooperation

Both the US and the EU need to foster deeper international collaboration to develop better economic resilience. It is just impossible for one country alone – regardless its size – to build economic resilience on the basis of national supply if the intention is to generate more economic prosperity. In the economy as well as in the military, an "alliance system" is a very effective structure to ensure stability and resilience.

Against the backdrop of global supply chain vulnerabilities, the pursuit of international collaboration emerges as a foundational pillar for constructing resilience. The establishment of partnerships and alliances with nations sharing similar values can lead to the creation of more robust and diversified supply networks, adept at navigating geopolitical vicissitudes. Such cooperation should transcend conventional diplomatic engagements, extending to collaborative ventures, shared research initiatives, and collective crisis management protocols.

Strategic Alliances and Multilateral Agreements

Building strategic alliances and strengthening international trade agreements offer a robust mechanism for pooling economic and political capital. By fostering a collective bargaining power, nations can better navigate geopolitical complexities and challenge economic aggressions by hostile powers. The practical steps include deepening trade agreements with like-minded and friendly countries and ensure they are based on institutions that enable trust and dispute resolution. With much more focus on standards and technologies in partnerships with each other, the (non-China) Asia-Pacific, and Africa, the EU and the US can achieve less dependence on China and mutual economic benefits, and use the leadership power to exert influence on the direction of economic policies in other countries.

Strategic alliances and partnerships emerge as pivotal in navigating the geopolitical complexities of global supply chains. By fostering collaboration on technology development, supply chain diversification, and security protocols, alliances can enhance economic resilience and strategic depth. Initiatives like the Quadrilateral Security Dialogue and the EU's strategies for connectivity underscore the growing recognition of collaborative frameworks as tools to counterbalance economic coercion and geopolitical rivalry.

Fostering Collaborative Ecosystems

The path to resilient supply chains is fundamentally collaborative. It requires a departure from zero-sum perspectives towards a recognition of mutual interdependence. In practical terms, this means forging alliances not just within industries but across sectors and, crucially, with governmental bodies. Such collaborations can facilitate the sharing of best practices, joint crisis simulations, and the development of standardized resilience metrics. The argument here is for a holistic ecosystem approach, where resilience is built not in isolation but through collective effort and shared vision.

This approach includes creating better cross-border ecosystems for innovation, also in supply chain management. Moreover, international efforts like building up more Western cooperation in defense technology and energy security will widen the ecosystems and make them more capable and flexible. With deeper developments of international standards, there is also going to be easier to move away from China or Russia dependent supplies and supply chains.

A Policy Agenda for the US and the EU

The EU and the US have a complex task to wean themselves off their economic dependence on China and Russia in strategic and important sectors. However, the task is not, to use the old phrase, "rocket science" and it is a perfectly achievable objective to improve the situation to such an extent over the next ten years that China has very little opportunity to weaponize trade flows for political purposes vis-à-vis the West. While it will take a decade for firms to adjust supply chains and reallocate resources, and for new public investment in industrial production to start delivering output, some of the results will start to come much sooner as economic actors adjust to anticipated change.

There are particular sectors that present more immediate needs. The energy sector is the most obvious one, and there the shift away from Russian gas has already started and led to significant diversification, albeit in a somewhat chaotic way. Rare earths and other critical raw and processed materials are another sector of priority. China remains dominant in these sectors and with these inputs being used for downstream products like batteries, China has the capacity to influence downstream output and competition in a way that is not acceptable. Ensuring new access to raw materials and their processing need far more urgency than Western governments shown so far, and adjustment needs to come much faster than in a decade.

It is a harder task to build the foundations that make the West capable to rely on the supply of ideas, technology, and innovation from own actors and those based in like-minded and friendly nations. These tasks require much more time to address and encompass many areas of policy and many parts of society. At the heart, it is about Western economic dynamism and the ability of the Transatlantic economy to foster technological change and rapid innovation. On both scores, the past decades have witnessed slowdowns rather than accelerations, leading to slower rates of growth in productivity and output. Allocating more resources to higher education and R&D will be equally critical, as is policies to allow such expenditures to be more effective than currently.

Where do we go from here? The themes discussed in this book, and outlined previously in this chapter, points to necessary improvements to be made. There is also an agenda for more direct Transatlantic cooperation, and we return to where we started, with the ten-point plan for the Transatlantic partners.

1. **New trade alliance.** The EU and the US should establish a new trade alliance for allies and free market democracies that eliminates tariffs and reduces regulatory friction and creates more stable and reliable supply chains. This is the best starting point for establishing new rules that effectively will discriminate Chinese and Russia goods and services in sectors of strategic importance. While it is unrealistic to go for regulatory harmonization across the board, it is perfectly achievable to establish mutual recognition agreements in selected sectors – building on already existing MRAs between the EU and the US. In the first place, such an agreement would reallocate substantial

amounts of trade with China to trade within the new alliance and generally reduce the economic significance of China for partnering countries. Moreover, on the basis of a trade agreement, the EU and the US could also give substantial trade preferences to each other – reducing the risks in a high trade exposure to China and other countries that are hostile to Western economic and security interests and creating alternative supply chains independent of hostile states.

2. **Constructive trade engagement.** The EU and the US should also seek and deepen constructive trade arrangements with other countries that will not be capable of joining the new trade alliance in an effort to strengthen a blue supply chain. It is of particular importance to do this in the Asia-Pacific region and void that China takes a leading role in the trade arrangements emerging there. For instance, both the US and the EU should apply to join the CPTPP – once an American initiative – and avoid China to take up a leadership position in the region's trade policies. Both sides should also deepen the relationship with India in strategic sectors, for instance telecom and energy policies. Signing (or, in Europe's case, approving) new trade agreements with countries in Latin America and Africa are also part of a programme for constructive trade engagement. The broader point is this: reducing the China threat cannot be done if the EU and the US continue to retreat into economic isolationism because

that will only embolden China and make it stronger in the global economy.

3. **A Transatlantic DARPA for research and innovation.** The EU and the US should establish a new body to collaborate on research and innovation for future technologies of core importance to national security – including materials, space, computing power, semiconductors, and advanced weapon systems. This initiative should be well funded and connect researchers across the Atlantic in coordinated and concentrated areas. It can build on already existing initiatives at Nato and generally draw in the Nato infrastructures, including the countries that are close partners of Nato. Moreover, it should include the expansion of universities across borders – for instance having leading US universities being invited to establish in European countries.

4. **Boosting R&D.** The chief long-term strategy to protect economic and security interests is to be at the frontier – ideally leading the frontier – of new knowledge and research. To that effect, the EU in particular needs to boost R&D spending – public and private – and halt the degradation of its universities. It is far away of reaching its goal of total R&D spending of 3 percent of GDP. This was a target established a long time ago, based on an economy that was less knowledge intensive than our current one. A better target now is to have R&D spending at least 5

percent of GDP by 2040. While the US spends more on R&D, it also needs to rise to the challenge.

5. **Global Gateway initiative is crucial in creating a new, reliable and secure supply chain.** The EU and the US should coordinate current and new efforts to have better control of key global trading routes and infrastructure. Building on existing resources, they can establish a new investment bank that is well funded to invest in new trade infrastructure in especially the Asia-Pacific and MENA regions. Stronger naval presence is also required in order to command authority over key sea routes – and it is especially important Europe rises to the challenge and become a supplier of protection and order of trading routes.

6. **Security principles for public procurement and system projects.** Both the EU and the US need to become more alert to security threats that are part of sectors strongly influenced by public procurement and system projects, including energy, telecom networks, and biomedicine. Companies that tender for these contracts should, at the minimum, be required to provide full transparency in ownership, links to governments, and received subsidies. Moreover, there should also be principles that apply to the security of supply for key products, including demands on when core, auxiliary or just-in-time facilitates need to exist inside the territory of

the procuring countries or close to it. This will add costs to public procurement, but there is no way around the fact that better supply security will entail higher costs.

7. **Ban China's SOEs from doing business in the West.** Of particular concern for national security in the economy is the influence of China's State-owned Enterprises (SOEs) in trade with the EU and the US. There is no reason for Western economies to accept the SOEs to operate in their markets and supply chains when it is obvious that they are strongly connected to foreign state interests in countries that are collision course with the EU and the US.

8. **Like-by-like mechanism.** China is pursuing aggressive trade policies and closing its markets to Western suppliers, and has already established a certain decoupling from western economies in its supply chains. The EU and the US should respond in kind. Reductions in market access in China will immediately be responded to by trade restrictions on Chinese or other exporters. A trade restriction warning system can be established in the EU-US Trade and Technology Council (TTC) to quickly flag new restrictions and coordinate the response. This also applies to cases when China takes coercive action against a single country: the EU and the US will respond collectively and will full economic force.

9. **Trade, climate change and green technology.** There
    is a dire need for the EU and the US to agree on what
    trade or trade-connected policies that should be allowed
    for the reduction of carbon emissions. Now the two sides
    are on collision course, with the US using distorting
    subsidies and the EU going for carbon tariff-like policies.
    A Transatlantic trade war is going to emerge in the next
    ten years unless there is a change of course. An accord
    on what trade measures that are acceptable, and on what
    grounds, should include maintained preferential access
    between each other. If, for instance, the EU is concerned
    about subsidy discrimination in America, it should also
    offer the US to be exempt from EU measures in its Carbon
    Border Adjustment Mechanism (CBAM).

10. **A high-tech alliance.** Finally, it is tremendously high
    importance that the EU and the US pursues a high-tech
    alliance that establishes common standards in key fields
    of technology. This alliance will have to include cloud, AI
    and quantum computing, and general rules for how data
    should be governed. Currently, there is strong divergence in
    the high-tech field, leading to less capacity for both sides
    to avoid growing dependence on technology supply from
    third countries – including China. The EU is shooting
    itself in the foot by trying to reduce the presence of US
    technology companies in the EU and eroding the power
    of industry-driven, bottom-up European Standardization

Bodies. Similarly, absence of policies in America and chaotic actions by its agencies create a wedge with all other countries that are attempting structured policy solutions to new and emerging problems. A new high-tech alliance should deepen current efforts in the TTC to establish better norms and policies on export controls.

This ten-point agenda presents an outline of action in an era where global supply chains are not just economic arteries but also strategic assets. The concluding insights of this exploration underscore the imperative for a visionary and resilient strategic framework. Drawing upon the insights from the detailed examination of GSCs within the geopolitical context, it has become evident that the future of global trade and security hinges on our ability to navigate the complex interplay of economic efficiency, strategic security, and technological innovation.

The analysis presented in this book reveals that the challenges facing GSCs are multifaceted and demand an equally complex response that will take time and financial resources to remedy. While useful as a theoretical construct, the dichotomy of engagement versus decoupling falls short of addressing the nuanced realities of global trade in the 21st century. Instead, what emerges is the urgent need for a strategic vision that is agile, resilient, and capable of navigating the fluid dynamics of global politics and economics.

This vision has called for an approach that balances the undeniable benefits of economic globalization—such as enhanced efficiency, innovation, and growth—with the strategic imperatives of security and sovereignty. It requires a recalibration of policies to prioritize not only the economic returns from GSCs but also their role in ensuring national resilience, technological sovereignty, and geopolitical stability.

At the heart of this strategic vision for global supply chains is the proposal for a renewed Transatlantic leadership. The United States and the European Union, with their shared values and economic clout, are uniquely positioned to spearhead efforts to redefine the governance of global supply chains. By deepening economic ties, advancing trade agreements, and leading by example in the pursuit of a balanced approach to globalization, Transatlantic partners can set a new standard for global trade—one that is rooted in fairness, sustainability, and mutual respect.

In conclusion, the challenges and opportunities presented by global supply chains in a rapidly changing world, the need for a strategic, forward-looking approach has never been more urgent. By embracing the complexities of the geopolitical landscape, fostering technological innovation, and building collaborative frameworks for resilience, we can ensure that global supply chains continue to be engines of growth and innovation, while also serving as pillars of stability and security in the international order.

This comprehensive approach, grounded in the insights from the detailed analysis in this book, have offered a roadmap for policymakers, business leaders, and stakeholders across the globe to navigate the future of global supply chains with confidence, vision, and a commitment to a more secure and prosperous world for all.

ABOUT THE AUTHORS

Niklas Swanström is the Director of the Institute for Security and Development Policy, and one of its co-founders. He is a Fellow at the Foreign Policy Institute of the Paul H. Nitze School of Advanced International Studies (SAIS) and a Senior Associate Research Fellow at the Italian Institute for International Political Studies (ISPI). His main areas of expertise are regional cooperation; Chinese foreign policy and security in Northeast Asia; the Belt and Road Initiative, traditional and non-traditional security threats and its effect on regional and national security as well as negotiations. Niklas Swanström has authored, co-authored or edited a number of books, including: *Eurasia's ascent in Energy and Geopolitics, Sino-Japanese Relations: The Need for Conflict Prevention and Management, Trans-national Crime: A security Threat?, Regional Cooperation and Conflict Management: Lessons from the Pacific Rim and Foreign Devils, Dictatorship or Institutional Control: China's foreign policy towards Southeast Asia.*

Niklas holds a Ph.D. in Peace and Conflict Studies from Uppsala University and degrees from Fletcher School of Law and Diplomacy, Beijing Languages Institute, Beijing University and Dalian Languages University.

Fredrik Erixon is a Swedish economist and writer. He has been the Director of the European Centre for International Political Economy (ECIPE) ever since its start in 2006. The Financial Times has ranked Erixon as one of Brussels 30 most influential people.

Fredrik is the author of several books and studies in the fields of international economics, economic policy, and regulatory affairs (welfare reforms, healthcare, competition policy, et cetera). His latest book (co-authored with Björn Weigel) was The Innovation Illusion: How so Little is Created by so Many Working so Hard (Yale University Press) and he has previously written books about the history of political ideas, the role of social capital for economic growth, and international economic policy. His research interests covers international economics, European relations with Asia and North America, trade and regulatory policy, philosophy and technological change. His next book, Saving Liberalism for the 21st Century, is about challenges from populism and other ideas to the open society.

Erixon has advised several governments in Europe and the rest of the world, and is a frequent speaker at conferences. He regularly writes for international newspapers and magazines. In his previous career, Erixon has worked in development policy, financial markets, business consulting, and academia.

Mrittika Guha Sarkar holds the prestigious SIS Dean's Award and the Mehdi Heravi Scholarship at the School of International Studies (SIS), The American University, Washington DC, USA, where she also serves as a Graduate Assistant. Additionally, she is an Associated Research Fellow at the Institute for Security & Development Policy (ISDP) in Sweden. Her previous roles include serving as a Young Professional and Ad-hoc Editor for the Asia Pacific Bulletin at the East-West Center in Washington, D.C.

Mrittika has been a Language Scholar at the Chinese Language Center, National Chengchi University (NCCU), Taipei, Taiwan, and a Research Scholar in Chinese studies at the Centre for East Asian Studies, School of International Studies, Jawaharlal Nehru University (JNU), New Delhi, India. Furthermore, she has contributed as a Research Associate at the Centre for Strategic Studies and Simulation, The United Service Institution of India, New Delhi and as a Project Assistant at the East Asia Centre at the Manohar Parrikar Institute for Defence Studies and Analyses (MP-IDSA), New Delhi, India. Her research predominantly focuses on policy analysis concerning South Asia, with specific interests in India-China relations and the broader geostrategic dynamics of the Indo-Pacific region.

www.ingramcontent.com/pod-product-compliance
Lightning Source LLC
Chambersburg PA
CBHW020528270326
41927CB00006B/487